The Smallest Objective

The Smallest Objective

Sharon Kirsch

VANCOUVER
NEW STAR BOOKS
2020

Author's Note: The names of some minor characters
have been altered for the purposes of this book.

 NEW STAR BOOKS LTD
#107–3477 Commercial St, Vancouver, BC V5N 4E8 CANADA
1574 Gulf Road, #1517 Point Roberts, WA 98281 USA
newstarbooks.com · info@newstarbooks.com

The publisher acknowledges the financial support of the Canada
Council for the Arts, the Government of Canada through the Canada
Book Fund, the British Columbia Arts Council, and the Province
of British Columbia through the Book Publishing Tax Credit.

Cataloguing information for this book is available from
Library and Archives Canada, collectionscanada.gc.ca

Printed & bound in Canada by Imprimerie Gauvin, Gatineau, QC

Cover design by Robin Mitchell Cranfield
Typeset by New Star Books
First printing, April 2020

In memory of my parents,

Rene Elissa Rutenberg

and

Dr. Archie Kirsch

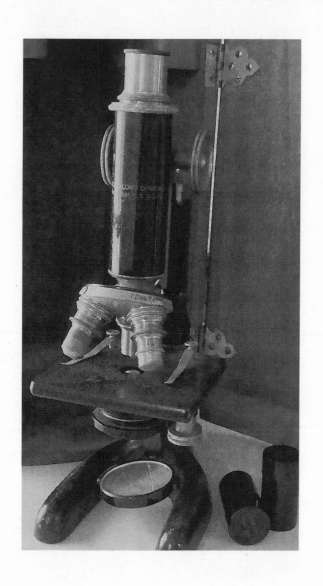

"... the telescope objective lens has to be wide to gather light and is of a long focal length, while the microscope objective lens is small, and has a short focal length.... The job of a microscope is to reveal fine detail to the eye."

— *Collecting Microscopes*, Gerard L'E. Turner

"WHICH EYE TO USE. The right eye is generally used for observations, but, while the manipulator may from habit be inclined to use this, it may be possible that in some cases the left can be used to the best advantage and with less fatigue.

Make it a habit at the outset to keep both eyes open."

— "Manipulation of the Microscope," Edward Bausch

Contents

CHAPTER ONE   *Treasure*   1

CHAPTER TWO   *Lantern Slides*   35

CHAPTER THREE   *Shut Out the Yesterdays*   83

CHAPTER FOUR   *The Right Part of Life*   101

CHAPTER FIVE   *Lake Pátzcuaro*   145

CHAPTER SIX   *Counterclockwise*   185

CHAPTER SEVEN   *The Possibilities Are Fantastic*   201

AFTERWORD   *Malibu Apr 02*   237

Sources   244

List of Photographs   254

Acknowledgments   256

CHAPTER ONE

Treasure

My MOTHER'S HOUSE WAS A PLACE OF PROHIBITIONS. ADMON-
ishments on scraps of paper, some in narrow ballpoint but
more in coarse crayon, obscured the walls and tabletops: *No
boots on rug. Don't mess with timer. Bolt basement door. Hands off
sheers. Don't leave black bedspread in the light.* Still, my mother had
failed on one count: She'd neglected to prohibit boring into
hardwood floor, not because she approved of the venture, but
simply because it had never occurred to her. Nor would her
blacklist have extended to a Highland Scots carpenter in her
bedroom or archaeologists in her wardrobe. Such improba-
bles, later realized, eluded even her frayed imagination.

My mother no longer inhabits that house. The brand-new
split-level to which she came as a lucid bride, she left without
warning and in confusion, appeased only by the belief that her
beloved daughter, her sole and cherished child, would never lie.
But that I did. The move to assisted living, I told her, was merely
a trial, a respite endorsed by her doctors. And in the months
that ensued I flouted my mother's strictures time and again, at
first with grief, and eventually with indifference.

Unbeknownst to my mother, the first assaults on her perfect
order began while she still occupied the 1950s semi-detached
with three bedrooms and two bathrooms, a spacious kitchen,
a formal living and dining room, a den, and an unfinished

3

basement supporting the whole — her house or, most often in her parlance, "the house." And yet, "the house" is misleading. In truth, my mother had withdrawn from most of her range, lumbering only between the master bedroom and bathroom or kitchen. Like a raccoon in winter torpor, she stirred grudgingly and merely to satisfy vital functions. Her adherence to the half-light made possible incursions that previously would have been unthinkable.

A martini shaker imprinted with *Skol* and *A Votre Santé!* The black ceramic bowl studded with gold bees. A never-sent letter my mother had composed for a friend about the ice storm of '98, the words on the envelope, *I wrote about the ice storm.* Not one was an obvious tool of transgression, but each was among the first objects I stole away.

Once I'd removed my mother from her house in Montreal, I could dispense with subtlety, but until then, stealth prevailed. Serge, the moving coordinator, agreed to survey the contents during one of my mother's several daily naps. With her hearing aid switched off and the requisite pillow over her head, my mother would detect little and suspect even less. Serge was ample, perhaps three hundred pounds, and that he itemized both the den and kitchen without rousing my mother was a measure of his grace. But as he hovered before the bedroom door, unwittingly he placed his full weight on a rogue floorboard.

"Who's there?" My mother came swiftly to the door.

The doctor's bride — in her now-standard uniform. Rene Elissa Kirsch, née Rutenberg, who wore for her wedding "a Simonetta of Rome original of white brocaded satin, with a high neckline, fitted bodice and a full flared skirt falling into a court train," stood before us in a ragged white shirt that barely grazed her upper thighs. Beneath the hemline, her legs were crisscrossed with varicose veins.

My mother squinted at Serge, then at me, her grown-up child and heir. "There's a man in my house," she declared, for once sure of herself. "Who is this man in my house?"

"A colleague." My voice faltered only slightly. "Go back to bed. You have nothing to worry about." She turned, stumbling along the well-trodden path to her bed.

The bride's "veil of tulle illusion was held by a cluster of apple blossoms. She carried a spray of apple blossoms."

Of late, I've been composing a memo for myself when I am old:
- Wear shoes with Velcro.
- Eat something other than cheese and crackers.
- Take charge of your own life before someone else does.

The morning of the move, a brisk October morning, I drove my mother to an apartment hotel with a newspaper, a nurse's aide, and a box of party sandwiches: cream cheese, gherkin pickle and smoked salmon pinwheels, double-decker egg and tuna. She'd once composed these herself, covering them in the fridge overnight with a damp washcloth to subdue moisture loss. Even now her appetite for party sandwiches remained unsated.

"I'm confused," she said. A familiar litany.

"Don't worry, everything's all right," I told her. I could scarcely believe I was following through on my own intentions, necessary as they were. Privately I reminded myself to keep breathing.

After I'd deposited my mother and her aide at the hotel, I hurried back to the house to dismantle her endeavour of more than fifty years.

By sundown, the kitchen, den, and master bedroom had been shorn of all that made them hers. The dozens of objects on my mother's dresser, arranged at precise angles and according to a highly evolved personal etiquette, I shoved randomly into a bag: hair clips, the Art Nouveau brush and mirror, a stopped watch, empty miniatures of Rive Gauche and Chanel No. 5. The family photos on the highboy, in recent months turned towards the wall, I reversed and put away. I pulled open the blinds.

Serge and his team executed the rest. They entered the house with their shoes on and tipped my mother's dresser on its side. They used my mother's toilet and sullied her towels. They fingered her Waterford crystal, they touched her gilt-rimmed glasses. The front and garage doors to the house, rarely disturbed in recent years, were thrust open, and the contents of the crucial rooms disgorged into the street.

"Where am I?" my mother asked later that day as I escorted her into her new quarters, where I'd arranged her sofas, bed, and chests of drawers to resemble home. "This is my furniture, but this is *not* my house."

"Everything will be all right," I said. "Let's watch Larry King."

Late that night, in the kitchen of my mother's house, I sat at the bridge table where my father and his friend George had played Clobyosh while snacking on Liquorice Allsorts. The kitchen, because it was the least violated of the near-empty rooms. Downstairs in the den, a black metal end table and a nubby brown footstool minus the matching easy chair were all that remained. Directly overhead, in the master bedroom, the pink plastic chamber pot thrust into a corner, the single dirty sock, and the scattered bed biscuits seemed more to the point — all that was missing was the yellow police tape.

The kitchen, in contrast, was barely disturbed, and here my mother's clippings, her notes to herself, mine to her, had survived the day. *Take two round white pills, wait 10 minutes, then eat,* read a reminder on the fridge door. Nearby, on the coral Formica countertop, my mother had smoothed out a newspaper clipping, "Days Start Getting Lighter in 16 Weeks." I sat inert on the hard bridge chair. Opposite me, on the top shelf of the otherwise empty cupboard, was a shattered glass, in the Jewish wedding ritual an expression of sadness at the destruction of the Temple in Jerusalem.

⟵⟍

My own home, a Victorian row house in Toronto, was built as narrow as my mother's was wide, as compact as my mother's was ample. I lived in an urban neighbourhood with cafés and shops within a few minutes' walk, my mother in the remote suburbs where buying milk or Tylenol most often involved driving to the shopping centre. Despite my home's small size, it had at one time served as a rooming house, accommodating a succession of tenants with their scattered histories. My mother's home, like each one on her street of near-identical mid-century modern houses, was conceived for a nuclear family. Hers — and mine. Whereas I'd ruthlessly discarded the belongings of strangers left in my own basement, I'd eventually exercise nothing but tenderness and curiosity towards the finds in my mother's lower level. For the moment, however, my attention was focused upstairs, on the promise of treasure.

After my mother's move and the ransacking of her house, I retreated to my own home, not returning to Montreal for more than a month. When I did venture back, I brought friends with me. But in the weeks preceding the visit, from my own home in a faraway city, I dreamt regularly of my mother's house. Not infrequently I woke believing I was there, momentarily mistaking my curtains for the Venetian blinds of my childhood bedroom, the horse chestnut tree outside my window for the flowering crabapple my mother chopped down because for a week in springtime the blossom stained the hood of her grey Nissan Altima.

More often, though, I dreamt of silver — my grandmother's tray chased with a seed pattern; the salt cellar with the cobalt glass bowl; but most of all the bacchanalian pitcher with the lion handle, the grinning lion with his monkey's eyes and kempt mane, his body fully extended, the hind paws forming the base of the curved grip and the forepaws the top. These treasures had existed — once — but now were vested only in dreams and memory. They'd been sold or lost or perhaps my mother in her confusion had given the items away.

No, silver didn't impel my return. I was in pursuit of a less articulated treasure, one hidden by my father years before I was born, when the house itself had only just come to be. The allure of this treasure lay not in its monetary value, if any, but in its significance as a last message from my father. There existed a kind of family precedent. Simon, my father's father, had issued a final instruction to his sons in a codicil to his will written almost a quarter century before his death. In it my grandfather had urged his three boys to *learn early in life that the only real road to true success is to work hard and earnestly at whatever pursuit they may choose for their life's vocation.* Almost thirty years later, my father had buried an object imbued with his own hopes and fears. To undertake the search for it would be to venture losses. If the treasure couldn't be found or failed to satisfy, it risked enhancing my sense of all I didn't and might never know.

After my father's death some ten years before, my mother had developed an obsession. "I want to rent a metal detector," she said, "to find what Daddy hid under the bedroom floor." My mother, by this time, no longer qualified as a "namby-pamby" — her preferred description of herself as a timid newlywed. At seventy she remained physically vigorous, opting for late-night TV in lieu of sleep, and without question knew her own mind, at least when it came to metal detectors.

My husband and I remained circumspect about her request. "Not now, with all that furniture in the room. Just wait. Wait until you're ready to sell the house."

"I'd like to do it now."

But she didn't, because we wouldn't lend our support. And instead, a decade later, I undertook the search with strangers to my parents' house while my mother, a few kilometres away, was engrossed in the final episodes of *Larry King Live*.

Several days after my mother's move to assisted living, my husband had joined me at her house, and, alone there, we shut ourselves into the master bedroom, closed the Venetian blinds, and with effort peeled back the white wall-to-wall. The tacks yielded up the carpet reluctantly, the sound of their forced parting like corn popping. Beneath the carpet lay a maple hardwood floor that had rarely been exposed since the house was built for my parents in 1955. Only the day before, we'd tried passing a metal detector over smaller areas of the same floor but quickly found the device reacted to every nail, of which there were multitudes. We resorted now to examination by feel.

Crawling across the floor, we palpated boards that were slightly raised, prodding the widest of spaces in between. Only one floorboard stood apart from the rest. On each of its four sides, space was generous, suspiciously so. My husband, a historian of gardens, seized a wrench. He forced it into a groove by the floorboard, got purchase, pulled, pushed, grunted, found no give. At least a dozen nail heads no bigger than lentils secured the floorboard to whatever lay below. My father's last gift, tantalizingly present but off limits.

Back home, I was quick to locate my friend David, a talented furniture designer and an able carpenter.

"David, how would you feel about a few days away right after Christmas?"

"What have you got in mind, then?"

"Maybe a stay at my mother's house," I said, "while I'm there clearing out. I've been wanting to hold a last supper round my parents' table — you know, give the house a final send-off. And you and Margaret could take some time by yourselves, check out the museums."

"Oh, aye." David was a Highland Scot.

"There's something else." I was about to betray my father's confidence, the secret he'd entrusted to me, my mother, and not least the house, decades before. "My father hid something under the floorboards, something special. I need to get it out."

David grinned. "Let me speak to Margaret — and we'll have to decide which tools I should bring."

"It should only take an hour or so. The rest of the time will be yours."

In her first months in assisted living, my mother never asked when or whether she'd be going home, never said she wanted to return home. But she asked about the house — whether it was safe, who was looking after it — as though the house counted as her protégé rather than she its. Quite reasonably, she presumed it to be unoccupied.

When David and Margaret pulled into the driveway at dusk, I'd just taken the last bite of a pistachio éclair. My mother's street, always quiet, was more so than usual, the silence a by-product of the cold and the holiday season. In the back yard that morning a rabbit had left prints in the snow.

"I'll just have a look, then, shall I?" said David, bounding up the stairs to the master bedroom. He knelt on the hardwood. "Seems like tongue and groove."

David and Margaret represented the first legitimate visitors to the house in years. The veto on guests had coincided with my mother's sudden indifference to crabgrass. From then on, she'd admitted no one into her home other than tradesmen, nurse's aides, her daughter and son-in-law, and the cleaner. And whereas previously she'd vetted strangers entering her domain, anticipating their arrival by laying newspaper on the carpets and shadowing the interlopers as they went about their business, her reply to outsiders had become withdrawal. From under the covers or behind the bathroom door, she occasionally queried the doings of personal aides or repairmen. But often they had the run of the house — a privilege denied decades earlier to our trusted cat, Suzie.

"This is the one, David." I pointed to the anomalous board. "It looks suspicious, don't you think?"

"Hard to say. It would help if we knew what we were looking for."

My father had left little in the way of guidance. Throughout my teens and early twenties, he'd referred every now and again to "something buried under the bedroom floor." More than that he never divulged, or if he did, I was careless of the details. And those confidences were now so remote that I might not have trusted my memory, except for my mother's validation following my father's death. With her entreaty to rent a metal detector, conjecture became conviction.

Beyond that, I possessed one tangible proof of my father's act — a scrap of paper I'd recently retrieved from a safe deposit box when searching for the deeds to the house. On it my father had written in a quivering hand, *If sell house, metal detector over bedroom carpet.*

"Let's have dinner, David," I suggested, "and then you can make a start upstairs."

I seated David and Margaret at my mother's dining room table, a polished cherrywood oval — her wedding gift from her parents — covered, in recent years, by a yellow plastic cloth edged with synthetic lace. In anticipation of David and Margaret's visit, I'd stripped the table of my mother's IGA receipts and dozens of notes to herself, her blank datebooks, scattered hair clips, and ancient toothbrushes in cellophane, the wreckage illuminated by a Second Empire chandelier. Similar to the house itself, this table embodied my mother's pride and fostered her anxiety. Her marriage to a war veteran seventeen years her senior had put her under strain when entertaining his contemporaries. Too frequently, the dark-haired, slender-legged newlywed incited jealousy among the older matrons, ever ready to deride her chicken à la King, zippy pineapple salad, and icebox lemon torte.

David ate his store-bought *Parmentier au boeuf* with enthusiasm and, when done, declared himself ready to address the floorboard. Margaret and I stood by in silence as David affixed metal clamps to the boards surrounding the one slated for removal and, with effort, leveraged them away from the target. We breathed tentatively as he picked up his small circular saw. From one of the few surviving photos on the wall, my earlier self, aged seven, looked on, my hair a croquembouche of curls festooned with velvet ribbons. To either side of me stood my parents, solemnly gazing outward.

"This is it," said David. "Let's go."

He created a neat incision across the top of the board, then lifted out a perfect rectangle of wood about 4 by 1.5 inches, exposing an indeterminate black matting. Leaning into what remained of the floorboard, David cut more aggressively along each side. The maple was brittle, desiccated. That this segment of tree had once sheltered birds and squirrels and run with sap in springtime was implausible, that a treasure lay beneath it even more so.

David frowned. "Whatever's there, it's got to be a wee thing. Look at that space between the hardwood and subfloor — it can't be more than a quarter inch. Not even."

He leveraged all his strength against the remaining segment of the board. Beneath lay the black matting, and below that the pine subfloor, rougher in construction, with wide planks on the diagonal, but intact. David flipped over the single board in his hands. Nothing.

"Was your father a joker?"

Yes and no.

My father, like his Uncle Mo, was a kibitzer, both honing their humour on the London Blitz and Normandy landings. While stationed in wartime London, my father, a medical officer, had arranged for a transatlantic call to his parents.

"What can I do for you, Canada?" queried the English operator. Phoning overseas was no easy matter, and this female telephonist proved more accommodating than most.

"You've been very decent," said my father as the operator prepared to withdraw. "Could I buy you dinner?"

"Listen, love, I'm fat, I'm forty, and I don't fuck."

My father, in his twenties, was muscular, unattached, and favoured tea dancing cheek to cheek at the Savoy Hotel. "Did I ever put down the receiver fast!"

But my father joked only in words, never in practice. In truth, he valued nothing more than loyalty — loyalty to Queen, country, and Empire, loyalty to me, my mother, and their imperfect marriage. Although my father cared little about other people's opinion of him, he'd brook no public criticism of my mother. When an acquaintance mistakenly accused my mother, a teetotaller, of drunkenness, my father called the man a "goddamn bastard" and made ready to use his fists in his wife's defence.

It was unimaginable, then, that my father should have encouraged his wife and daughter on a search for treasure that would yield nothing. Not he himself but his war experience almost certainly furnished the motive for his stealth. For a man

who'd nearly had his head blown off on the Normandy crossing and then witnessed the execution of one of his stretcher
bearers on Juno Beach, the idea that not merely your person
but your home, too, could be ravaged or violated was entirely
plausible. My father buried what he did as a wager against an
uncertain future. The only certainty he allowed himself was
that his wife or as-yet-unborn child would one day excavate
his secret.

My mother also harboured secrets, one being that she continually hid provisions in the kitchen roasting pan. Her reasons were twofold: to prevent my father snacking excessively,
and to enable her own gorging, customarily after midnight. My
mother's stash tended to nuts and candy, especially rocky road
chocolate. Her binges were solitary and went unacknowledged,
though I was wise to them, and my father, too.

The more burdensome secret was that my father and mother
sparred continually as she evolved from his submissive young
acolyte into his most unsparing detractor. No one was to know
about her set-tos with my father nor her struggles with depression that periodically confined her to bed until noon. Both
counted as private matters she had no choice but to entrust
to me, and both she expected me to conceal. In hindsight, I
realize the secrets I guarded so fiercely as a child were public
knowledge.

"Here's a thought," David said the morning after the
non-retrieval. "I don't see how your father could have hidden
anything much in between those two floors — there's just not
enough space. The way I figure it, underneath the subfloor
would have been a better bet. There's got to be loads of room
down there."

"What are you suggesting?" I hadn't slept well and lacked David's resolve to carry on.

"Well, it's like this, isn't it? We couldn't get anywhere from above, so why not try from below?" He hesitated. "I'd have to drill some holes in the den ceiling."

"How many?"

"If we don't get lucky, maybe sixteen."

I left David readying himself to drill. My mother's apartment building was barely two miles from the house, half an hour on foot, ten minutes by car, but for her the geography of the two had become insurmountable.

"Where are you staying?" she asked as I placed my boots on a sheet of newspaper in her narrow front hall. Throughout my life my mother had nurtured me, encouraging me with praise and small, gentle tokens of affection, so that even now, with so much forgotten, this love and solicitude endured. At the same time, she'd always kept track of me, and in her middle adulthood went so far as to tail me in her car on my first date — a vigilance that encouraged in me the habit of evasion.

"At the house."

"At my house? The house I lived in?"

"Yes."

Over and over she scraped the nail of her pointer finger against her thumb. "Did you set the alarm?"

"Yes."

She began searching for her remote control. "What am I doing? I don't know what the heck I'm doing."

There was a chronology to my mother's forgetting: first, the symptoms of my father's illness, then bill payments or going to a friend's or relative's funeral; later, that her son-in-law worked in Boston, which days the garbage went out, how to open the trunk of the car, what she'd eaten for dinner, that she'd eaten dinner, that she'd phoned me ten times, that she couldn't remember. She might have benefited now from the aide-memoire of an acrostic poem, such as the one an early suitor composed for her:

> Ravishing lips that draw me near,
> Eyes so soft, tender, clear,
> Nearly stops my heart with love,
> Enticing angel from above.

I settled my mother, a shopworn angel, in her chair and gathered my coat, patting her on the shoulder for reassurance. "I have to go now, but I'll see you soon."

"Oh, I'll miss you so much." As I stepped into the corridor, she didn't retreat into her unit but instead surveyed me until I'd entered the elevator with the door about to slide shut. "Be careful," she said.

Back at the house, David was stacking up plaster rounds from the den ceiling. Thick, and with crumbling edges, they resembled the plugs of grass dug from lawns in springtime to promote aeration. Plaster dust coated the plastic sheeting David had flung over the end table and footrest, and more plaster dust clung to the exposed built-in with its small liquor cabinet backed by a mirrored wall and lit from above. Although the cabinet displayed a range of offerings, my mother had disliked spirits and my father had drunk only to "cut the fat" when he ate *piccata al limone*. Here in the den, however, they'd poured generous libations for their friends. The evenings of entertaining began with "Tremendo Cha-Cha-Cha" and "Whoop Dee Dee," Xavier Cugat and Bobby Dukoff.

"Nothing so far," said David.

"Call me if you get a hit."

A level below, in the unfinished basement, other tasks awaited me. Whereas my mother or, in later years, her cleaner had kept the upstairs of the house immaculate, here dust was allowed to proliferate, dead potato bugs to moulder. In this room I wore jeans, a long-sleeved lavender T-shirt, thick argyle socks, and a white cardboard mask ridged like a nautilus.

In a dusty brown box that promised old photos, I found an array of chignon bows from the 1960s: one a filmy black mesh with a velvet heart, two muscular bows glittering gold and silver, a white bow with a leatherette finish, another a delicate bone like the points of a Siamese cat. Elsewhere was a nosegay of dried bulrushes coated in dust and a flour-and-water relief map of Chile.

Upstairs the phone rang.

"I'm not sure what I'm doing." Against all odds, my mother had remembered the second phone number at the house.

Once, for just a moment, as David shone his torch through the private spaces of the house that had gone unlit for fifty-five years, he glimpsed metal in the hand-held mirror that enhanced his view. But what might have been a gold bar or coins was soon revealed as nothing more than a joist hanger, there to support a short beam, a sloppy cut. "The work of an apprentice," David speculated.

I was deliberating over the fate of a stuffed baby alligator when David made his way down to the basement. The reptile, already dead when my parents bought it in Florida, had been denied its life for the passing entertainment of a child like me. With a tenderness that came too late, I stowed the forever-young alligator in a shoebox.

"That's it," said David. He stood awkwardly in the thick of several marionettes suspended from the basement ceiling. Their faces were the colour and shape of persimmons while his was closer to the heft and contours of a durian fruit and dusted in plaster powder. I was still sporting the nautilus.

Little was said as David and Margaret readied their van, loading in several bottles of single malt I insisted they take from the house. It was Christmastime, after all, and missing treasure aside, the recipient of a gift had been not David but me.

After David and Margaret's visit came winter, and the snows denied objects, even buildings, their contours. In blizzard conditions my adopted and native cities — Toronto and Montreal, respectively — the first a succession of ravines emptying into an inland sea, the second a sequence of hills with the kudos of a mountain, were near-indiscernible. I decided to return to my adopted home.

An archaeologist friend, schooled in the excavation of treasure, had an idea for me — one that merited a winter trek to his office. Sodden but hopeful, I hung my parka in the entranceway. Two men bedecked in kilts and sporrans nodded as they walked past, and in the nearby kitchen several archaeologists were debating how best to microwave a sheep's stomach. Preparations for Robbie Burns Night were under way. As the singer and bagpiper rehearsed a stop-start rendition of "A Man's a Man for a' That," I made my way down the corridor to Ron's office.

"Tho' hundreds worship at his word . . ."

I knocked.

"He's but a coof for a' that."

Ron swivelled round in his chair. "Young lady," he said excitedly, "I think I have just the thing for you. With your permission I'll call in two good young lads, and then we'll talk."

I nodded my assent.

"John, Sharon. Sharon, John. Sharon, Blake." The men sat. Ron continued. "I've taken the liberty of telling these worthy gentlemen about your little problem. Now Blake here did his fieldwork on battlegrounds in the UK — we're talking layers of buried treasure — and he's confirmed what you need is a GPR."

"GPR?"

"Ground-penetrating radar," interjected Blake. "A technology for detecting near-surface objects. If you're looking for gold bars or coins just below the floorboards, this would be your machine."

"Can I buy one?"

All three men chuckled.

"You'd be looking at twenty thou minimum," said Ron. "But we have a couple of ideas. One, we've located a company with both the technology and expertise to do the job. They have an office near your mother's house and the ability to collect and analyze the data — for a price, of course. Downside is you'd have to let them in on the secret. The second option" — Ron paused — "is that John and Blake here make the trip with you. They rent a small GPR from a local company. You cover the rental cost, and John and Blake do the work, gratis."

"Let me get this straight. You're offering me my own private team of archaeologists?"

"You bet. I can spare them. We're outside the digging season."

"You're an amazing friend."

A blizzard delayed the expedition. More than a week after the planned departure, John and Blake finally picked me up at my house. As they loaded my duffle bag into the back of the van, I glimpsed the case containing the GPR — square, matte black, and in the style of mid-century Samsonite luggage, with rigid sides and hasps. Taped to the lid were two red vinyl strips bearing yellow letters: *Conquest*.

Although the three of us had met only once, we chatted easily. By the time we stopped for Mama Burgers, root beer, and rings, I'd learned that Blake's grandfather had made a name for himself crafting fishing lures and that Blake, an avid fisherman, was dating a woman he'd recently met online. John's wife excelled at Highland dancing.

I didn't need to thank John and Blake for making the journey to my parents' house. They clearly were excited by the prospect of a *Boys' Own* adventure, restless to begin the quest and exhilarated by the mere getting there after months of winter confinement in the office. As the mountains came into view, I talked of my father. The D-Day crossing and his ensuing reserves of anger and seasickness (he shunned even glass-bottom boats for the rest of his years). His love of kittens and fledgling birds. His obsessive collecting of seashells. How he boiled the whelks alive.

We reached the city just as the windows of the patisseries and *traiteurs* were beginning to glow in the half-light. Although I'd spoken to my mother the previous afternoon, I hadn't told her I was on the way. Largely without memory, she could recall being entrusted with something to remember even as the thing itself eluded her. To announce my visit in advance would produce not pleasure but anxiety and vexation.

"This is it, guys," I said, pointing to my favourite purveyor of cakes. "Your choice."

John and Blake hesitated before the twenty-odd cakes encased in glass, some Meissen yellow and others deepest magenta, some as dark and lustrous as resin — and like it, neither fully liquid nor solid — others scattered with gold dust.

"Too hard," said Blake.

John wandered towards the opposite end of the shop with its baskets of croissants, crusty and burnished from the oven. Summoning the server, he pointed to a brown heap.

"That one."

"Why that one?" I was taken aback by his choice.

"It's authentic."

We carried the boxed sweet back to the car. "John, do you know which cake you chose?"

"What do you mean?"

"It's the *galette des rois*, the cake with the buried treasure."

We were a week shy of Valentine's Day and long past Epiphany. This cake, a remembrance of the three wise men from the East who bore gifts for the infant Jesus, should have been retired towards the end of January. Before making their selection, John and Blake had never heard of the *galette des rois* nor its treasure — traditionally a small figurine in plastic or porcelain — enfolded in puff pastry and frangipane.

We drove the route to my mother's house, the *galette des rois* compliant on the back seat, and once inside began to unpack the GPR. Although the Conquest System rented for $197 per day, it didn't impress. Not at first glance. What John and Blake revealed when they popped open the worn case was an ordinary, if oversized, computer monitor. Given a choice between it and the single other object of value in the master bedroom, a lithograph of a resting fawn, I would have chosen the latter. It was never aging, whereas Conquest, I imagined, would soon be superannuated.

Flowers bloomed perpetually in the wallpaper of the bedroom, pale pink, taupe, and ivory flowers with neither foliage nor stems but centres the brown of dried autumn leaves. The décor revealed little about my parents. My mother had employed an interior designer to determine how the house should look and to negotiate costs with my father. Although endowed with a fine aesthetic sense (she was often asked by friends to design crocheted Kleenex box and toilet roll covers for their sons' bar mitzvahs), my mother suffered from indecision and lacked self-confidence.

In their fake bower, John and Blake began to lay X's in green painter's tape at intervals across the bedroom carpet. One by one they marked off the known but invisible triggers for a GPR or metal detector — joist hanger, junction box, pipes, pot lights.

Afterwards, Blake measured out twelve squares on the carpet, deftly marking the corners of each with painter's tape. Then he and John unfurled a clear plastic sheet overlaid with a grid of lines an inch apart. This grid, when placed over the squares marked with tape, would yield the exact coordinates of any hit. But only with the help of a scanner. John unpacked the three-foot black shaft attached to a mobile yellow box with a stubby black antenna to one side.

"All we need to do now," said John, "is connect this here scanner to the monitor and we're good to go."

"Done," Blake confirmed, retreating from the now-lit screen. In stocking feet, he stepped delicately onto the plastic sheeting and began to guide the scanner along Grid 1.

Song lines, laugh lines, clothes lines, lines of reasoning, lines in the sand. The lines before us qualified as none of these. Maybe, if we got lucky, trap lines. If less so, the end of the line.

John sat cross-legged in front of the monitor, surveying the images and manipulating the controls as Blake slowly traced each of the lines with the scanner. On the upper right of the monitor showed, in red, the grid number, and below it a representation of the grid itself, with numbers assigned to each line on the vertical and horizontal axes. The image on the left was as fluid as the other was rigid, as fugitive as the other was declarative. Here, John explained, we were looking into a cross-section of the floors and joist space that corresponded to a precise point on the adjoining grid.

The hardwood floor and subfloor I could recognize at the top of the image as the two dark bands set apart by a margin of light. Beneath these defining lines, the shapes appeared more amorphous, the blacks and whites confused in shades of grey.

"*This* may be a nail," John said, pointing to a sequence of thrusting broken lines, "and *this*," he motioned towards a blackness scattered with almost-familiar pale shapes, "is air."

I smiled politely. To me the near-crescents, stars, and oblongs evoked the small, frayed organisms of the deep sea — bioluminescent worms, krill, and jellyfish that together, in the depths of the ocean, radiated more light than the sun. They were beyond apprehension.

"Is this as clear a reading as we'll get?"

"Probably. It's all a matter of interpretation."

My father, into his eighties, recalled vividly the Second World War and especially his passage to England after his wounding on D-Day:

> When I got back ... I began to walk towards the ambulances, and one of the soldiers or the corporal said, You can't walk. ... you're a stretcher case. So I said, Look, I can walk; and he said, Sorry ... you'll have to get on the stretcher. So I got on the stretcher with my 65-pound pack and my revolver. ... they walked about three feet and one of the sides of the stretcher broke, and I landed on the ground. So I said to the fellow, If you don't mind, I'm going to walk.

For decades my father stored that revolver in the drawer of a wooden table in the unfinished basement. If while spring cleaning my mother had to touch it, she wore rubber gloves. My father had other more lasting relics of the war: athlete's foot, a scar on his lower right leg where he was hit by shrapnel while tending to a wounded comrade on Juno Beach, the ability to be content with very little, and self-reliance. The first three he kept for life; the last he lost at some untraceable juncture as dementia claimed him in his final years.

My mother was a stranger to shrapnel and occasionally knew contentment. After I left home, she came to believe happiness would be attainable only if she abandoned her house for a condominium. "I can't cope with this house anymore. I want to move," she told me continually, declaring herself to be ready for "easy living." She favoured a building with a multi-storey atrium festooned with climbers originating in subtropical broadleaf forest. My father, her husband, would hear none of it. Once he'd died and my mother occupied the house alone, she relinquished her interest in leaving, suddenly attributing her bouts of unhappiness to the loss of her husband and not her failed quest to live all on one level. In her waning years, she held fast to the house as a repository of beloved memories she could no longer remember.

Losses are rarely solitary. My mother had lost first her ambitions and later her recall of them, my father had lost his memory, and I in turn had lost my father and the memory of precisely where the treasure lay, *if* I'd ever possessed it in the first place — and here my own memory failed me. Now, having seen the indistinct images produced by the GPR, I wondered for the first time whether I'd lost the expectation of retrieving the treasure itself. And yet the hazy shapes were like incipient things. Promises. Hopes.

From downstairs I called my mother on the single phone still connected to the land line.

"Where are you?" she asked.

"Home." I was no longer sure whether this amounted to the truth or a lie.

"And where am I?"

"In your apartment."

"Does it matter if I know where I am?"

For the second time that evening, John, Blake, and I assembled around the bridge table in the kitchen. Here, too, the decorator had opted for a floral wallpaper in lieu of the more complex backdrop to my mother's early marriage — the one-time array of coffee and tea pots, flightless birds, bulrushes, open scissors, and a pocket watch stuck at three o'clock.

The team had news: The GPR was not going to yield instant results. Because the targets appeared so numerous and their silhouettes so elusive, the men would need to analyze the data in their office, disqualifying one by one the hits least likely to be coins or other non-ferrous objects. Whatever the findings, I knew I could disturb no more than several floorboards beyond those David had already raised and then repaired. Time, cost, and the integrity of the floor imposed that limit.

"I think we're ready now for that *galette des rois*," said John.

I cut a first slice of cake and peered inside. Both the upper and lower crusts were firm, while in the middle wisps of puff pastry and dollops of almond cream flanked pockets of air. I cut two more slices, like John and Blake scrutinizing each wedge for signs of treasure. We sighed. Apparently the *fève*, the treasure, lay undisturbed in the remaining half of the *galette des rois*. I handed round the plates.

"Mmmm." Blake was the first to take a bite.

"Yum!" said John.

"Ouch!" I'd crunched down on something hard — a fragment of tooth, a rogue filling, maybe a gobbet of plaster. Into a napkin I let slip the foreign object coated in saliva and frangipane.

"Wow!" Blake's voice radiated excitement. "This is no tooth. Look, it says *Pain de campagne*."

Porcelain or plaster, and no bigger than a quarter, here was a rounded country loaf, brown, with a shiny latticework top and a single triangular slice missing. To its right sprouted a blue-green wheat sheaf with a red poppy at the centre, and immediately above the loaf, in capital letters against a yellow ground, were the words Blake had uttered: in French, *pain de campagne*; in English, country bread.

"It can't be," I said.

"But it is," replied John. "It's an omen."

Closets are where we hide some of our most intimate things, what we don't want others to see. As a child I rarely ventured into my mother's closet, whereas my own, not merely a place for Barbie dolls and the complete Enid Blyton, doubled as my reading room. On the low shelf that served as my bench, I joined the boarders Pat and Isabel O'Sullivan in their antics at St. Clare's — thrashing opponents at lacrosse, fitting up apple-pie beds, being sent to Coventry. An only child, in my closet I became one of the multitudes.

My father aside, no men were ever admitted into my mother's wardrobe. This space was once the domain of the bespoke black brocade maxi coat and matching sleeveless gown, the smoke Perspex sandals with the red leather uppers, the *postiche* that gave my mother's beehive hairdo the thrust of a model skyscraper.

During my early childhood, my parents regularly attended cocktail parties, weddings, and bar mitzvahs designated "black tie." They left me at home in my puffin pyjamas, returning after midnight with morsels for my breakfast — bites of fruitcake or a chocolate mint in a crumpled napkin. From an agency, they employed mature single women to ensure I brushed my teeth and went to bed on time. Some of the caregivers were unnerving. One told me how she'd sleepwalked out of her burning house as a little girl, carrying a favourite desk that even a grown man would have struggled to raise off the ground.

In recent years the sitters had been hired for my mother, and her wardrobe now was filled with New Balance orthopaedic shoes and racks of faded housedresses all of a sameness. That the team of archaeologists would enter my mother's closet was preordained. Inside lay the only bit of bedroom floor still to be mapped, and David hadn't explored the joist space below. I opened the accordion door, motioning to John and Blake. "After you."

The space was compact, the task urgent, and John and Blake's time running out. I retreated to the kitchen, where I began to pack up my mother's crystal, bone china, and curios. Along with the ding of crystal and the clank of china could be heard the by-now-familiar clicks and whines upstairs. The GPR at work. Then, more unusually, a staccato. Steps. From the hall adjoining the bedroom. On the main staircase. In the downstairs hall. Thud — the kitchen door was flung open. Blake stood before me, half exultant, half restrained.

"I think we found something."

The two of us sprinted up the stairs and into the bedroom, where John was fingering a floorboard until now hidden beneath the shoe shelf in my mother's closet.

"See this bulge here?" said John.

I nodded.

"Feel."

Undeniably, something was pressing against the underside of the board.

"Did you get a reading from the metal detector?"

"Big time. What do you want to do?" John spoke the words, but both men looked at me expectantly.

The floorboard was in the closet. The closet floor in general was under carpet. This section of closet floor was beneath a shoe shelf. At issue was a single board.

"Let's go for it," I said.

John angled a hefty screwdriver against the swollen board and began chipping away at it with a hammer. We had neither a drill nor a wrench, no circular saw, level, or pliers.

"Shit!"

The wood had splintered under the pressure of his blows, breaking into slivers as sharp as shards of broken glass. A single nail, the upper half of its shaft driven flat into the pine sub-floor, now lay exposed.

Once again I heard David's words: "Was your father a joker?"

"I'm so sorry," John said to me. He turned to Blake. "We'd better start loading the car."

"Not to worry, I'll clean up after you go." To allow enough time to close up the house, I'd booked my return on a late train.

"Wait," I implored them. "Before you leave, you should have a memento of my father — a seashell." I led them into my father's office and to the aquariums where kissing gouramis once brushed up against angelfish, and guppies bore generations of transparent young that were all eyes and tail fins. From the arrangement of shells in the drained tanks, John chose a mollusc, Blake a tulip.

I waved the team off, collected a green plastic garbage bag from the garage, and made my way back to my mother's closet. Gingerly, I began to pick up the shards of wood, taking care not to draw blood.

$\longleftarrow$

Illness shows no hesitation, not even illness that ravages memory. It needs no reminder, proceeding with certainty to its next move.

On my way to the train station, I stopped briefly at my mother's apartment. She wore what I'd come to consider her uniform: brown trousers with an elastic waistband, one of two pink polyester shirts, and a cardigan. She seemed more tired than usual. As I prepared to leave, she followed me to the door. "Where are you going now, to Granny's?" Her mother, my grandmother, had been dead for more than twenty years.

Eighty years earlier, my grandparents had returned home from the hospital with a bundle, my mother, eight weeks premature. When the doctors judged the baby had grown enough in an incubator, they released her to my grandparents, who placed her in an apple basket on their kitchen table and hoped for the best. My grandfather had nervous hands. He dropped the baby on her head. The year was 1932, and my grandfather, residing in Montreal, the Canadian city most ravaged by the Great Depression, had recently lost his prized Chevrolet. He hoped for the best. A second daughter, Carol, born six years later, was carried to term.

For the moment I was unsure of what happened next. My father's charge to me had become an obsessive one, undermining my attention to my work as an editor, my willingness to poach eggs or Dustbust. Visions of coins, joist hangers, incisions in floorboards, messages in an unsteady hand continued to impose themselves upon me, especially at the threshold of sleep. In a last-ditch attempt to find a way to recover my father's confidences, I googled "hoards *and* memory." The results directed me exclusively to sites about birds and their food caches: Woodpeckers, shrikes, titmice. Pine nuts, peanuts, acorns. My father wasn't of that ilk. Whatever he'd buried, it was old and not perishable.

My husband often remained at home during my excavations in Montreal, tasked with caring for our cat and hindered from travel by the demands of his profession. Although supportive, he understandably didn't share my obsession and was beginning to lose faith in the enterprise. I had to regroup, replace the pursuit of treasure with another obsession — any obsession — that would subdue unbidden thoughts about my mother's forced departure from her home.

Snow came every day now, mostly flurries — and no thaw, not for days. Not always, but often, I thought of the empty house enfolded by winter. More often I dreamt about it. Dreams strewn with sea urchins, marionettes with red aprons, crystal decanters, pitchforks, cheese bells, torn paper patterned with notes.

To occupy myself, I began making my way through a yellow box of old buttons that originated with a cousin's spinster aunt. Rhinestone and Bakelite. Plastic and rubber. Years ago, when settling her aunt's estate, my cousin had procured the buttons for me, a child collector. My mother had introduced me to the hobby so I'd be occupied while she pursued her own "antiquing." In their favour, buttons generally were hygienic — unlike chamber pots — and took up little space. My parents never conceived of the collecting as a child's pursuit. I was permitted to own buttons that had belonged to courtesans or even an officer in the Nazi guard. I quickly outgrew my hobby, and the buttons sat for decades in my mother's cedar closet until I excised my mother from her house. Soon after, I moved the collection to my own home and my own closet.

For nine days I dismissed all ideas of treasure, concentrating on nothing but buttons. On the tenth day, John and Blake summoned me to their office, where they handed me a twelve-page report, "Ground Penetrating Radar and Metal Detector Survey." Privately they referred to the exercise as "John and Blake's Excellent Adventure." The document contained, among other things, nine pages of slice-depth and cross-section images generated by the GPR, plus one certainty.

It can be stated with confidence that no objects of greater than 2 cm in size can be located within the floor boards; and any hidden objects of that size were previously removed.

The best bet by far remained Grid 13. My mother's closet.

The false target was located in the closet space, in Grid 13. . . . However, the space under the middle floor board was not fully investigated due to the need to preserve the integrity of the floor.

I remember little of the second trip with David, my carpenter friend. It was midwinter, when travel is better postponed. Before I boarded the train to join David in Montreal, leaving my husband once again in the company of the cat, I couldn't help asking him the obvious. "Do you think I'll find the treasure?"

"To be honest, not really."

"Why not?"

He shrugged. "Just an instinct."

Almost everything I'd valued in the Christmas trip — fine food, wine, jokes, anticipation — had fallen away. All that survived was my purpose.

That night, David raised a few more floorboards. The outcomes were too familiar — a misshapen nail, a nail with a larger than usual head, nothing. I was in no hurry for the certainty the morning would bring, for David planned after breakfast to cut into the subfloor below the middle board in Grid 13, my mother's closet, the final and most suggestive of targets.

That morning I decided to absent myself. While I made a quick visit to my mother, David would undertake the excavation alone.

"Do I still have another place? The house?" my mother asked by way of greeting.

"Yes."

On the round glass table by my mother's TV, four carved wooden figures from the Windward Islands, two women balancing loads on their heads and two men in the throes of the dance, lay on their sides, inert. I could rely always on finding them thus. Such was my mother's practice, the fulfillment of her energy.

When I returned to the house, David stood in the front hall, his face impassive. "Come upstairs, will you," he said. "Have a look."

He'd opened up a section of the joist space about eighteen inches by eighteen inches. As always, his cuts were deft and his tools arranged neatly, with a compact hammer to one side of the incision and a cluster of nails and a trowel to the other. The space revealed was unlike any already seen. About eight inches down, underneath the middle floorboard and between planks in the subfloor, could be glimpsed a secure nook — just big enough to contain gold bars or a bundle of coins.

David stood by with his legs apart and his arms folded. "I reckon something could have been in there. But if it was, it's not there anymore."

I'd told few people about the treasure. Those in the know harboured an abundance of theories. The treasure had been stolen, most probably by a workman when the bedroom carpet was replaced and pot lights installed in the den ceiling. My father, anticipating the possibility of theft, had removed the treasure in advance of the 1980s renovation. My father had removed the treasure even longer ago, once the fear of invasion by the enemy had abated. Decades later, in his old age, his mind addled, my father had remembered his burying of the treasure but not his retrieval of it. The note he left in the safe deposit box was an expired truth — a non-deliberate lie. Or there never was any treasure. My father was a joker.

"What now?" I asked my husband upon returning home. I was spent — and broke.

He considered. "Finding the treasure would have been the better outcome, but this is the better story."

I was inconsolable. Yet I now possessed one thing, the certainty I hadn't found the treasure, and in this, in a small and far less commanding way, I was not unlike my father as he stood on the shore before the D-Day crossing. "Look, if I got killed, I got killed," he said some fifty years later as he recalled steeling himself for the battlefields that lay ahead. He had accepted the certainty of not knowing what awaited him on the other side.

My mother, for her part, moved from one day to the next in a perpetual state of unknowing. Although, when required to by the geriatrician, she could spell *world* backwards and convene the hands of a clock at precisely ten to three, she mistook spring for winter and 2012 for 2002. But the gift of her memory loss meant that none of this mattered. Much of the time she felt at home in her uncertainty. If I didn't aim to join my mother in her overall state, I could at least aspire to this single rare attribute.

There was one more uncertainty I had to endure — that my father had retrieved the treasure and I, with no means of recognizing it, had possessed it all along.

CHAPTER TWO

Lantern Slides

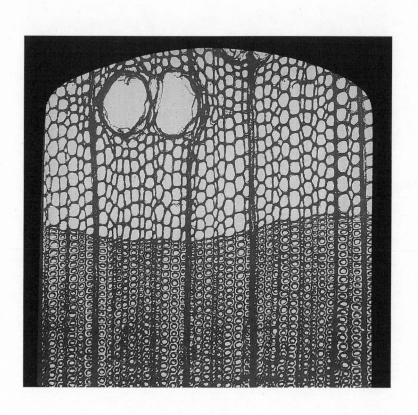

THERE HAD BEEN COMFORT IN FOLLOWING MY FATHER'S POST-
humous directives to excavate treasure, rendering me once
more the child with a parent in command. Now, as I was prim-
ing the family home for sale, I was learning to submit to the
revelations of the house itself — the obsolete devices, spattered
photographs, postcards, and first editions my parents had chosen not to forfeit but to conceal. While the days tentatively
grew longer and my mother gradually was vanishing from my
life, her house was delivering to me through its objects a family
I'd never known. Not least among them was Simon Kirsch, my
paternal grandfather, a Lithuanian-born Yiddish speaker who
immigrated to Canada in 1890, aged six, later to distinguish
himself as an expert in a fern called common bracken.

My father remembered his father through a decision and an
achievement, neither of which was enacted when my father
would have been present or old enough to remember it first-
hand. All the same, my father periodically reminded me of
how Simon had picked the site of the Jewish General Hospital
in Montreal, how he was appointed one of the first Jewish faculty members at McGill University. The criticisms my father

withheld from his father he too often unleashed on my mother, who in turn berated the father-in-law she never knew.

My mother [to me]: "Simon was a dictator, a little Napoleon. Beware of short men."

My father [to me]: "My father used to take us boys out shopping. He always bought wholesale. We didn't buy one chicken. We bought a dozen. Not two tins of tomatoes. Twenty-two."

Eddie, Simon's eldest son [to my father]: "Simon wasn't so great."

My father [to no one in particular]: "He was a brilliant man."

My aunt [to my father upbraiding my mother]: "Stop acting like Simon."

And so, in exploring my grandfather's life, my starting points involved a handful of pronouncements now ten, twenty, thirty years old, together with the objects I recovered from the shelves in my parents' basement — the lantern slides and optical microscope, my grandfather's instruments of light. Both perhaps still bore Simon's fingerprints. But if traces of my grandfather's papillary terrain survived, a compendium of fats, loose skin cells, and sweat, I lacked the means to see them. As when excavating my parents' house for buried treasure, I was engaged in an act of retrieval. This time, however, I wasn't searching for objects, which I already possessed, but for how they elucidated their owner and might inform his past.

The decision to undertake the searches was mine, my activities unauthorized by either my parents or my objects of study.

Simon's belongings had come into my possession haphazardly, because my father had retrieved them from *his* parents' house. The microscope once belonging to my grandfather was stored, for now, in this house destined to change owners, with a vendor, my mother, who could recall neither the existence of the said apparatus nor its lineage. Without a doubt my grandfather would have appreciated the irony in his single unrealized grandchild becoming his accidental heir. Born eleven years after his death, I'd counted as nothing for my paternal grandfather, not even an expectation.

t⁓

"Don't touch that!" No matter that my mother was languishing a couple of miles away in assisted living, I could hear her nonetheless as I reached for the microscope. Whereas the basement — the location of the microscope — in some ways had evaded the careful scrutiny my mother applied to the upper floors of the house, it remained the space, too, where she'd enacted some of her most cherished rituals: those of cleanliness and decontamination.

Late each night, from my teen years, my mother made her way down the six unfinished wooden steps with minuscule loads of laundry in a red plastic basket simulating wicker. She paid no heed to the photographs of her parents laid out on my father's old wooden desk, nor did she pause to study my childhood artwork on the walls — the trumpet in yellow Bristol board dotted with black glitter or the silhouette of a horse in fragments of broken eggshell. Instead, my mother headed straight into the laundry room, donning the appropriate pair of rubber gloves for her soiled quarter load before delivering it into the capacious washing machine.

As the garments were churning, my mother, in backless white terry cloth slippers, retreated to the den. There,

ensconced in a white plastic garden chair with a padded cush-
ion, she watched the late-night news: announcements of road
closures, purse snatchings, car thefts, near-death experiences
of cats stranded up telephone poles. She found the coverage
of horrors and calamities strangely tranquilizing, as she did
the progress of the garments through the washing cycle, but
if my father or I ever ventured to touch anything in the laundry room — the array of carefully assigned rags or the clothing
hangers suspended from a hot-water pipe — my mother never
faltered in her response. "No!" For my mother, panic could be
induced by an insult as slight as her own spouse or child touching an undergarment fresh out of the spin dryer. It wasn't until
I began dismantling the basement that I became aware of how
this space most burdened by exposed and buried memories
also was the one where my mother's most intense cleansing
rituals occurred.

As I overrode the sense of prohibition honed over decades,
daring to examine my grandfather's microscope, I was confronted with opaque surfaces — the blackness of the horse-
shoe-shaped metal base, the array of notched brass dials and
cylinders like the mechanism of an elaborate clock. The device
possessed a reflector mirror in which I could see nothing but
my finger, and a glass eyepiece through which I could see nothing at all. When I slipped my fingers through the handle, it was
cool to the touch.

The microscope came as a surprise, the lantern slides less so.
Decades before, when the man who would become my husband first visited my parents' house, my mother retrieved the
slides for him. Quite rightly, she supposed they would intrigue
this British-born landscape architect and historian of plants.
The three of us gathered in the basement — always the basement — my mother in one of her faded pastel housedresses,
my boyfriend and I in T-shirts and jeans. Then she located the

box of slides in the laundry room, in the same table in which my father kept his revolver wrapped in decommissioned boxer shorts. His stash, her territory. We glanced at only a few slides, each one a glass plate imprinted with a positive image overlaid with a glass cover, each slide a perfect square edged with black tape. One depicted an embryonic plant with a single seed leaf, the others abstract patterns seemingly alien to any living organism. A rectangle of paper, black and unmarked — a paper mask — filled the empty space within the frame to either side of each imprint.

I later understood the ink impressions were designed to reveal themselves fully by means of a magic lantern, a wooden box with a flame chamber and a condensing lens to concentrate the kerosene light on each slide. But none of us would grasp that day how a microscope, with all its powers of magnification, could lack the capacity to elucidate these images. Instead, untroubled by speculation, we went away and ate egg foo yung.

My father didn't join us in the basement that day, and I don't recall him ever showing me his father's objects. He conveyed his father's legacy in other ways, by subscribing to *National Geographic* magazine and remarking upon how deftly the squirrels buried nuts on the ninth hole at the golf course; by presenting me with a kitten when I turned five — the runt of the litter. The kitten, my father, and I lay on my parents' bed watching Mutual of Omaha's *Wild Kingdom*, my father invariably in floppy boxer shorts, his fitted grey socks the only suggestion of his weekday identity as a physician. My mother deplored our watching TV in the bedroom and feared my father would impart his bad habit to me, which he didn't. Still, whether through teaching or heredity, he left me with a responsiveness to the natural world so strong that it continues to overwhelm almost every other impulse.

I wasn't sure I'd be able to recover my grandfather's slides until I held both boxes in my hands. My father had been dead for more than a decade, and the slides no longer lay in the drawer from which my mother had retrieved them with such confidence in her powers of recall. But on the back shelves in the basement, during the fiercest snow squall of winter, I found them, my grandfather's legacy in glass.

The first of the boxes had a broken clasp. Inside were arranged fifty or so slides, all botanically themed and some depicting non-native species. The Engelmann spruce, for example, was a tree of high altitudes common to western North America. Other species, though familiar, concealed their own personal dramas — like the red pine, which may have suffered a near extinction in its recent genetic history. But whether exotic or indigenous, the slides manufactured by my grandfather rendered the familiar unrecognizable to any other than an expert gaze, and certainly to his own granddaughter. Dissected and radically enlarged, segments of fibre, bark, and stem were reduced to vertical and horizontal lines, some undulating, others straight, some sequences uninterrupted, others perforated by lacunae.

To my inexpert eye, Engelmann Spruce, slide 3219, was a fine mesh lightly torn, a screen door punctured by cats' claws. Slide 2297, Fibres of the Oak, a canoe with thwarts. Balsam Fir, magnification unknown, the cascading beaded backdrop of a painting by Gustav Klimt. Red Pine X 25, a cardiogram. Simon, as my father called his father, had assimilated the teachings of his mentor at McGill University, Professor David Pearce Penhallow: "Internal structures must always have precedence over those of external morphology in questions of classification." My father's father was a student of concealed minutiae.

Until that moment in my parents' basement, when, by default, I became the custodian and accidental heir of Simon's possessions, I'd thought little about the grandfather I never knew. And yet my parents had appointed me his namesake: Sharon, akin to Shimon, my grandfather's Hebrew name. It was a popular name of the era. At school, to distinguish one Sharon from the next, our French teachers resorted to calling us by our surnames, so that I became Kirsch — in their pronunciation, *Keersh.* That the family name originally took the form of Kirz I didn't discover for almost a half century. In spite of my grandfather's accomplishments as a community leader, a developer, and a scientist, he remained largely invisible throughout my childhood — almost as invisible as if he'd never lived. Or as if his life had been curtailed.

The latter undoubtedly would have been Simon's fate if he'd remained in Lithuania. As Dan Jacobson observes in *Heshel's Kingdom,* during the Nazi occupation, "in towns and villages scattered all over Lithuania, a country roughly the size of Ireland, 600 years of Jewish life were brought to an end over a period of ten weeks only."

Simon's native town, Vilkomir — thought to mean *she-wolf* — was during his boyhood 55 percent Jewish. Even so, by the end of my grandfather's lifetime, the Jews of Vilkomir had been rendered invisible. In the woods of spruce and pine, the Nazis shot them and other undesirables in the head, then burned their bodies and buried their remains. Had Simon Kirz stayed in Lithuania, he'd have been murdered in the shelter of the trees that became his life's work.

My mother had shifted her preference from orchids to cyclamen. In her several rooms of half-closed blinds, grip bars, and soft food on trays, they presented as the only organism capable of photosynthesis. Whenever I came to visit, which I did every day or two for my mother's reassurance and as a respite from toiling in the house, I disturbed the soil to ensure adequate moisture.

"I don't want this," my mother said to no one in particular, meaning not the cyclamen but the indistinct fish on her plate. I set the new plant, a white one, in a saucer of water.

"She's excited because you're here," said Darlene, my mother's helper. "Usually she eats everything."

That it was dinnertime held no imperative for my mother. She now occupied her own time zone, in the way my grandfather had given himself over to geological time. In 1902, Simon, the son of a jobber, had secluded himself in McGill's Redpath Museum, with its herbarium of plant specimens, paleontological collections, and hall of rocks and minerals. There he examined desiccated ferns and their fossil antecedents. Later he engaged in prospecting and left behind an array of rocks as opaque as the lantern slides were transparent. These, too, had come into my possession.

$$t \longrightarrow$$

"Here's what we've got for you," the archivist said to me too cheerfully. I was sitting opposite the museum in the McGill library building where I'd composed my undergraduate thesis on *Pearl*, a Middle English poem that begins with the narrator's loss of a precious gem worthy of a prince, followed by his immersion in a dream world where he chances to recover the peerless treasure.

The archivist set down before me all she'd found on Simon Kirsch: a 1907–08 annual calendar the colour of green beans, and the registrar's copy of the 1910 convocation booklet.

Sensing my disappointment, she said, "We don't always have complete records for your grandfather's era. It's pretty early." I couldn't disagree. Nineteen hundred and six, Simon's graduating year, coincided with the era when Einstein introduced his theory of relativity.

The calendar and booklet yielded little of interest about Simon. Only as I was preparing to leave did I notice a shelf of *Old McGill* yearbooks behind the table at which I'd been seated. I had seen other photos of my grandfather, always black and white, but none so early as this 1906 graduation portrait. Whereas in later years the face appears angular, even Russian in cast, and the eyes defiant, alert in the way of a fox or vole, here Simon Kirsch merely looks sleepy. His brows are heavy; his hair, parted in the middle, is wavy and thick with two intricate coils, like snails' shells, stranded to either side of his forehead. The recent graduate has neat ears that would never be the butt of jokes, a full mouth with just a trace of a smile.

The same volume, under "Arts' Scalps," featured a pronouncement on my grandfather by his fellow graduates. It began with a desecration of his name — not Simon Kirsh but "Simon Halftone Kirsh, the 'terrible Armenian'" — then went on to celebrate Simon's prank at the freshies skating party. His voluntary soaking by several "gentleman waiters," his inevitable reprimand before the authorities. "O that he had been massacred," lamented the scribes of *Old McGill*, concluding with the observation, "Daffy's leading characteristics are his assurance and grin. He would look well under a descending pile driver."

Simon's was an imperfect encomium. A peer of Lewises and McLeods, Daffy gained notoriety as a stranger in their midst, a boy of exotic origins, in their estimation neither black nor white — a government document later described his complexion as "swarthy" — from a country renowned for its abundance of storks. In the same yearbook he countered the teasing with a motto of his own, designating himself "One of nature's living jokes."

Nevertheless, while the "terrible Armenian" was impersonating a fool, Simon Kirsch was pursuing "herbarium work and the systematic study of the seed plants with reference to the determination of species, their environment and mutual relations." In his spare time, he served as staff secretary of the Jewish Free School with an enrolment of seven hundred.

As I left the archives, I turned towards the mountain behind, where the once-crystalline anatomy of the leafless trees now was misted by snow. Simon had collected specimens into the cold season, ferns and flowering plants in the neighbourhood of Montreal. My grandfather might be irretrievable, but his objects of study survived up there on the mountain, in frozen groves where woodpeckers tapped relentlessly for the insects they knew to be alive beneath the concealing bark.

Methodically I persisted in ordering the finds in my mother's house, my attention now on photos. When I returned from the archives, I reviewed the few pictures of my grandfather in my possession. Simon at the ground-breaking ceremony for the Jewish General Hospital, a short man barely discernible beneath a top hat. Simon at Old Orchard Beach, still muscular and in a one-piece bathing costume, with the first of his grandchildren between his spread legs. Simon at the annual meeting of the Federation of Jewish Philanthropies, a man in a suit among other men in suits, writing busily. Simon grown old, a wraith of a man, fleshy only in the middle, with a leather belt wound twice around his waist to hold up his draping trousers. Always he appears middle-aged or older and in company, defined by kinship or position. Always he sports a moustache. Rarely, in public, is he without a tie. His attire, most often a suit, is invariably black and white. The photos themselves are black and white.

There can be no doubt, however, that Simon Kirz, born, by his own account, in late November or early December, the near-darkest days of the year, originated in colour — in the saturated blues of the rivers and greens of the larch and pine he renounced in the Baltic. *Vald*, he would have called those woods, or perhaps *les*, if his family were among the quarter of Jews in the Pale of Settlement versed in Russian as well as Yiddish. He would already have been in command of those words at age six, when he could first distinguish day from night and his left hand from his right and became capable of thinking about the future.

In Hebrew, Shimon means "heard." I was listening to my grandfather, listening hard, but through the medium of sight, not sound, for he'd ostensibly left behind almost nothing personal in the way of words spoken aloud or even those silently articulated on paper.

"Stop being so goddamn verbose," my father would too often say to my mother, for whom life's minutiae — the depth of chartreuse in a damask dress, the extent to which curtains should be drawn to admit the light — were endlessly compelling. My father's distaste for elaboration, this economy of words, originated perhaps in his father. I have only one letter authored by Simon, but it bears witness to his deliberateness of speech:

> *My great and good friend:*
> *It has been my good fortune in the early days of my life to have associated with a man of your caliber, and now in the autumn of my life I am about to consolidate my position so that the fruits of my labour for many years past can be allocated to my heirs.*

Amidst the assets that I value most is your friendship and I find that there is also a bill which has been outstanding for a great number of years . . .

The letter is dated March 18, 1947. I found it among the folders assembled by Simon's executors, a yellowing paper, soft around the edges from handling, with defiant black type that asks more than it answers.

⟵

My search for my grandfather had begun with a loss and an acquisition, my mother's removal to assisted living and the retrieval of the microscope and lantern slides months before her house was to be opened up for sale. Although the winter solstice had passed, this arguably counted as the darkest time of the year. The Christmas illuminations were gone, the silhouettes of trees strung with lights no longer visible in other people's houses. My mother had liked nothing better than to trawl the darkened streets in her car, looking for evidence of Christmas. Floodlit snowmen garnished with tinsel. Luminous fat plastic Santas. On these excursions she'd spoken little, her lips settled into a relaxed smile. Now she spoke only in response to questions and during interludes between sleep.

"You're feeling all right?"

"Yes."

"You've had enough supper?"

"Yes."

"You'll watch some TV now?"

"Yes."

I didn't think to ask my mother about Simon's microscope and lantern slides, nor did I tell her I'd retrieved them. Whether I had a claim as their rightful owner, a mere custodian, or their legitimate heir, I couldn't have said. But it didn't take me long to discover the irony of my grandfather's unknowing gift — that these objects made of glass were not transparent.

Though undeniably my grandfather's own flesh and blood, his namesake, I needed another, an outsider, to interpret his belongings. For this purpose I'd have to suspend work in my mother's house and return briefly to my own city. There I'd arranged to consult with Dr. Suttie, an antiquarian and a retired academic, a guide with careful fingers and a well-disciplined dog.

"Come this way." Dr. Suttie pointed to a flight of stairs leading to his basement as the dog hovered above ground. We entered a room lined floor to ceiling with leather-bound books, their spines engraved with gilt lettering. More books and manuals were stacked on the floor, and not a corner of the central table was exposed, so dense was it with files and the accessories for old microscopes. Black boxes for the even distribution of light. Tin cans concealing lenses. Bottles of brown translucent glass with medicinal-like droppers.

Dr. Suttie shoved some folders aside. "Now, let's see what you've got."

"Ah, it's a Jug Handle." He eased the microscope from its mahogany case. "This is a good-quality general science microscope," he continued, "used in histology among other fields."

"Histology — that was one of my grandfather's areas of interest." In preparing himself for the study of plants, Simon had enrolled in courses on anatomy and the microscopic dissection of tissues.

"Well, that makes sense, then. Your grandfather's Jug Handle was produced by Bausch & Lomb."

"How old would this microscope be?"

"If your instrument has a number ..." — he pulled out a magnifying glass — "we can look it up." I glanced over his shoulder as he read aloud. "One-four-eight-seven-eight-eight." Dr. Suttie plucked a volume from one of his shelves, undeterred by the hundreds of others surrounding it. "Ah yes, the year of production would have been 1919, maybe 1920."

The microscope dated from my grandfather's final years in academe, when already he must have been pondering a shift to real estate, a turning away from the advancement of knowledge to the development of land.

Dr. Suttie smiled encouragingly. "And now you ask me some questions, and I'll answer. I'm a believer in the Socratic Method."

"Can we look at the parts and how they work?"

First came the oculars, or eyepieces, in size and shape like rolls of old Kodak film, but with silver, not yellow, surrounds and glass peepholes at the top. "See that?" said Dr. Suttie, indicating that I should look through the eyepiece. "Your ocular has a pointer in it. That's an extra beyond the basic model." The eyepiece flowed into the cylindrical extension tube that determined length of focus. Next came the nosepiece, the dull silver disc that held in place three objectives, or lenses. These were suspended over a square of black metal — the "stage," Dr. Suttie called it — with two moveable clips to secure the glass slides.

"I'm going to fetch a light box," said Dr. Suttie, returning with a small black box resembling a miniature TV set. "If this doesn't work, I have another one. If not, you can see a grown man cry."

For several minutes he tinkered with purpose. As the box cast an even light over the microscope, we prepared to examine a micrometer slide, among the easiest of the period slides to see.

Magnifying through the larger and middle objectives was relatively simple, through the smallest of the three — perversely, the most high-powered — less so. Without droplets of balsam oil applied to the glass slide beneath it, the smallest objective would reveal nothing. Dr. Suttie reached for one of the translucent brown bottles, unscrewed the top, positioned the dropper over the slide, and squeezed. Once. Twice. Three times. Then he touched his nose to the sleek rim of the open bottle. "It smells like the forest after rain."

The slide we were about to view was rectangular, the width of an average Band-Aid. At Dr. Suttie's urging I put my eye to the ocular. The micrometer slide consisted of a minuscule ruler, each notch and corresponding value bold and uncompromising. It disclosed everything about the power of the microscope, nothing about my grandfather.

I began to gather up my belongings.

"Ah, now here's something of interest," said Dr. Suttie, lifting a metal wheel from a vertical slot in one of the trays. The wheel was the size of a silver dollar, the thickness of a paper doll. "This is a 'spot,' and it's not a common accessory for a microscope. It fits into the condenser to make the light oblique."

"I don't understand."

"It provides indirect lighting, or a dark field. It's useful for viewing small living organisms."

"You mean animals?"

"Perhaps."

As I prepared to leave, the silvery light outside was slipping away, the darkness leaching in. In the basement, the light had been uniform; clues to the time of day, none. I beckoned to the dog, who nuzzled me with her moist dark nose, then bestowed a parting slobber. Dr. Suttie grinned. "She's never met a human she didn't love."

I grew up with specimens. In the plastic drawer in the fridge where most households stored cold cuts and Kraft Singles Cheese Slices, my father kept vials of urine and coagulated blood, samples he extracted from patients who came to his home office. My mother, for whom even a worm casting in the cold storage represented a threat to hygiene, became oddly relaxed about the fluids of strangers in her fridge.

The specimen plants my grandfather might have viewed under his microscope would have been more benign, but only lantern slides — no slides for microscopes — had survived among the few boxes retrieved from my parents' basement. With no diary belonging to my grandfather, no letters nor even working papers, my only hope was to recover a more public treatise, and in midwinter, alone in my mother's house, the windows taut with frost, I found my opportunity. A quick Google search located my grandfather's master's thesis, communicated before the Royal Society by Professor D.P. Penhallow on May 15, 1907. Two double-clicks and the thesis downloaded without hesitation.

On the Development and Function of Certain Structures in the Stipe and Rhizome of Pteris Aquilina *and Other Pteridophytes* was foreboding, the title a succession of multisyllabic words, Greek and Latin in provenance. But as I skimmed the pages, I understood that the tangibles underlying the research, stripped of the embellishments of language, were primary. Simon was writing about ferns, among the most ancient of plants. The sensitive fern. The royal fern. Common bracken. Things that could scratch, change colour, obscure your way. Things that arose in swamps and fens, along the damp borders of streams, on sandy hillsides and in open woodland. The spring specimens, gathered on May 29, 1899, belonged to the collections of

Simon's mentor, Professor Penhallow. The autumn ones dated from 1906 and had been gathered by Simon himself as the first frosts were setting in. The stipes, or stems, of the smaller ferns had already wilted or were easily ruptured, so Simon took as his samples ferns with stipes of vigorous growth. Upon returning to the lab, he preserved his specimens in 5 percent formaline and sectioned them by means of the freezing microtome. Then he coloured them, his fingers stained with Bismarck Brown.

From the outset, the basis for Simon's research was an irregularity. In his study of ferns at the McGill laboratory, Dr. Penhallow had noted patches of large, anomalous cells in the vascular bundles — the conducting vessels, in this instance, in the stem — of common bracken. He needed a promising young scientist to investigate.

Bracken is among the toughest of ferns and, with its reservoir of root-like stems snaking below ground, a first colonizer after fire. Its generous fronds shelter field mice and rabbits from foxes and sharp-clawed kestrels. Indigenous peoples draped it over their heads to repel black fly. For Simon, my grandfather, the draw of *Pteris aquilina* lay elsewhere — in the fern's secret commerce with itself, the canals piercing its vascular bundles and the outgrowths choking the canals, made real only through the objective of a microscope, magnified two hundred, two hundred and thirty times. It was an unlikely preoccupation for the son of a peddler.

In Dr. Penhallow, however, Simon found a guide who'd ranged widely in places little known and barely attainable. From 1876, several years before the birth of Simon Kirz, David Pearce Penhallow had served as professor of botany and chemistry at the Imperial College of Agriculture in Sapporo, Japan, on the mountain island of Hokkaido. When on leave from teaching, he'd lived among the aboriginal Ainu, the first Westerner ever to do so. Three decades later, no longer young and several years away from a nervous collapse, Professor Penhallow shared his microphotographs of ferns with a young Jewish student from Lithuania. They were reproduced, enlarged, in my grandfather's MA thesis. Beside them Simon hand-printed the corresponding names of the fern anatomy in a serif font, each of the many capital and small letters perfectly uniform in size. C for "Intercellular canal or remnants of it." *Sp.tr.* for "Disorganised spiral tracheids of the protoxylem." *Th.* for "Thyloses."

Two photographs appeared on every page, always circular and depicting a black-and-white section of a stipe, outgrowth, or vascular bundle. As with the lantern slides, I found it easier to understand the images by what they were not. The very young stipe of the king fern, *Todea barbara*, the full moon mottled with patches of light and dark. The stipe of the royal fern, *Osmunda regalis*, insects no bigger than pin heads swarming in crescent formation. Other microphotographs resembled X-rays of teeth.

$t \longrightarrow$

While my obsession with Simon was prompting me to cultivate a close focus, for my mother, observation was losing its appeal. In the past she never hesitated to tell me "You need a haircut" or "Without lipstick, you look like you're asleep." Now, however, if she'd ceased to appraise me, equally she shunned visual stimulation. On a recent expedition to Gibbys Restaurant in Old Montreal, where my mother for years had devoured the garlic salad and grilled scampi, she repeatedly squeezed her eyes shut, daunted by the glint of jewellery and elbowing of waiters, the brazen red of lobster claws and insistent flickering of candles. "I want to go home," she implored before having finished her meal. An out-of-town friend who accompanied us to dinner said to me afterwards, "Mum's sweet." But this didn't seem to be "Mum" as I'd ever known her.

From now on my cold-weather interactions with my mother would take place either in her apartment or at a doctor's office. Meanwhile, my own focus was narrowing as whatever time was not absorbed by my mother I invariably spent thinking about Simon and his study of irregularities.

For me to follow the intricacies of my grandfather's argument proved impossible. But although denied the details, I could grasp the essence — or so I believed. In the blackness of midwinter, my computer monitor a reliable source of light, I read.

First came Simon's statement of purpose: to discuss "the formation of a more or less regular canal in the vascular bundle" and a "more or less complete blocking up of this canal by outgrowths ... found in many trees and grasses ... and which have also been described for some fossil Pteridophyta."

In living ferns the outgrowths were thought not to occur. But my father's father, by examining the concealed minutiae in the stems and rhizomes of common bracken and other ferns, vied to disprove this belief. He examined all the phases of development of common bracken and then its petrified imprint from the Carboniferous and other ages. Considering the outgrowths, or thyloses, within the expanse of time, as well as close up under the microscope, Simon concluded, "different appearances at different levels represent consecutive stages of the same structure."

I'd been surprised on my visit to the McGill archives to learn that my grandfather had been awarded a prize in moral philosophy. And yet the methodology informing Simon's thesis was prescriptive. From it I could deduce a philosophy of ways of seeing, a belief that underlying the study of irregularities prevailed a system of norms:

- Consider all stages of the life cycle.
- Never dismiss minutiae. The smallest section may enable understanding of the whole.
- Recognize that like structures may differ in outward appearance.
- Practise a close focus. Look beyond what can be seen with the naked eye.
- Examine the individual within the context of the group, both species and genus.
- Take into account the ancestral past.

For Simon, such tenets led to identifying not only the presence of thyloses throughout the lifespan of common bracken, but also their purpose: "For, it has been clearly proven, that thylose formation is essentially only a disposition on the part of the plant to restore a disturbed equilibrium, the activity ceasing as soon as the equilibrium is obtained." Put simply, the structures afforded a means of closing wounds.

Dr. Penhallow's origins were in the cattail marshes of the Maine coast, where plovers skittered through tidal pools and sea spray hung generously in the air. In October 1909, while Simon was completing his PhD thesis on *The Origin and Development of Resin Canals in the Coniferae*, David Penhallow began to suffer from a nervous disorder. His death, in October 1910 on the *Lake Manitoba* crossing from Montreal to Liverpool, took place at sea. The sudden loss of his mentor marked the second of several ruptures in Simon Kirsch's life, along with the exit from Lithuania; the forthcoming death of Abraham, his natural father; and his eventual renouncement of academe.

Someone, possibly my grandfather, wrote of the vanished botanist, "History, whether written upon the rocks or buried in forgotten volumes, was particularly attractive to Professor Penhallow." Through his work, Simon upheld his mentor's valuing of the past. In his external life he kept moving forward. Within a year of the professor's death, Simon had relocated to Madison, Wisconsin, suddenly an expert with the U.S. Forest Service, a husband, and a father to a son.

Coinciding with the onset of Professor Penhallow's illness, Simon had become engaged to Malca Cossman, a Russian-Jewish orphan two years his junior. She furnished the fat to his leanness — no taller than he, a woman of ample breasts, a solemn face, and full lips with a penchant for dresses of striped silk, feather boas, and hats augmented by the mating plumage of snowy egrets. In between their marriage ceremony and the move to Wisconsin, the newlyweds honeymooned in the Western states — a luxury that distinguished them from their peers, for whom a honeymoon typically amounted to no more than a few hours in Montreal's Dominion Park.

Lithuania is a country of pine trees, of arid sandy forests where, in June, toothless peasant women gather wild strawberries among the pliant needles on the forest floor. Spruce and birch are also known, but not redwoods. The redwood, *Sequoia sempervirens*, surely accounted for Simon's choice of the Western states for his and Malca's honeymoon. From the start, he led, she followed — a pattern that reasserted itself throughout their lives as evidenced by photographs, Simon up front, Malca in the rear, he defiant, she pensive. Only in their final years together did both occupy the foreground.

A century ago, as now, the redwoods of California extended from the valleys to the upper slopes, growing more than three hundred feet tall and living more than five hundred years. In the shaded understory, Simon and Malca might have glimpsed elk, fisher, even black bear, sword and lady fern. The canopy often would have been engulfed in fog, the life within it remote.

This lofty community Simon may have read about before his visit — the entanglement of crickets, wandering salamanders, woodpeckers, marbled murrelets, fern mats, and centipedes. My father's father, as he stood beneath the redwoods, was twenty-six and short, a PhD, a husband, an expert for the prestigious U.S. Forest Service, a Jew. In the ancient redwood forests so resistant to fire, he encountered the threshold of the probable. One of the most abundant plants beneath his feet, though only in forests not exceeding middle age, was common bracken.

$t\frown$

I found no direct evidence in my parents' home of my grandfather's tenure in the U.S. Forest Service. To fathom Simon's years in Wisconsin, I had to consider the remaining box of lantern slides, the box of unspecified wood that smelled both sweet and musty and exhibited precisely twelve dull silver nails on its unpolished lid. This set lacked the consistency of the first. Here Simon had arranged similar abstract images of individual plant specimens but also boilers, ladders, lathes, pulleys, and spigots. An unspecified machine is labelled #13 *Max Load 62000 at 1st Failure*. Mixed in amid the many depictions of industry were isolated diagrams of crustaceans, one with a double-ringed enlarged eye.

In Wisconsin, Simon was employed not in the field but at the newly opened Forest Products Laboratory in Madison. The wildfires of summer 1910 had ravaged more than three million acres of woodland in Montana and Idaho, adding urgency to the enterprise at the lab. A thousand miles away from the western devastation, the staff were to investigate the fundamentals of wood from specimen trees: the relation of strength to weight and strength to height, the relation between strength and rate of growth.

Winter in Madison and throughout Wisconsin was unsparing. In the woods, the loggers wore padded suits and wide-brimmed hats, the horses, blankets and blinders, as the sleds for them to haul their unseen loads were stacked with frozen trees arranged into tight pyramids. The mist of snow was sometimes so thick, the felled trees so plentiful, that the mist might have been mistaken for smoke, the splintered trees for the aftermath of a forest fire. To subdue the cold, the men played the squeezebox. They drank beer from opaque bottles, a dog of indistinct provenance by their feet.

In the shelter of the lab, Simon continued to draw on the techniques learned from Dr. Penhallow — preparing microscopic slides for standardization of wood-pulp samples, creating microphotographs of American woods — but with the goal of identifying commercially viable species. His slides showing radial, tangential, and cross-sections of tree species provided the foundation for further undertakings at the lab.

Malca, my grandmother, likely was lonely in Wisconsin, partnered with a scientist whose pursuits she couldn't fully share and without long-time women friends or kin. Her husband, though devoted and a provider, showed little regard for his wife's intellect in the same way that he showed a general disdain for the inconsequential. An older cousin, the offspring of one of Simon's younger brothers, recently told me, "When I was a kid, my dad used to take me to see Simon. You didn't play around in front of him, I can tell you. He always carried a cane. Oh yes, Simon — he didn't suffer fools."

"A cane. Was he lame?"

"No. It was more of a walking stick."

"Part of his wardrobe, then?"

"Yeah, something like that."

That Simon could both frighten and repel children didn't preclude his having them. From the Montreal *Jewish Times*,

May 21, 1911, "At 181 Esplanade Ave., Montreal, a son." Edward, the first of Simon and Malca's three sons, was born in Malca's sister's home on the level ground east of the mountain. Simon travelled from Madison to Montreal for the occasion but was required soon after to return to the lab. On the Manifest of Alien Passengers Applying for Admission to the United States, he's described as a Class E Passenger, a forestry expert, son of Abraham. He was bound for Wisconsin alone.

By October 1911, Simon Kirsch, expert in the Forest Products Laboratory, had taken unpaid leave. Several months later, his appointment was terminated. In Canada an immigrant, in the United States an alien, the Lithuanian-born Jew elected belonging over displacement, family and community over professional solitude.

Only by way of two lantern slides can I understand at all my grandfather's disposition upon leaving Madison and returning to McGill. In the first, in the middle ground, a young man sits on the trunk of a felled pine, several bruised logs before him. To his rear is a simple A-frame cabin amid a scrappy but intact stand of conifers, maybe lodgepole pine. The young man is alone, the house is alone, the trees, despite each other's presence, are alone. In the second slide a dozen or so men and women, even a child, inhabit the foreground. It's harvest time, and they're picking. The women wear the flowing patterned waists of the Edwardian era, the men, pale loose tunics and trousers. Hats are more in evidence than faces — shallow wide-brimmed straw hats for the women, higher narrower-brimmed hats for the men. The community, on an unspecified island in the Caribbean, has gathered for the flowering. The crop is the crepe paper–like hibiscus. Or maybe it's only okra. As always, I view the slides as they're not meant to be seen — without a magic lantern, each glass square edged in tape held up to the natural light, my right eye fixed to the amber-rimmed magnifying glass that was my father's. As always, I view them alone.

Simon's research had furnished me with a methodology for my inquiries but left it to me to determine what was genuine. What was valid. As I became better acquainted with my grandfather's field of study and the thrust and drag of his personal advancement, I began to infer his values and priorities, many of them unlike my own. Whereas I shared Simon's fascination with the non-human world, I inclined more to the solitary. Unavoidably, the more time I was forced to spend alone in Montreal, distant from my husband and circle of close friends, the more my tendencies were confirmed. My grandfather, an immigrant from Russian-occupied Lithuania, not surprisingly sought out family and community, principally in the company of men.

"Your grandfather Simon didn't like women," my mother continually told me in my young adulthood. His wife, Malca, whatever her native wisdom, lacked Simon's extensive education, her tastes tending to bridge and 500, charity teas, and family idylls in the Laurentian Mountains. More than anything, she approached vigorously her role of homemaker, of *balabusta*. My father adored his mother's noodle kugel and schmaltz herring yet continually derided her, claiming "she wasn't too bright." Throughout my childhood, my father's pronouncements on his mother were perhaps the closest I came to hearing my grandfather's voice.

Within Simon's household, no girl children proliferated to speak in Malca's defence. To my grandmother's disappointment she bore only three sons, the first and second, Edward and Leonard, in the lead-up to the Great War; the third, my father, Archie, when Bulgaria and Italy joined the conflict. She named her youngest son after her Uncle Archibald, the Russian doctor who brought her to Canada, and in spite of small Archie's assertive masculinity — with two older brothers, he discovered his fists early and used them — she kept his ringlets uncut and dressed him in impeccable suits.

"Malca was desperate for a girl," my mother told me when she could still remember such things. "She treated your father like a daughter."

My father himself never commented on his resistance to being outfitted in white stockings and an oversized spherical hat. Instead, as I was growing up, he continually quoted a favourite pronouncement from the medical literature: "Every exaggerated reaction is a mask for a person's defects." My father applied the dictum selectively, referring to my mother's obsession with minutiae and not his own response to the subduing of his masculinity.

In my efforts to understand my paternal grandfather and his bearing on my father, I'd assembled a succession of nouns: Wood, forestry, smoke. Self-assurance, progress, integrity. Severity. Resolve. Each was indivisible and strangely intangible. What my father related to me of his father continually hinted at esteem rather than intimacy. Even so, through his medical practice, my father willingly bore Simon's legacy of hard work and resilience, rising in the night to tend sick patients long after most doctors had stopped making house calls. He maintained, too, his father's regard for the non-human world. In his college yearbook my father cited as his favourite pastime "love of the great outdoors."

Of Simon's inheritance from his own father I know even less. When Abraham died on March 28, 1917, Simon was thirty-three, about the same age as Abraham in the only photograph of him I've seen. The father clearly was the forerunner of the son — the same leanness in the face, same fecund moustache, same insolence of demeanour — only with unsuppressed ears. Abraham Kirz likely started out as something other than a purveyor of broomsticks and nylons. Possibly he even worked in the timber trade, a métier open to Lithuanian Jews in late nineteenth-century Russia. In the early years in Montreal, his was a life of numerous addresses, the sale of goods not his own, packages travelling through his hands, chicken, prunes, and pike consumed as soon as they were brought home, logs in the fireplace quickly turned to embers. He died a merchant — Kirsch, not Kirz — in the same month and year that the Russian Tsarist government collapsed.

The closest I could get to Abraham would be his burial place in Montreal, and before venturing there I made a routine stop to see my mother. I found her in the dining room, alone at her usual table by the back wall, with the rabbi in his black habit muttering Hebrew approbations nearby. My mother's metabolism had remained level throughout the winter. Now, with the advent of spring, her lips were coated in sugar crystals, her fingers glazed with sugar and saliva. Mistakenly, one of the kitchen staff had furnished my mother, a diabetic, with sachets of sugar for her tea.

"What are you doing here?" My mother looked up at me, more puzzled than gratified. She wore no lipstick. Her face was pinched, her hair combed flat, her once-flawless complexion marred by two red pimples.

"I'm here to visit with you," I said too brightly. Her silence was broken only by the clattering of dishes in the kitchen and the groan of the swinging door as the servers elbowed it open, their arms piled high with dirty vessels.

My mother squeezed her eyes shut, then opened them. "I want to go to my room now." As she prepared to withdraw to her apartment, supported by a care aide, she issued no invitation to her daughter nor did she inquire where I'd be going instead.

"There's still something bright about your mother," the geriatrician had recently told me. "Enough quality of life that it's worth trying to preserve." Although on better days my mother continued to surprise me with her sense of humour and mental agility, today neither was in evidence. I recalled how on a trip to Ireland years before, an innkeeper had suggested to my mother that I'd make a lovely nun. In response, my mother had laughed heartily, whereas now, her core identity unchallenged, she could barely force a smile.

The De la Savane Cemetery turned out to be close to the Orange Julep, a citrus-shaped drive-in where in the 1960s my parents had regularly taken me for an orange drink made from both the pith and the rind.

Abraham's grave was tucked away in a forgotten corner, with more spring foliage than the rest but without the expansive views of the newer burials. With no evidence of how Simon had mourned Abraham, I wondered about the wording on his gravestone. *A beloved father? A dear father? Beloved in life?* As I approached the row where Abraham was buried, surnames came into view: AXELRAD, ABRAMOWITZ, SEGAL, BOLOTIN, WIGDOR. Only when I stood little more than a foot away did KIRSCH, carved in relief into the base of a granite headstone, catch my eye. The remainder of the headstone, the rectangular slab bearing the inscription, lay face down in the soil.

I dropped to the ground, grasped the monument by its scratchy edges, and tugged. That I was five foot four with little-girl shoulders and weighed no more than a Bouvier des Flandres — a cow-herding dog reported to be sober and thoughtful — never even crossed my mind.

At the cemetery office I waited impatiently for the clerk to conclude his meandering conversation with an older woman in a dark skirt suit and tortoiseshell glasses hinged in gold. "Fine," he said to her at last. "*Zol zayn mit mazel!*" And then to me, "You, what do you want?"

I explained how my great-grandfather's headstone had fallen face forward to the ground. "Can I have it repaired, or at least turned upright?"

"It's doable — at a price. Give me your contact information and I'll be in touch."

I never heard from him. But when I returned to my mother's house and viewed the images I had taken of Abraham's grave, enlarged on my laptop, I became aware that in my efforts to read the headstone I'd overlooked the fractured base, by design a secret part of the stone, here exposed. A dark image — a silhouette — was clearly visible on the opaque white surface. A vertical section of a complex leaf or frond, the irregularly sized blades extending left from the stem. Whether the image had been fostered in light once the headstone had split from its base, or proliferated in darkness from a specimen trapped between two slabs of granite, I couldn't tell. I could conclude only that the methodology was non-deliberate, and if it had occurred during my grandfather's lifetime, would have escaped his notice.

$t \frown$

Impressions of fern in rock as part of the fossil record played a central role in Simon's research. Moreover, non-fossilized rock — minerals in particular — held for my father's father both scientific and commercial interest. In summer he went prospecting in northern forests of balsam fir and black spruce, attired in lace-up boots with striped socks, padded leggings, and a button-up shirt with generous breast pockets. The matching hat was wide brimmed, the face beneath it thickly bearded. If not for the inscription on the back and the grin, my grandfather as photographed in the field would be unrecognizable.

In Simon's objects, I was searching for waymarks to places that had shaped his character and purpose. Lithuania — for Simon a place remembered, for me a place imagined — remained for now out of reach. Leaving my mother to travel abroad when she so depended on me to reassure her and oversee her care simply wasn't an option. At any rate, I'd recovered no physical evidence from my grandfather's first childhood in the Pale of Settlement. Measured by possessions alone, his life began in early middle age when he acquired lantern slides, a Jug Handle, rocks. I resolved to confine myself to journeys nearer to home and an itinerary to be specified by my grandfather's box of minerals. The Mineral Clinic at Toronto's Royal Ontario Museum apparently was free of charge and staffed by experts who could pinpoint the origins of specimens.

As I readied my mother's house for sale, I'd been discarding her own collections — the lists Scotch-taped to the wall, with reminders to buy Smucker's Concord grape jelly, rocky road ice cream, and Metamucil; her outfits, one of them a pale green summer suit with a neck like a chicken's ruff; the mouse puppet she and I had made together, its head a red plastic ball to which we'd added whiskers and rounded black cardboard ears. With little to sustain me other than the memory of surrendered objects, I boarded the train for my own home in Toronto, now the repository of my grandfather's forgotten minerals. Secured in my travel bag were books from my first library: *The Cat in the Hat, Green Eggs and Ham, Snow, One Fish, Two Fish, Are You My Mother?*

⌐

The Mineral Clinic took place in the Brown Bag lunch area — an artificially lit, near-colourless room in the museum basement. Most of us seated there were cradling one or more specimens in an unlikely receptacle — a Salada tea canister, a dog dish, a microwave container for pad thai.

"Rock or fossil?" the coordinator asked me. The two fossil experts were grey-haired men wearing necklaces of orange ribbon with monocles attached. The mineralogists, seated farther away, were squinting into microscopes.

"Rock, I think." The cardboard box on my lap secured by jute string concealed, among others, a slick wafer of mineral tinted the blacks and greens of mould; a hexagon of beryl; and a powdery white rock like an imperfect square of Turkish delight.

A middle-aged man in a baseball cap and sweats had just learned his treasure rated as no more than a pseudo-fossil, by God-given coincidence an arrangement of molecules that looked like a claw. "I knew it wouldn't be totally unique," he told the expert, "but I'm still calling it 'the devil's claw' — for the kids' sake."

"Rock 7," announced the coordinator. The mineralogist beckoned me to approach his table.

We examined first under the microscope my small hexagon of beryl, a rock that can yield precious emerald or aquamarine. "There are two deposits in Ontario, northeast of Bancroft in Quadeville," said the mineralogist, twiddling the stage, "but those deposits are coloured and this is white." He withdrew his eye from the ocular, focusing instead on me. "This may come from Maine."

The Maine coast alone measured some 230 miles. "Can you be more specific?"

"Sorry, no."

My next offering, the powdery white rock, was identified as sodalite — like lapis lazuli, a silicate. My sample exhibited quality and might have originated in the Princess Sodalite Mine in Ontario, named for a British royal who commandeered 130 tons for her ancestral home in England. Sodalite was found elsewhere, too — in Africa or Brazil.

Instead of clarifying my grandfather's movements, the rocks were confusing his whereabouts. The trail I'd imagined

— by Greyhound bus through Quebec hamlets ringed by pert spruce trees — was now encompassing whole countries and continents, savannah and rainforest, with impediments like lions and bullet ants.

The expert beside me was addressing his remarks to an eight-year-old boy. "It sticks itself to the sea floor. Like this." He held one of his liver-spotted hands upright, wriggling the fingers.

This man has a grandson, I thought. To the mineralogist I said, "Here's the last of my rocks." Without even placing the sliver under the microscope, he concluded, "This is serpentine. There's lots southeast of Montreal in the asbestos mining areas, and some east of Timmins."

"Asbestos?"

"Yes, asbestos runs in splits of serpentine, but serpentine itself isn't dangerous. It dissipates in the body."

The correspondence detailing my grandfather's asbestos land claims was drab, the paper grey to yellow. Old man's colours. Simon wasn't old when the Porcupine-Destor geological fault began to yield significant ore in the 1940s, but he turned out to be, unwittingly, in the final decade of his life. He had a wife, three grown sons, two daughters-in-law, the beginnings of grandchildren. He had one son, my father, in active service. He had asbestos. As an adviser to the Jewish Laurentian Fresh Air Camp, he spent time among the wives and offspring of men at war, watching the children of others dance and sing, or listening with them to stories by Sholom Aleichem. But Simon was travelling also to Destor, Quebec, eyeing asbestos showings and prospects, a Jew among the francophones and Algonquin, an interloper in the land of pine marten and bear.

For sixty-three years the records of Simon's mining invest-
ments survived in my father's highboy, longer than my father
himself, longer than my mother's tenure in the house she
shared with him. The highboy eventually accompanied my
mother to assisted living, its contents unaltered. In his middle drawer my father had safeguarded extensive records of
his father's posthumous assets, a blueprint of the shares
and claims Simon held in his lifetime, as intangible now as
they were then, words on paper indicating holdings of ore
so remote, so vast, their essential physicality could only be
expressed through numbers. The showings of serpentine, at
four thousand feet long and eight hundred feet wide, merely
suggested wider and longer deposits. The thick paper of the
stock certificates was printed with borders and laurels of acan-
thus leaves, symbols of everlasting life. Before my grandfather
could divest himself of these holdings, he was gone.

On November 5, 1949, Simon died suddenly, one might say
"decisively." In the bulletin of the Congregation Shaar Hashomayim synagogue published on November 11 that same year —
Remembrance Day — a tribute described Dr. Simon Kirsch as
"an indefatigable communal worker and a universally esteemed
and highly respected personality in our Community." My
father merely said to me, "Simon had a stroke in the bathtub."

My father's father was sixty-five at the time of his death,
roughly within the life expectancy for the era. No doubt the
war years had aged him, as they had so many others, and not
merely the pervading horror or the worry of a father with a son
in the overseas theatre, but also the news of the extermination
of European Jewry and Canada's obstinacy in refusing asylum. Throughout the Second World War, only four hundred
Jews were admitted into the country — and these temporarily.
Simon also had lived long enough to learn of the Nazi depreda-
tions in the country of his birth, not least the massacres in the

forests of pine and spruce. The damage to his recollection of those woods would have been irreparable.

⌐⌐

My father never explained to me how the duties of executor at first were awarded to Leonard, the middle brother. In his efforts to close down his father's business, Leonard, in October 1950, had dispatched a G. Spence to Abitibi-Témiscamingue, a near wilderness south of the tree line and populated largely by the Algonquin. It was in my father's highboy that I discovered Spence's yellow rental agreement from Tilden Drive Yourself Company, 900 miles guaranteed. A receipt from Lalonde & Fils for one locker and one flashlight. The blue-marbled Crown Expense Book with its log of hotel stays at both Senneterre and Macamic: breakfast $3.00, lunch $5.00, dinner $4.00, incidentals $2.90.

The thousand miles driven by G. Spence on behalf of the Estate of Dr. Simon Kirsch were along the Trans-Canada Highway, through granite outcrops, matted bog, and stunted woods of spruce, birch, and tamarack. Simon Kirsch was fourteen and a mere schoolboy when Quebec assumed ownership of the vast lands that were being harvested for wood and where rights to fur-bearing animals — fox and beaver — would be contested. He was forty-eight when the mining town of Destor arose in the wilderness, fifty when the town of Val-d'Or followed. In the arithmetic of the North, neither was far from Lake Simon.

Lake Simon wasn't named after a Jew from Vilkomir, but I believe nonetheless that my father's father travelled there and to the even more remote settlements of Macamic, Destor, and Senneterre, foreshadowing the journey that G. Spence later made on his behalf. The impetus for Simon's travels were stakes in the beginning ore extraction of the 1920s, '30s, and

'40s. Gold and copper in Malartic, Rouyn-Noranda, Val-d'Or. And in Destor, asbestos. Upon his death, Simon left behind no precious metals but instead burlap bags containing lumps of asbestos and sheet mica of high reflectivity.

Simon didn't merely hold shares in the new concerns but also interests in land that showed promise for mineral extraction, hence the need for first-hand surveillance. Macamic, a stopover on the route to Destor, is even now within miles of where the main road north ends. Its name — from the Algonquin *makamik* — is thought to mean "limping beaver."

The felling of trees, the splintering of rock, the opening of traditional hunting and fishing grounds to tourism — from the vantage point of business, a triumph — had begun ruthlessly to undermine the indigenous way of life. Perhaps my grandfather remained unaware that the harvesting of pulp and paper, the mining of copper and gold, the milling of asbestos fibre, weren't merely sources of wealth but also violations of the forest and rock and their inhabitants — sudden noise to their stillness, exposure to their stealth. Or if he knew, he rated profit before empathy.

On his way north, Simon would have encountered common bracken. Spence, travelling in October, when Simon had collected his fern samples, would have seen the same. By mid-autumn, common bracken has turned the milky taupes, subdued oranges, and misty browns of unroasted cocoa beans. Each individual, whether growing alone or in groves or thickets, exhibits its own pace of senescence. Some fronds are erect, even pointing skyward. Others, more desiccated, can be bent without breaking. It is these latter, the early frail, that on windy days rattle like paper in silent woods. Whatever treasure my grandfather was seeking in the forests and bedrock of Abitibi-Témiscamingue, he must have seized upon the rustle of *Pteris aquilina* and taken comfort in the familiar.

In January 1952, for reasons unknown, the Estate of Simon Kirsch renounced all asbestos claims at Destor, thereby abandoning the realization of one of Simon's final ambitions. My father had replaced his brother Leonard as executor in November 1951, two months before the withdrawal of the claims. The recent war veteran wouldn't have used asbestos to woo my mother, a belle who'd already spurned several proposals of marriage when she first met my father on a double date at the Normandie Roof nightclub. As a teacher of small children, she'd have understood little of the business dealings that undoubtedly preoccupied him at the time, and my father, in his wisdom, took his young companion to Grossinger's Resort in the Borscht Belt and entertained her with stories of his encounters as locum physician to Al Alberts and the Four Aces or Alan King. That he chose not to share his worries as executor doesn't undermine the burden he bore. It's fair to say that my parents' courtship began amid the disposition of a dead man's assets and that I was born in the wake of the surrender of the claims in Destor.

The magnolias now were in full flower, the birches in full leaf, and more of Simon was to be found in my father's highboy, but only on those occasions when my mother rose from her bed and joined the other residents in the communal dining room. Though perplexed, she'd still notice me rifling through her bedroom drawers. And object.

In the dining hall, my mother sat at a corner table with three women, but whereas the others were tucking in to mounds of egg and salmon salad, my mother's place setting was empty.

"She's already eaten, even if she doesn't remember," a curly-haired woman told me. "She eats fast."

My mother looked longingly at the others' plates. "Am I supposed to have one of those?"

"You've already had yours," I said. "Soon they'll bring your dessert."

She was dressed in faux denim — a tunic and matching trousers.

"What's the matter with her?" the curly-haired woman asked loudly.

"Memory problems," I whispered. My mother smiled, hearing but not comprehending.

The woman nodded. "It's very common. But what can you do? That's life. Does she have a husband?"

"Not anymore. He was a lot older, seventeen years."

"I used to have a big store. What do you do?"

"I'm a writer and editor."

"My grandson does that. He moved to Minnesota."

"I brought my mother some blueberries from Atwater Market," I said.

"My daughter's a therapeutic nurse," said the curly-haired lady, "and she tells me to eat blueberries. They're very good for you."

Suddenly my mother pushed back her chair, determined to get up from the table. "Stay here," I urged, placing my hand on her arm, "I'm going to tidy up your room."

$\longleftarrow$

I can only guess what my father, a diagnostician, made of his father's unfinished business. At the time of Simon's death, the asbestos claims ranked as a small holding in an estate that encompassed parcels of land in the hundreds, some within walking distance of my grandparents' house in Lower Westmount, others tens or hundreds of miles away. Simon wasn't exclusively an owner of property but also a conduit or expert witness for land transactions. Clearly death had caught him out, the apparent finality of the transactions on paper misleading. These weren't stable assets but notions in flux with land as their underpinnings: negotiations, recalibrations, claims, options, evidence of debt, risk of default, wins, gambles, plays, and manoeuvres. *What about mortgage — Duggan — Latt? ... 913 acres of high, dry and level land ... The option, if not exercised, shall become null and void,* ipso facto. They were alive, survivors of Simon's own life.

The origins of my grandfather's landholdings dated back to 1917 and earlier, when Malca persisted in believing my father was a girl. That year was notable, too, for the publication of *The Rise of David Levinsky,* the first novel to memorialize the Jewish immigrant experience in America. Simon's original edition of this novel by Abraham Cahan, now in my possession, has survived intact for more than a hundred years. On the dust jacket, a young man is rendered entirely in black and white, his clothing patched, a carpet bag in hand. Behind him rise the silhouettes of Manhattan's early skyscrapers, but stunted, scarcely reaching above his elbows.

David Levinsky, my grandfather's unwitting mentor, was born in Antomir, Lithuania, inland from Juodkrante, the black shore, and due north of Kaunas. Simon Kirz was born in Vilkomir, Lithuania, marginally southeast of Antomir and closer to the border with Belarus. David was born in 1865, Simon about 1884. David, the son of a mother who peddled pea mush, was without siblings and for much of his childhood an orphan. Simon, although himself one of many siblings and the son of a peddler whose first vocation remains unknown, married an orphan. Simon was real and David a fiction, but Simon, like David, showed a flair for self-invention, and here's where their stories converge.

David himself had no need of real estate. Already a wealthy industrialist by means of the shmatte trade, he accepted the lure of trading in properties against the advice of his mentor,

Mr. Nodelman. "Take pity on your hard-earned pennies, Levin-sky," he'd say. "Else you'll wake up some day like the fellow who has dreamed he has found a treasure. He's holding on to the treasure tight, and when he opens his eyes he finds it's nothing but a handful of wind."

Simon Kirsch, my father's father, was thirty-three when he first read *The Rise of David Levinsky*, and mindful of Nodelman's prediction. For David did lose a portion of his treasure in the collapse of New York's real estate boom — a catastrophe he found to be in "the nature, or rather in the unnaturalness, of the 'get-rich-quick' epidemic." He didn't begin, like Simon, with an understanding that nature and quick frequently aren't synonymous. A botanist grasps that common bracken is of vigorous growth, rebounding rapidly after fire. The redwood, in contrast, may take six centuries to mature and, though not quick to grow, is slow to be destroyed.

Nineteen seventeen, the year Abraham Cahan published his novel, took shape for Simon as a year of unbidden change. His father, Abraham, died that spring, his sister Bessie Victoria six months later. In Montreal, as in New York, a real estate boom was under way. With the city expanding, Simon's con-temporaries acquired property for resale or, if they lacked cap-ital, enlisted as real estate agents paid by commission. Simon himself had begun a sideline in real estate as early as 1912, but during the boom he resisted the enticement of obvious wealth, choosing instead to remain in academe. Before her death, Bes-sie Victoria had delivered a son, a now-motherless boy with only a bereaved father to raise him. The real estate boom would lead to a bust. Simon occupied himself for the most part with the fossil record and the exigencies of family.

Seven years later, when my grandfather had assimilated the lessons of David Levinsky, he moved. From the east to the west slope of the mountain. From a red-brick and wrought-iron tri-plex on Durocher that now serves as a multi-family dwelling for darkly clad Hasidic Orthodox Jews to a single-family row house on a genteel street where life happens indoors. From a forestry expert and long-time demonstrator in botany with a propensity for real estate to a full-time purveyor of buildings and land. To say the new life betrayed the old would be too simple. There were continuities and evolutions discernible, but only when examined close up, beyond their evident proportions. Throughout it all, Simon didn't discard the Jug Handle.

The reasons underlying Simon's departure from academe, aged forty, were complex and, as I understood from the little my father told me, voluntary. In early 1925, however, the year Simon resigned his position at McGill University, the dean of arts had begun investigating the presence of Jews in the faculty. Throughout Simon's roughly two decades at McGill, half his working life, the number of Jewish professors in Canada was minuscule. Already in 1919, the president of Queen's University was bragging about how the faculty included only five Jews, a necessary restriction since they "lowered the tone" at universities. In the 1920s, Ira Mackay, dean of the McGill arts faculty, said unreservedly, "The simple obvious truth is that Jewish people are of no use to us in this country." By 1926, shortly after Simon's departure from McGill, the university adopted an "informal ban" on "Hebrew" students from outside Quebec, and in the later 1920s, McGill began escalating the grade requirements for Jewish students in particular because they were thought to be too "academically concentrated." By 1931, Jewish faculty in the whole of Canada numbered eleven, of which only five worked in Quebec. Simon no longer ranked among them.

If hostility towards "Hebrews" contributed to Simon's resolve to leave McGill, nor did he gravitate to a second profession that invariably welcomed Jews. Statistics revealed Jewish realtors in Quebec to be even more uncommon than Jewish insurance agents, the latter accounting in 1931 for only 3.59 percent of insurance workers, including clerical staff. In Winnipeg during the same era, only 0.27 percent of gainfully employed Jews held positions in real estate. For those few who succeeded, the financial rewards presumably exceeded those in academe. Simon's earlier forays into real estate, dating mostly from the nineteen teens, likely had been inspired by the need to supplement his academic salary.

For my father's father, the need for profit wasn't slight. He had three schoolboys and a wife to keep, a Russian wife who favoured opal starbursts and thrusting hats from bespoke milliners. For my father's bar mitzvah in 1928, Malca wore a French gown of green transparent velvet with gold lace and a corsage of orchids. Proceeds from the study of common bracken wouldn't have sufficed for Malca's couture, nor the arrangements of mauve and gold chrysanthemums, autumn foliage, and pink roses and pompoms she commandeered for her youngest son's coming of age. These my grandfather presumably funded with earnings from real estate several years after he'd launched his second career.

Finally, a more subtle motive might have informed Simon's move into land development, an urge discrete from profit. In Vilkomir, and throughout Lithuania, cultivation and ownership of land by Jews had been prohibited. Consciously or not, Simon would retaliate, signing the deeds for his own home while at the same time purchasing or advising on the acquisition of buildings and lots for public institutions. In each land purchase, perhaps, he was repudiating the entitlement that had been denied Abraham, his father.

Simon couldn't have guessed that two of his three sons, Archie and Leonard, would grow up tall. When their father assumed the presidency of Camp B'nai Brith, a venture demanding the acquisition of land, the middle and younger boys hadn't yet attained their full height. The camp provided for sons unlike Simon's own — boys confined to the city, naïve in the ways of the bush, fatherless or with fathers lacking in means.

In 1929, Simon and his brothers at the B'nai Brith Mount Royal Lodge had acquired 300 acres of virgin forest at Lac Long. The property was classic Laurentian and indistinct — scrappy conifers, low mountains sloping one into the other, a lake that didn't conform to any known geometry. That autumn Simon felled trees for the new beach. Eventually all three of his sons — Edward, Leonard, Archie — would serve as counsellors at Camp B'nai Brith.

Not only the landscape, but also the materials of the camp returned Simon to his Baltic origins. In the photographs of Camp B'nai Brith belonging to my father, almost everything is made of wood. Canoes. Raised tent platforms. The dining hall with its two rows of tables and benches neatly aligned. Totem poles. The obstacle course of downed logs. In all probability, my grandfather Simon as a child had lived in a house resembling the camp cabins — a house of wood on the edge of woods, perfumed with resin.

Invested with permanence ten years before the Nazi invasion of Poland, Camp B'nai Brith evolved as a summer place, a property of hope. The lone photo of my father's father at camp, in shirtsleeves and seated in a canvas tent alongside his fellow directors, is notable among his photographs in middle age. In it he's not amused, not smirking, not defiant. Merely content. Unguarded. It's here amid the black spruce and balsam fir that the forestry expert made peace with the realtor. Here that his youngest and middle sons grew taller than the smallest of trees.

To the untrained eye, the wildlands around Lac Long and Prefontaine appear all of a sameness; in late spring the sloping mountains a monotony of green, thick with conifers, the clearings splashed with woolly blue violet. To see through this jumble to the contours of the land, to distinguish one thicket from the next, a person would need to be familiar with rock, leaves, sap, and soils. This expertise Simon had. For him, trees weren't merely trees but evergreens, black spruce or balsam fir, their trunks conduits for resin, the lifeblood of conifers, the anointing oil for slides viewed under the smallest objective of the Jug Handle. Granite wasn't merely an obstacle to construction but an igneous rock with secret pockets — druses — of quartz and feldspar, a host to veins of porphyry and pegmatite. Fresh water not merely a byway for loggers but a medium for crustaceans and man alike. Nature did not, would not, stand still. Nonetheless, of the wilderness near Prefontaine that was to become the new Mount Sinai Sanatorium, Simon said "subdue." Simon said "build." Daffy's leading characteristics were his assurance and his grin.

Instead of submitting to a guided tour of Camp B'nai Brith, once the pride of the Mount Royal Lodge and now nearing its centenary, I'd opted for a private wander through the barren lands of Mount Sinai, a demolished sanatorium for tuberculars of any faith. Whereas the boys camp as Simon had known it survived only in photographs, the grounds of Mount Sinai Sanatorium were reverting to the wildlands my father's father might once have surveyed.

Dr. Simon Kirsch, a director of Mount Sinai and a key member of the house committee, was present for the opening of the sanatorium on October 5, 1930. The patients, mostly working-class Jews from Montreal's needle trade, likely never had been exposed to such splendour. Grander and more beautifully situated than many hotels, the Art Deco palace consisted of two wings arranged on either side of a central tower, each one sheltering a solarium with views onto a formal garden of sinuous paths emptying into a small lake. There, at land's end, a bridge led to an island with a gazebo. Nearby were to be found staff quarters, a chicken farm, a potager, and a network of walking trails through the forest. Inside, the sanatorium offered up-to-date X-ray and operating facilities, along with quartz lamps, a medical library, and a continuous supply of hot water. That the complex was opening in times of economic crisis as a refuge for the gravely ill and dying was alluded to neither in its cosmetic appearance nor its setting. Like Camp B'nai Brith, Mount Sinai proclaimed optimism.

Close to a century later, no plaque identifies the site, nor are there signs declaring ownership or prohibiting entry. Just a few rocks bigger than pumpkins and, beyond, the remnants of a path that might have led to the sanatorium. The gravel path edged by spruce gives way to a vast vacant space, defined, at the rear, first by woods and then forested mountains.

Only on my way back to my car did I come across the engraved parking curb at the southwest corner of the site — "Nurses' Home / Mount Sinai Sanatorium." Of concrete and with no date, the slab both announced the site and created a barrier to it. I wasn't the only recent visitor. Someone had placed two stones and a sprig of wildflowers, already desiccated, on the reminder of the nurses' residence. Defenceless as they were, I chose to leave them in place.

On the return journey from Mount Sinai, I stopped briefly to check on my mother.

"Where were you?" she asked plaintively.

"On an errand." As so often in her presence, I felt shame at my engagement with the world outside. Beyond my mother's half-closed blinds, the waning of the day was luminous, the apple blossom and pollen-drenched bees intent on renewal. I didn't tell her I'd become obsessed with Simon, nor that she and he shared more than I might have imagined.

My mother had just narrowly missed knowing her father-in-law, who died several years before her courtship with his son began, but like Simon, my mother had studied biology before abandoning dissection for pedagogy. In her younger years, she, too, could have distinguished an icthyoid from a sporophyte. Moreover, both my mother and Simon were partial to the unrelenting cleanliness of laboratories, and both in their later lives gravitated to water.

When perennially anxious but not yet memory impaired, my mother had been explicit about her wishes for her declining years. "Just put me somewhere by the water," she said. In the end, it was Simon who died in the bathtub while my mother's only late-life exposure to the ocean came via a BOB's Cruise to Alaska after my father declared himself too old to travel. For my mother, the ten-day boat trip along the Inside Passage proved to be "phenomenal," one of her happiest times in the years preceding her widowhood. On board she was photographed holding hands with the chef, whose starched white tunic and toque blanche spoke of careful hygiene. The buffet table behind exhibited a windmill made of profiteroles and a pineapple with bulrushes sticking out of it. My mother wore an orange life jacket with FRONT in block letters.

Among the stops on the cruise were old prospecting sites, one of them a cemetery with an uncut boulder identified as "The largest nugget in the world." My mother brought me a rock from that trip, a small, hard nodule of glitter that mimicked one of my grandfather's finds. Iron pyrite, more easily recognizable as fool's gold.

CHAPTER THREE

Shut Out the Yesterdays

WHEREAS SIMON KIRSCH HAD SOUGHT OUT AND FOUND minerals and ore, both fake and genuine, he'd sequestered none of these in his own home, leaving nothing there to retrieve. My grandfather's house, where he and Malca raised their three sons, thus had escaped the reputation of treasure.

I never thought of it as my grandfather's house. From as early as I could remember, my father's middle brother, his wife, and several daughters had inhabited Simon's one-time home in Lower Westmount — a brick Victorian with generous bay windows on each of the principal floors. This house, where French poodles skittered and children played Spin the Dreidel while adults gathered in the parlour to argue and eat and dance and laugh, was as ebullient as my parents' house was hushed. It also, once, had served me as a place of refuge. Whenever my mother and I approached the linear street in her white Volvo, she recalled how we'd sheltered there during the great ice storm of my infancy. "For days on end," she said, "there was no heat at home. You were only just beginning to walk."

Before I was old enough to want to remember my grandfather's house, my aunt and uncle had sold it and moved to Florida.

Throughout my teen years, once my aunt and uncle had become well established in Miami, and while Quebec was threatening to separate from the rest of Canada, my mother was fond of telling me she didn't know where I'd come from. She meant by this that she failed to understand why I was resisting her desire for me to become a lawyer or a doctor and, as perplexing, why I'd announced I was searching for a man with a beard, a model of masculinity for which no family precedent could be found. That I felt uncertain about having children of my own only reinforced for my mother how I scarcely qualified as her daughter. In *Bride and Groom*, the manual for marriage presented to my parents by the rabbi who would oversee their union, two books in particular are recommended for the bride: *The Three Pillars* and *The Jewish Home Beautiful*. The first, written long before the feminist movement of the 1970s, when I came of age, outlines the fundamentals of life for Jewish women, including the birth of children. The second, which my mother received as a bride, relates how, into the "small, pink ears" of their offspring, "Jewish mothers crooned desires and hopes, dreams and yearnings." Motherhood, for women of my mother's generation an inevitability, became for me a matter of preference. My mother never subdued her enthusiasm for me but puzzled over her unconditional love for a daughter whose instincts and aspirations marked her out as a stranger.

In a more basic understanding, however, where I'd come from remained clear and incontestable. I'd originated in my parents and the home they'd provided for me from birth. This split-level where I grew up, with its lavishly carpeted staircases and confusion of floors, spoke to my father's ardour for his fiancée. He himself would have favoured a house similar to the one he grew up in — a brick Victorian close to downtown, with a partly submerged office space for his medical practice. "But I was a new bride," my mother explained to me decades later, "and I wanted a new house."

And so my parents chose a house with no history and brought to it no history of home ownership. My father, until his marriage at nearly forty, had lived with his widowed mother in her apartment hung with prints of European cityscapes and Corinthian ruins, or overseas with the military on borrowed estates or in army barracks. My mother had remained at home with her parents and sister in a red-brick midrise apartment block until she married and moved into the purpose-built house, where, unbeknownst to her, her husband would bury a treasure for her to find when he'd nothing else left to give. The house without a past was situated west of downtown and thus afforded better views of the sunset.

In other ways my parents' house, the house that now, more than a half century later, I was aiming to sell, had satisfied the newlyweds' shared vision for themselves: the stability of their own home in the place they were born. During the years of my parents' courtship, the Jewish community in Montreal, the second largest in the British Commonwealth, was coming to terms with the annihilation of Jewish life in Europe. Many Yiddish-speaking artists and intellectuals from the Old World had already settled in Montreal and were joined from 1947 by large numbers of Yiddish-speaking refugees, distinguishing the city as an international centre for Yiddish cultural life. By 1951, roughly a quarter of Jews in Montreal counted as recent arrivals from Europe, whose remembered home had become irretrievable. This sensibility remained foreign to my parents, both Canadian born. Throughout their lifetime, neither ever imagined living elsewhere than Montreal, a city of opaque greystone nunneries and shimmering tin spires, where earlier generations of Russian Jews had made landfall after weeks at sea. In the final year of my father's life, when he was in hospital recovering from pneumonia, he took part grudgingly in a non-competitive quiz. The animator put a question to him: If you could travel anywhere in the world, where would that be? My father, from his wheelchair, replied without hesitation. "Montreal."

More than a decade after my father's death, my mother's house no longer met the criterion of a house without a past. A developer had already made me an offer — one I refused because the would-be buyer planned to gut the interior and, by extension, the outline of the life we'd led there. With overheads for maintaining the empty house mounting, I couldn't risk rejecting a next bid. I was months away from agreeing to relinquish this house where I grew up and my parents grew old.

$t \frown$

The size of the void next door was startling. You could imagine a whole apartment building or shopping mall had been razed, not merely a single house on the corner lot. I'd been away from Montreal for several weeks, and having arrived there after dark the night before, I'd initially been spared a first glimpse of the desecration of the familiar house next door. Instead, by lamplight, I'd discovered in my father's desk drawer a crumbling butterfly's wing from a red admiral. When I slipped it into the palm of my hand, the once-hardened protein and scales, the machinery of flight, turned to dust.

I half expected someone to appear and expel me from the house. In my mother's final years there she'd had to be persuaded to grant my husband and me access. Invariably, she came to the front door in gaping white running shoes and a housedress fastened with snaps, her exposed calves narrow but sinewy, her still-thick hair unkempt. "I'm not ready for you yet," she'd say, evaluating us through the peephole, or "I wouldn't have minded if your train was late" or "I was hoping you wouldn't be here so soon."

"Do you mind if we come in?" I'd say. "We've come all this way to see you."

And grudgingly she'd acquiesce, but only if we laid our suit-cases on newspaper and hung our coats at the far end of the closet, at a safe distance from her own garments. Despite my mother's fretfulness, I had no doubt she loved us fiercely and inexhaustibly — this love a gift from her to us. We in turn counted as her prized possessions — the things she'd tried to keep hidden but instinctively exposed to the light because to do otherwise would have brought about our end. As a consequence of that exposure, my husband and I posed a hygiene threat.

That my mother no longer commanded the family home since her forced departure was evident from the disarray in my old bedroom, the black quilted bedspread askew, the yellow over-sheet to counter fading from sunlight incorrectly placed, the white corduroy and yellow faux fur pillows sloppily over-lapping. In other ways my mother's presence remained palpa-ble, the lack of renewal pervading her final years at home still obvious. The scant furniture, most of it purchased in Manhat-tan with help from Aunt Rae, Simon's sister and an interior designer, harked back to the 1950s. In the kitchen, no fresh food was to be found — no fruits swollen with seeds or roots moist with earth — only frost-tinged bagels and expired vegetarian shepherd's pie. Yet outdoors, in the L-shaped back yard where my father had planted plum and apple trees, and where, when I was old enough, he taught me to grow carrots, the peonies were blooming, their smooth petals trembling with the move-ment of polished black ants. On my husband's instruction, the gardener had filled the central beds beside them with red salvia.

I walked the couple of miles to my mother's residence and found her cheerful, although, as usual, in her uniform of stretchy brown trousers and a pink blouse, her hearing-aid battery dead.

"You know," she volunteered after I'd restored her hearing, "a setup like this is ideal for someone like me. At home I was lonely wandering around those eight or nine rooms, but here I have company."

"You can stay here," I told her. "You don't have to go back home."

She frowned. "Wouldn't I have to sell the house? I suppose I could get a good price. My car's there."

"At your stage, you don't need a car anymore."

My mother most likely couldn't recall any longer the trips she and I made to the car wash on Decarie, which had uniquely combined two of her most appeasing pastimes: driving and hygiene. She began always by aligning the front wheel with the conveyor track, shifting into neutral, then turning the key in the ignition. As we lurched forward in the sedan, the steering wheel spinning, suds released from electronically controlled brushes obscured the view from the windows while the screech and roar of machinery impeded conversation. At the car wash, temporarily immobilized, my mother sought and found relief from her anxiety.

If I'd become my mother's memory now, I was selectively so. She didn't need to recall that, months earlier, I'd sold her Nissan Altima for a pittance. It bore numerous gashes from my mother's diminishing driving skills, not least from a minor collision with a minibus brimming with schoolchildren. When the new owner, a slight grey-haired man fluent in the patter of buying and selling, came to collect the Altima, he discovered the battery had died long ago. "This affects the deal," he said. I dropped the already low price, and my mother's prized possession — her "life" as she called it — left the house for the last time on a tow truck.

Before I became an adult, nothing enthralled me more than the prospect of leaving my parents' home. Alone.

The first time I left for an extended period was for sleeping camp. I was twelve, one of the oldest novice campers ever admitted to Camp Pripstein's, evidence of my mother's reluctance to part with me. I learned how to somersault backwards into the lake from a dock and how to portage a birchbark canoe. In letters to my parents I expressed no homesickness but directed my mother and father to forward packages of jawbreakers, PEZ, and Oh Henry! bars.

When I returned from camp, fatter and more mature, I found my parents unaltered. Always the central drama that unfolded in the house was their conflict, to which my growing up seemed secondary. "That's enough, kids," I said too often as my father called my mother "a goddamn idiot" and my mother my father "a selfish bully." I no longer remember the essence of the arguments, only my mother's loud, deep-pitched voice projected to the full intercepted by my father's nasal but crisp diction. The conflicts arose most likely from numerous small slights and annoyances — the common complaints and grievances outlined in the marriage manual *Bride and Groom*. In her copy my mother had underscored, among the complaints levelled by husbands against their wives, *nagging, slovenly appearance,* and *interference in innocent pastimes*; for grievances claimed by wives against their husbands, *touchy, refusal to talk things over,* and *differences in age*. Amid the frequent bickering, I enforced civility when I could. In our family of three — in Judaism a number symbolizing harmony of opposites, completeness, and stability — I served as the witness, the peacemaker, and the captive.

From a young age I learned to fit myself into a small space and to be either solitary or conciliatory. My best friend and I began a secret society headquartered in my parents' basement of which the membership consisted of two. My friend's home was mysterious in its own right. Her uncle was missing part of a finger the Nazis had sliced off for his ring, and her senile *bubbe* wandered the halls after dark in a fraying paisley housedress, the milky film over her eyes muting the distinction between day and night. But we chose my house to hide our letters and documents, all of them ending with *Shhh . . . it's a secret*. It could be that my search for treasure or a hidden past originated somehow in those early habits of subterfuge, in a notion that those things most worthwhile exist in silence.

As I grew older, I continued to leave the house and my parents for entire summers. At sixteen I enrolled in a cross-Canada camping trip, where the group leader with the ginger beard explained around the campfire how hard it was to bring his wife to orgasm, and black bears sniffed around our tents at night. The next year I spent the summer in Winnipeg, where a boy called Larry, with bad skin, told me I had beautiful eyes, and his friend Liz advised me never to waste time on speculation.

$\longleftarrow\mathrel{\rule[0.4ex]{0pt}{0pt}}$

As the months passed and the need to sell my mother's house grew more urgent, I rarely gave thought to the buried treasure. When I entered the master bedroom, my concerns were to ventilate, run the taps in the ensuite bathroom, and flush the toilet. A timid groundhog had set up housekeeping under the front steps. At the back, under the balcony roof, wasps were nesting, their porous hive oozing moist white pearls like tapioca balls. The robins had already vacated their nest over my mother's outside front light. The birds must have endured the chill and rain — the storms of late spring and early summer, the demolition of the house next door.

My parents' circle of friends and neighbours on the street had mostly departed long ago. The jeweller from Czechoslovakia.

The CA with a spouse from Yonkers. The owner of a car dealership and his vivacious French-Canadian wife. Life on the block had evolved, for the most part, predictably. The neighbourhood was defined by wading pools and lopsided snowmen, kids slurping popsicles on front stoops, mothers who frequented the hairdresser weekly and sat for hours under the dryer, their strands of hair looped round fierce metal rollers.

Although I'd ceased to look for things in my mother's house, I continued to find them. My mother's fold-up rain ponchos; my father's golf clubs; my uncle Eddie's eightieth-birthday ode to his uncle Mo, with a note at the top in my mother's hand, *Worth remembering*.

I became a regular at the dump. In particular I frequented Metal (Zone 2), Wood (Zone 5), and Unsorted Items (Zone 9). Heaving no-longer-wanted objects into the said containers felt strangely emancipating. By the time I was done, the house would be stripped of my mother's belongings and, with them, her habits and gestures, the patterns of her anxiety. Many of these she herself had lost or forgotten, so that now only I — and maybe my husband — remembered. I had become the keeper of her anxieties.

In late summer I once again returned to my mother's house on my own. The weather was both warm and cool. In the back garden, squirrels picked at the detritus of raspberries, but the white phlox were blooming and the Queen Elizabeth roses flowering more abundantly than in midsummer. I took my mother two roses in her twin bud vase. "These are from your garden," I said before settling in for *So You Think You Can Dance*. As with so many aspects of my mother's house, the garden she'd cherished and tended as a new bride became, in middle age, a source of anxiety, even hostility. If she'd had her way, she might not have planted annuals at all, except that the gardener, a purveyor of vital snow removal in winter, demanded summer employment.

As I prepared to leave my mother smiled, pointing to the blush-pink roses. "These are from my garden?" Lately she'd begun once again to refer to my father as the "love of her life."

A week later a buyer emerged for the house. He asked to keep my father's workbench in the basement, since he, too, liked to tinker with wood. He and his wife expressed a desire to preserve the den with its built-in bookcases, turntable drawer, and mirrored liquor cabinet.

Although the new owners wouldn't take possession until December, I began to say my goodbyes to the house, to the street, to the few remaining people I knew there. "I can't take any more of this noise," one of the neighbours told me, motioning to the construction site beside my mother's house. The approval to "demolish and rebuild" had been granted the year before. On Valentine's Day. As I was gradually letting go now of my own home, this new house rose from apparent nothingness, casting a shadow over the split-level of my childhood. Memory itself, according to some recent theories, affords no permanent, unassailable home but rather is a house perennially under construction; each memory retrieved is rebuilt using more immediate experiences and perceptions.

I thought of all the animals that had occupied my parents' house, and how, for some, the ceilings furnished their sun, moon, and stars, the rooms their cities, countries, and continents. Hank the South African soft-shelled turtle; the kissing gouramis, green in their native Indonesia, and tinted pink only in aquariums; the slippery turtles I kept in a kidney-shaped plastic bowl — like my mother in her later years, none of them ever left the house.

I hired movers. I held an estate sale. I invited over my mother's cousin to take what she liked of the unwanted objects. As we sat at the bridge table in the kitchen she said, "Do you know, your mom told me your dad hid something in the house, something under the bedroom carpet."

Recently I'd taken comfort in the belated realization that the treasure never was intended for me, or only latterly. Because my father had buried the treasure before I was born. Although I'd come to think of it as mine, it was mine only to retrieve, not mine in its inception. The treasure didn't count, then, as my father's final communication to me, didn't harbour a note addressed to me, would even, conceivably, be meaningless to me. If my mother was losing her memory, I qualified as the one making things up. What's more, even if I'd found the treasure, what could be more impersonal than a gold bar, or coins intended as a medium of exchange to pass through countless hands, to travel. And yet I desperately didn't want someone other than me to have it. My father buried the treasure with his hands, the way he planted seeds in the back garden, the way a cat scrabbles in the soil to bury its excrement. His was a private act.

Throughout the removal of my mother from her house and my search for treasure, my circle from Toronto, my husband and friends, had responded generously to my appeals for support. For their presence I'd always be grateful. However, I alone harboured the memory of growing up in my parents' house, and for this reason I resolved that I alone should be the one to let it go. I chose to make my final trip to the house unaccompanied.

Upon my arrival, on the cantilevered black lacquer table in the downstairs hall, I found the gilt lampshade with the bronze lady base glowing bright. The lamp persisted in operating on the timer my mother had set when she still understood the transition to Daylight Saving Time.

The temperature was dipping below freezing now, the nights drawing in, as I prepared to breach the last of my mother's filing cabinets. I wasn't expecting to find anything significant, and I didn't. Stamps, hearing-aid batteries, swatches of white brocade brighter and more unblemished than their used counterparts, small-format black books with accounts of who paid for what and, if my mother, how much of her "allowance" remained. The birthday, Mother's Day, and anniversary cards I packaged up in a shoebox to be stored in my mother's unit. I was determined that she should have memories, if not memory.

My mother was watching PBS fundraising when I arrived at her apartment. She sat with her mouth slightly ajar, her chair at a right angle to the TV set. When urged to "Pledge now, or important stories might never be told," she remained impassive, but a half smile formed on her lips when the fundraiser begged her to endow Sesame Street and At the Minnesota State Fair. "I have to go," I said as the pledging concluded and the donations were tallied up. "I have things to do."

Until now, my most momentous departure from the house had taken place when I left to study in England. A friend's father, a cartoonist, had presented me with a sketch of myself in a flouncy tartan sports skirt and ankle socks, wielding a lacrosse stick. A delegation saw me off at the airport, family and friends. I can't remember saying goodbye to the house, only to them, but I soon became aware that I was far from home. By happenstance, I'd ended up renting a room from a German alcoholic with an old dog that smelled rank, and I sometimes caught my gaunt, pale-skinned landlady running naked down the hall when her boyfriend was visiting. I fed 10p coins into the gas fire in my bedroom and tried to mind my own business. I ate too many scones with clotted cream and didn't tell my parents what was happening to me. I wrote letters home, but never letters to the house itself. In my absence my grandparents began to fail, and my mother assumed the same responsibilities of care that now were falling to me several decades later. In the house I was about to vacate, I recovered a letter from one of my mother's contemporaries, at the time tasked with supporting an elderly parent: *We're all the same as ever,* he wrote, *though maybe a bit older and a little more worried.*

Several decades ago, then, willingly, deliberately, I'd left my parents and the house behind. Now my mother and the house were leaving me. As I prepared to lose both, I cherished the familiar in them. I readied myself to live the rest of my life in a strange place.

Although I could have spent my final night in any of the now-vacant rooms, and I'd considered the dining room for its warmth, I chose the red room, the so-called spare room, in which my husband and I had slept together since he'd first entered my parents' house. It was the room of my maturity, and my choice a betrayal, almost certainly, of my childhood bedroom. It was also the room my mother frequently had retreated to in the later years of her marriage when my father snored.

Neither of my parents was aware, when leaving the house for the last time, that it would be the last time. My father, having suffered a small stroke, was taken to the hospital where he'd interned and later volunteered. In his final days, before he lapsed into a coma, he mistook the intensive care unit for a resort in the Florida Keys. "My, it's very nice here, isn't it?" he said before succumbing to unconsciousness. My mother left under the guise of a lie, in the belief she was engaging in a trial departure and could at will exercise the prerogative to return. My family had been the first to own this house built expressly for them, and I would be the first knowingly to forsake it. Dispensing with the prospect of return came to feel like a form of extinction.

More reassuringly, I wouldn't be leaving behind the objects I'd retrieved from this house nor the people who'd laid claim to them with tenderness and vied to keep them safe. The awareness of my hidden ancestors, brought about through their possessions, was beginning to furnish me with another kind of home. In my mother's final years, she possessed a home in the simplest, most concrete meaning of the term but failed to understand where she was. In turn, I was developing a more intangible base from which I could orient myself. I looked to my lost family the way all of us do to distant stars, which, although not identical to us in composition, share many of the same elements.

As I prepared to relinquish the house, my mother had lost track of the relationship of her bedroom to her bathroom, but also of what constituted home. And yet place ultimately didn't preoccupy her. What concerned her most was her purpose. On a recent trip to the shopping mall, a place previously so familiar she knew the exact whereabouts in the IGA of Maxwell House decaf and Smucker's Concord grape jelly, she'd mislaid her intentions.

"I don't know what I'm doing," she said, at first quietly and then loud enough that passersby began to look.

Quickly I guided her towards a table of sale books in front of a store and arranged her hands firmly to either side before putting my arm around her shoulder. "I'm taking care of you. You can trust me."

"Yes, but I don't know what I'm doing."

She and I wouldn't need to make another trip to the IGA anytime soon. My mother's understanding of coffee entailed a few granules of freeze-dried decaf dissolved into a cup of hot water. This replacement jar would last her close to a lifetime.

The final night in my parents' house I slept on an extended footrest with no sheets but just scratchy wool blankets. For a night table I had a chrome footstool topped with black rubber. In the morning I found the emptying crew had carried off both the toothpaste and deodorant I kept for use in the house. I sucked on a mint teabag and dabbed perfume in my armpits. I swallowed a banana.

The task now fell to me, the last occupant of the house, to make sure it was genuinely empty. I went from one room to the next, dragging the chrome footstool with me so I could grope the unseen places — the overhead storage in cupboards, the upper pantry in the kitchen, the most inaccessible of bookshelves in the den. There, on the highest of shelves and almost beyond reach, I felt what I couldn't at first see: a leather-bound chapbook. *A Way of Life* by William Osler, professor of medicine at McGill and Johns Hopkins universities and sometime physician to Walt Whitman. On the inside front cover was an inscription to a medical student, my father, dated 1937. The book fell open at page 4, and I read, "'Life is a habit,' a succession of actions that become more or less automatic. This great truth . . . lies at the basis of all actions, muscular or psychic."

Down in the basement I stroked the familiar ridges of the oil furnace, peered into its monocular pilot light where the flame leapt reassuringly, and checked the pressure gauge, a ritual my mother had practised so assiduously until her own forced removal from the house. Next to my bedroom closet and the kitchen, the basement felt the most reassuring of rooms, only dirtier, its dust like a tarnish on my skin.

In my father's office I paused to consider Osler once again. This time an exhortation on page 14 caught my eye: "Shut out the yesterdays, which have lighted fools the way to dusty death, and have no concern for you personally, that is, consciously.

They are there all right, working daily in us, but so are our livers and our stomachs."

There is no absolute way to strip a house of its inhabitants. Even when you've accounted for every object, odours linger — confusions of chicken soup, Chanel No. 5, and talcum powder — as do stains, scratches, worn grooves on stair treads that belie the habits of a lifetime. All these the house retains, ownership aside.

The last of my father amounted to several seeds nestled against the cool marble floor of his office — *Dolichos lablab*, the purple runner bean, the planting of them his old man's project. And a mollusc shell. My mother's last belongings to evade the emptying crew were hearing-aid batteries buried in the pile of the red carpet in the spare room, and also one on the office floor. The silver batteries, akin to seeds in size and shape, I left in place. The remnants of my father I would take into the garden. I hadn't brought snow boots and slipped on instead an old pair of women's rubber waders from the garage. The companion pair, my father's, had disappeared. I walked the entire L shape of the garden, then stopped in the southeast corner where my father had trained his runner beans up their stakes, numbering the poles and later itemizing his harvest — 127 large seeds and 114 small in his bumper season. Next door the workmen were hammering in windows. Glancing sideways to make sure I was unobserved, I sowed the last of my father's seeds in winter.

CHAPTER FOUR

The Right Part of Life

ALTHOUGH THE SURRENDER OF MY MOTHER'S HOUSE HAD happened weeks before, I remained in vital ways an inhabitant of my childhood home. My obsessions returned me there, sustained by the finds I'd taken away. Not least among these were some clippings confined to a single business-size envelope I'd recovered from an overnight bag in my parents' basement — their subject, my great-uncle Jockey. The family black sheep and a doubtful celebrity of mid-century Montreal, my mother's uncle often was described as a "Runyonesque character," akin to Dave the Dude, Nathan Detroit, and The Seldom-Seen Kid — the Broadway con men, minor thieves, and marginal eccentrics brought to renown by the New York writer Damon Runyon. By all accounts, Jockey Fleming's chosen pastimes involved fantasy and obfuscation. Whereas my grandfather Simon was a fact, my great-uncle Jockey was a rumour.

My scrutiny of the few keepsakes in the envelope dedicated to my mother's uncle took place in my own home in Toronto. The first of the carefully folded newspaper clippings I recognized to be an obituary, its headline: "Passing of horseless Jockey leaves void on sports scene." My mother or her parents had cut out the same item in triplicate. And from a rival paper, in a single version, another eulogy, "Jockey Fleming rides no more." This more expansive obituary offered as a second-page headline a quote from Jockey himself: "Everybody is nobody unless they know me."

My mother and her parents seemingly hadn't thought to keep and archive stories about Jockey until his death on April 18, 1974, when, possibly, they experienced a moment of posthumous pride. This, or they'd divested themselves of earlier clippings. And no family member, but rather a janitor, had found Jockey in his apartment — the fixed address of his final years — dead, apparently, of a heart attack. To confuse my task, the few photos of my great-uncle that spilled out of the same envelope depicted a man in early middle age sporting an army cap and gathering to him three small boys — Sandy, Frankie, Danny. The photos and obituaries didn't agree. Jockey Fleming, a civilian Jew, was reputed to be childless.

Mine wasn't the only confusion precipitated by Jockey. In truth, my great-uncle confounded some of the best newspapermen of the postwar era — the sportswriters Jim Coleman and Dink Carroll, gossip columnists Fitz and Al Palmer, and humorist Don Bell. Whether by design or by accident, Jockey lived as a man without personal history. Left to describe his own lineage, he cited as distant and unknowing ancestors One-Eyed Connolly from Massachusetts and Pittsy Blackman from Cincinnati, both expert gatecrashers. In an homage to their example, Jockey reportedly gatecrashed Madison Square Garden by masquerading as a peanut vendor in a barber's white coat. My mother's uncle thus allowed to his chroniclers no more than spoofs, one-liners, carefully curated stories, and hearsay. Although written down, his telling belonged to an oral tradition. Stories about Jockey were frequently related more than once, sometimes in his own words, more often than not with playful variations or perversions of fact.

Jockey's escapades, whether told by him or his fleet of newspapermen, often have him coming out on top. But there's another strain in the literature of Jockey — the occasional ridiculing of him by his own admirers and, as an element of his repartee, a belittling of himself. As early as 1921 my mother's uncle recited "How I became a bum," his autobiography in brief, for a benefit at the Gayety Theatre. Jockey soon after befriended Eddie Cantor, Mickey Rooney, and Al Jolson, "all great guys," he said, "and most are on top today, but the old Jock is still at the corner of Peel and Ste. Catherine, shoving his two hockey tickets." My grandfather, Jockey's brother, continually lamented that the family had no luck.

As I slipped the clippings and Jockey's few personal photos back into their envelope, my father's emptied aquarium, now in the basement of my own home, caught my eye. Most beloved among its occupants had been the kissing gouramis. Their kissing didn't imply, as I'd long believed, a declaration of love, but rather a challenge between males.

It was nearly dark and time to make the daily long-distance call to my mother. I imagined her in her half-lit room as she reached for the receiver, her face for me ever present — a dulled, hurt thing after the brash vivacity of the day.

"You've had your dinner?" I asked.

"Yes."

"It was good?"

"It was okay."

"You're feeling comfortable?"

"Yes."

"Are you resting now?"

"Yes."

"You have a good evening."

"You too."

I couldn't remember when she'd last uttered a complex sentence.

I didn't ask my mother about Jockey, nor did I tell her I'd investigated the envelope in the faux leather overnight bag where her mother, my grandmother, had also put away for safekeeping a pink-and-blue-gingham apron string. In the space of an afternoon, Jockey had become my reluctant inheritance. It would fall to me, an unclaimed great-niece, to reconcile Jockey Fleming's personal history with his reputation.

⟵

I had little in the way of first-hand knowledge to support my inquiries. In truth, in the nearly fourteen years that Jockey and I might have got acquainted, I glimpsed him only once — a rumpled figure in front of Ogilvy's department store, occupying a spot on the sidewalk more typically reserved for quadriplegics selling pencils or blind men playing the spoons. He struck me as someone I wouldn't know. Before I could appraise Jockey further, my mother, having recognized her estranged uncle, grabbed me by the arm and pulled me across the street. "He's not a bad man," she said once we were safe on the other side, "but his family are ashamed of him." That's all she ever told me about her father's older brother, even though the two men shared the same face.

My near meeting with Jockey took place in the 1960s, when he was approaching late middle age and I was crayoning my ambitions on the walls of my parents' basement. I AM A QUEEN, I wrote in lopsided block letters. I AM A RABBIT. My great-uncle had fostered other aspirations. In his prime he earned his principal living as a ticket tout, holder of bets, and unbidden mooch, with more respectable sidelines as a failed comedian, singing waiter, and performer at stags of the hockey elite. His only fixed dwelling was a Montreal lamppost doubling as an office for his several lines of business. The cheques for his old age pension he reportedly collected from a downtown strip-tease joint.

Let me be clear that I don't come from a censorial family. When I was ten my father acquiesced to my plea for a first alcoholic drink, a tantalizingly pink strawberry daiquiri served up with a maraschino cherry at the Bermuda Castle Harbour Hotel. Two years later, one of my aunts asked me straight up whether I was still a virgin. "What are you saving it for?" she demanded in response to my barely audible reply. When it came to my great-uncle, however, my parents and grandparents shared a rare, if not premeditated, urge to silence. That I lived in the same city and frequented the same streets as Jockey without ever wondering about him not only testified to the careful omissions by my mother, her parents, and even my father, but also was wholly remarkable. Because among the few facts circulating about Jockey, one in particular laid claim to being more than a partial truth: Jockey Fleming was famous.

In Jockey's lifetime, sports and gossip columnists called my mother's uncle "The Jimmy Durante of Peel Street," "a famed raconteur and close confidant of hockey players and statesmen," "King of the Moochers."

Repartee with my great-uncle furnished material for journalists, and they in turn embellished his persona. The Montreal columnist Al Palmer, in his 1950 book, *Montreal Confidential,* opened the chapter "Characters, Characters — Never Any Normal People" with a word portrait of none other than Jockey Fleming, and this opinion: Jockey's "rise to fame as one of the town's official meeters and greeters has been meteoric — whatever that means." Palmer's Montreal chronicle sold upward of twenty-five thousand copies. And so most everyone in Montreal read avidly about Jockey Fleming, except his own family. As Jockey would have said, his family "played the ignore for him."

In my adult imaginings, Jockey engaged in nothing more than an outré version of his brother's, my grandfather's, pranks. As I was growing up, my mother tried to impress upon me that her father had suffered a hard life, having been sent out to work as an errand boy when he was merely seven or eight years old. Perhaps because he was denied play when young, he adored tomfoolery, and I, a solemn child prone to unbroken hours of reading, continually resisted his roughhousing. On family visits to Murray's restaurant, an Anglophone enclave beloved by Jews, my grandfather would point me out — a runt in white leotards, my cheeks engorged with steamed fruit pudding — announcing to the waitress, "This kid's gonna do great things!" Jockey's own actions, I expected, made for a more exaggerated form of my grandfather's, tipping over into misguided capers or bad taste.

In fact, my assumptions about my great-uncle were soon upended as I discovered how much of Jockey's truth turned out to be worthy of deletion. Although the Jock not infrequently was described as "kind" — even "harmless" — his pursuits were too often unwholesome. As Jim Coleman said of my great-uncle, "The difficulty in writing about The Jockey lies in the fact that some of his most interesting adventures cannot be related in print." Equally perplexing, much of what made it into print was "as hard to believe . . . as to disbelieve."

It's alleged that the first of several biographies of Jockey Fleming — a publication now untraceable — appeared in 1946, when my great-uncle's life was squarely *in media res*. That same year my grandparents went more than once to the feted restaurant Au Lutin Qui Bouffe, where my grandmother, in a pillbox hat and elbow-length silk gloves, bottle-fed a live piglet wheeled to the table on a silver trolley. She must have been aware of the transgression — a rare position she shared with

her brother-in-law Jockey Fleming, whose misdemeanours
were many and unrepented.

Her brother-in-law's *mishegoss* went something like this:

*A customer approaches Jockey at his lamppost or in his
secondary office, the foyer of the Mount Royal Hotel. The Jock's
slight, only 125 pounds, and in that regard, not an inappropriate
candidate for his name. His telltale ears and nose, the first gently
protruding, the second forthrightly bulbous, make him easy to
pick out in a crowd.*

"Hey, Jock, got any tickets for tonight's game?"

*If outdoors, Jockey straightens his herringbone coat. If inside,
he adjusts his headdress, on at least one occasion a World War
One helmet. "Sure, for you I always got spares. Hey, ya heard this
one? Parallel lines have so much in common, it's a shame they
never meet!"*

*The customer slips Jockey the ticket cost, plus commission, plus
a little extra for the unsolicited laugh.*

*The Jock summons Maxie the Goon, a one-time house painter
and factory worker who covers the afternoon shift. Jockey runs
about thirty men, some mooches — in Jockey parlance, "receivers
of gratuities" — others procurers of tickets they acquire legiti-
mately and then hawk "for a commission." Maxie hands over a
percentage of his take to cover the Jock's "expenses."*

*Jockey heads to nearby Dankoff's Steak House for a well-de-
served rib-eye and baked potato (he never frequents "creep-joints").
Whatever or whomever Jockey sees at Dankoff's, he will note,
remember, and transmit to the appropriate sources for a legitimate
fee.*

*Jockey is Jockey Fleming. He returns at night to no fixed
address.*

Had Jockey vanished betimes in those postwar years, his
family scarcely would have noticed. The Jock was by nature

a dealmaker, but whether his remove from his younger brother, my grandfather, happened by mutual agreement or was induced by one side or the other, I can only guess. Yet I wouldn't be surprised if Jockey and my grandfather occasionally spoke, Maurice in his stock trader's headset at Oswald & Drinkwater, Jockey pressing coins into the phone box by the Mount Royal Hotel. Possibly they even met. "Your grandmother didn't want to know from your grandfather's brother," a family friend recalled, but an older cousin, when I asked him about Jockey, said without hesitation, "Of everyone, your grandfather understood him best."

Only weeks after I'd examined the envelope with the clippings and photos of Jockey, I was threatened with jury duty in a murder trial, then released owing to a plea bargain the day before juror selection was to take place. I celebrated my sudden freedom with an assertion about my great-uncle:

Jockey Fleming is not Jockey Fleming.

My great-uncle, born on January 3, 1898, was never genuinely Jockey Fleming. By all accounts my grandfather's brother was mountless, with a sloping posture, flat feet, and a paunch. Jockey, his given name, which he gave himself, originated in his machinations at the track, when in the nineteen teens he nurtured a career as a ticket tout at Blue Bonnets Raceway. As for the surname Fleming, it signalled a tip of the hat to Frankie Fleming, Jockey's sometime employer in the same era. At five foot six and 112 pounds, Fleming for several years held the title of Canada's featherweight boxing champion, and Jockey, for his part, held Fleming's towel. In assuming made-up names, my mother's uncle was fashioning no less than his greatest gag: the invention of his legitimate self.

By 1921, Frankie Fleming had been out of the ring but was prepping for a comeback, whereas Jockey was hamming it up in a brief boxing career of his own. At least twice my mother's uncle was matched against the gangster Kid Baker, and on at least one occasion knocked him out before the ref Benny Cohen declared the round over. Simultaneously, and by his own telling, Jockey was launching a career as a singing waiter. In reminiscing about this era, the Jock rapped to newspaperman Baz O'Meara that he waited tables at The Frolics alongside famed entertainer Texas Guinan. Another newspaperman thought Tex appeared not at The Frolics but the old Venetian. By the time the discrepancy was noted, Jockey's mainstay during the early Prohibition era had become unverifiable. Throughout his life, he preferred to begin accounts of himself mid-narrative, excluding the nineteen teens and twenties.

In my frequent trips to Montreal, those I undertook alone, I began to experience in a small way Jockey's freedom of self-invention. My mother no longer made for a reliable witness to my past, and without my husband or friends on hand to confirm my identity, I found myself released from expectations. This rare solitude allowed me the freedom to satisfy my obsessions — for the moment, my fascination with my great-uncle Jockey.

When I travelled once again to Montreal to visit my mother, I elected to stay below ground in a gentrifying neighbourhood by the Lachine Canal where Jockey himself might once have frequented rooming houses. The cement walkways by the canal were dappled with ice. In the electric fireplace of my basement apartment, the soundless movement of flames was not unlike the flicker of a TV screen for someone unable to follow the contours of a story or grasp the words.

Una, a care aide, was arranging my mother opposite her TV in a hard-backed chair with a green leatherette seat when I arrived. My mother recently had turned eighty, although, by her own reckoning, she was but sixty-eight. She smiled as I presented her with flowers: apricot chrysanthemums for the Lucite coffee table and bold pink Kalanchoe for the galley kitchen. On TV, Piers Morgan was interviewing Hugh Hefner, then eighty-four, alongside his twenty-four-year-old fiancée, Crystal Harris. When faced with an indiscreet comment about her and Hef's sex life, Harris replied, "We have the best time together no matter what we're doing."

"I want to go to bed now," said my mother, although I'd only just arrived. And so Una grasped my mother's two hands and, taking backwards baby steps, guided my mother to her bed, where she curled up on the diagonal — her preferred position. I stepped out of the tropically warm, dimly lit apartment into the indifferent cold of the Montreal night.

I brought out my notebook and ventured a second assertion about the uncle my mother for decades had deliberately forgotten and now could no longer remember:

Jockey Fleming is Moses Rutenberg.

In sharing this entry, I'm disclosing a fact that remained largely hidden until after my great-uncle's death — Jockey Fleming had another name, and it was biblical.

Moses Rutenberg, my great-uncle, originated in a neighbourhood of meagre streets near the St. Lawrence River and the Courts of Justice that was later demolished for an expressway. It served as an enclave for immigrant Jews from Eastern Europe, their numbers to increase fourfold within the decade or so following Moses Rutenberg's birth. Jewish children themselves weren't especially abundant in my great-uncle's growing-up years. The newly arrived immigrants, many of them married men, struggled to become financially established before sending for their wives and children in Europe. One of the first English sayings they learned at the Baron de Hirsch night school for new immigrants was "Time is money."

By 1911 the Rutenberg family, along with many immigrant Jews, had moved farther north to the Plateau, a neighbourhood of English-inspired row houses not far from the abattoir and the public livestock market for hogs, sheep, and cattle. Horses, too, played a crucial role, a mainstay of business for the better-off Jewish peddlers who could afford wagons.

Montreal's Jewish community now numbered twenty-eight thousand, and Yiddish had become the third-most-common language spoken in the city, after French and English. In his formative years, then, Moses Rutenberg — the middle of three sons and a brother to a half-dozen sisters, all of whom acknowledged the Rutenberg name conferred by their father, Casper — was undeniably Jewish and versed in Yiddish with at least a smattering of Hebrew. In the apartment at 743 St. Dominique, a street named after a Catholic saint, Casper would have tutored his rebel son in the ancient words of the Kaddish prayer.

Yet only occasionally in the chronicles of Jockey Fleming is Moses's Jewish background acknowledged, whether because it was so widely known as to be thought unworthy of reporting, or because it was considered unseemly, or because Moses himself had chosen to obscure it by electing an ancient Irish surname with even older origins in Flanders. Certainly, during Jockey's childhood, being recognized as a Jew carried some risks — jeers and taunts or, worse still, the possibility of being beaten up by street gangs galvanized by anti-Semitic "Jew comedians" in the burlesque theatres.

In other respects, too, even before Moses Rutenberg voluntarily became Jockey Fleming, a degree of anglicization would have been enforced. For Jewish immigrants, the language of advancement necessarily was English, the mother tongue of the Quebec business elite. Jewish children were sent not to the Catholic school board but to selected Protestant schools in the Jewish lower city, where in the era of Jockey's childhood the small Yiddish speakers were registered as Protestants.

Generally, the Jewish immigrants from Eastern Europe were versed in several languages, demonstrating higher degrees of literacy than the population at large, all of which enhanced their academic achievement. In this respect, however, as in so many others, Moses Rutenberg stood apart from his milieu. By his own account he was a bad boy, "so dumb in school" he couldn't spell his own name. For his brief tenure as a formal student, Moses attended Aberdeen School on St. Denis, a palatial stone building with a mansard roof, Romanesque arches, and exactly two turrets. Despite the building's splendour, many of the immigrant children within, Moses among them, came from backgrounds so poor that their parents could scarcely afford to clothe them.

Academe didn't suit Moses, nor he it. Too soon, he walked away from Aberdeen School, having discovered an alternative grandeur. On the eastern slope of Mount Royal, beneath the summit cross, dark horses hauled sleighs that sliced a clean path through the undisturbed snow. As the mares drew close to the expansive arch of the Ice Palace, the small passengers in the sleighs thrust their fists deeper into their rabbit fur muffs. Although mere blocks from St. Denis, this winter palace at Fletcher's Field, built on the remains of a disused racetrack, offered no view onto Aberdeen School.

Soon after the rupture with academe, Moses Rutenberg devised his first scam. According to Kid Oblay, Jockey's lifelong rival, Moses was ten when he commandeered resources from Kid's mother. On Jockey's instruction, Kid — genuinely Lazarus Goldberg — borrowed thirty cents from Mrs. Goldberg. The loan was for pencils, a tin cup, and sunglasses from a nearby Woolworth's. Then Moses led Lazarus to the corner of Craig and St. Lawrence Main, where Moses put on the sunglasses, holding the cup in one extended hand and the writing implements in the other. "Please help me," he said to all and sundry. "I'm a poor boy who can't see." With a slyness that foretold mastery, Moses instructed Lazarus to throw pennies into the cup so that passersby, watching a mere boy engaged in an act of charity, would feel "like a rat" and maybe donate even more.

How did Moses, the wayward son of respectable, if cash-strapped, Orthodox Russian Jews, escape his origins in Esther and Casper — a mother bound to plucked chickens and imperfect dresses, a father consumed with Hebrew learning and other people's sons? The makings of Jockey Fleming presented themselves from early on, but that Esther died too soon, in 1918, the year of the great flu pandemic, no doubt destabilized the household. By the 1921 census she'd vanished from Casper's precarious band.

The single photo that survives of Jockey's mother is from the leatherette overnight bag once kept in my mother's basement, from an album saturated with a black dye that leaves its dark trace on my fingers. Esther Rutenberg, née Susnitsky, appears uneasy before the camera. Anxious. Her eyes don't meet the photographer's in the defiant gaze common to portraits of that era. Instead she looks sideways and, I'm certain, is focused on nothing outside herself. She's a woman preoccupied, the lips of her smallish but full mouth parted, hesitant. Only the loose brown curls piled high on her head are unguarded. The white lace collar of her dress envelops her neck right up to the earlobes, a stain, a tatter, or perhaps just a shadow on the left side above her heart. Immediately before her, obscuring her bosom, is a feature I first took to be part of her dress and only later realized to be discrete — a quadruped, more probably a dog than a horse, sporting a beret and serving as a mount for a diminutive rider, a female doll seated English style and wearing a jaunty hat. The photo is sepia, the age of the subject impossible to discern. Whether I'm looking at Esther Susnitsky, Esther Rutenberg, a mother, or a woman who's barely surrendered her own childhood, I can't say. I know I'm looking at fear.

Esther's middle son, Jockey, from the age of majority and coinciding with the era of his mother's death, revealed himself to be oddly impartial to the female sex. In his world the feminine was relegated to doubtful jokes — "I tell the waitress when I pay my cheque, 'Can I take a couple of hard-boiled eggs out?' She says, 'Sorry, mister, we don't get through till five.'" — or rumours — "Jockey claims his girlfriend has given him the frigid clavicle and he threatens to come to TORONTO to forget about her." Women thus rated among Jockey's exclusions, as did crewelwork, animal husbandry, and every troubling aspect of his personal history.

And yet Moses grew up one of several boys in a family of six girls, a position that conferred demands as much as entitlement. Casper, the patriarch, never enjoyed a surplus. Not for him the gold teeth, blue serge suit, pointy-toed shoes, and gold rings that for his peers bespoke affluence. A Hebrew teacher of limited means, and in the Old Country a rabbi, he looked to his sons to engage in commerce. Max, the eldest and the only one of the children born in Lithuania, under the Russian Empire, obliged by becoming a salesman; Maurice, the youngest son, eventually secured work as a telephone operator and broker at the stock exchange; Moses, whether through inherited disposition or misplaced ingenuity, found his natural milieu in make-believe.

Although not missing in the way of Jockey, my grandfather's siblings remained markedly invisible throughout my childhood. "Something in that family was broken," an older cousin recently confided to me, but she could offer no more. I realize now that, like my grandfather, the half-dozen sisters vied for respectability. They lived by their appointed names, some of them forging lives as independent women and adopting professions worthy of printing in *Lovell's Montreal Directory*: candy maker, milliner, attorney. Still, as a child I simply took for granted that my mother's aunts and uncles roused little interest, whereas my father's clan was both familiar and abundant.

Throughout the winter, as I sorted items from the Montreal house in my own home in Toronto, my mother continued to command my days, mostly in the form of a voice-over. Even so, she said little. I'd just come across her parents' yellow vinyl cooler, sour smelling from traces of smoked meat and dill pickle, when the phone rang once again.

"Do I still have another place? My house?" she wanted to know. "I'm confused."

"Do you have everything you need?" I asked.

"Yes."

"Then *carpe diem*. Just live for the day." My mother's literal understanding of language remained perfect. More than most, she simply felt at a loss for meaning.

This lack of assurance pervaded even my mother's younger years. When laying plans or expressing hopes, she'd invariably prefaced or concluded her statements with "God willing" or "All being well." My mother didn't believe wholeheartedly in God, although she wanted to, but she feared his wrath. The mezuzah she'd placed by our front door to designate a Jewish household was upside down.

The day Moses Rutenberg became Jockey Fleming — arguably, the day he compromised Lazarus Goldberg at the corner of Craig and Main — he'd already lost faith in the foregone conclusion. In 1907, during an economic depression and when Moses was a mere nine years old, he learned the essence of the maxim he was to repeat throughout his life: "There ain't no such thing as a sure thing." The early evidence lay in the person of his Uncle Hiram, the eldest of Casper's brothers and hence the patriarch of the family in exile.

Hiram belonged to the set with gold rings, gold watch fobs, and gold teeth. He'd demonstrated his acuity by leaving Sereje, Lithuania, in the 1870s, during an economic downturn, and later by dispensing paper money to Litvak expatriates while securing the loans with their treasures — their mother's wedding band, their father's pocket watch, the silver kiddush cup from the Old Country.

But there must have been more to Hiram. To Chaim. We know the facts. What's missing is the rumour. From *The Canadian Jewish Times*, November 29, 1907:

RUTTENBERG, Hiram, 67 Shuter St., Montreal, died Nov. 24, 1907, age 53.... The rash act which caused him to take his own life is quite unaccountable as he was a man of considerable means and there was no occasion, with the exception, possibly, of a temporary annoyance, to cause him to terminate his life as he did.

Perhaps Hiram was anguished by the ongoing financial crisis, when both established immigrants and newcomers lacked work, the latter without means to send money home to their wives and children in the Old Country. Whatever the reason for taking his life, Hiram defied the expectations of actuarial science as, eventually, did Casper. In the single rusty photo of Casper in middle age in my possession, he wears a bowler hat and too-loose coat, a white shirt and subtly dotted cravat. The pupil of one eye has retreated to the inner margins of its socket while the other holds steady dead centre. A splendid candidate for suicide — penniless, prematurely widowed, with a son who renounced the family name — the luckless brother persisted into older age and died a natural death.

Almost two years before Hiram's suicide, when Moses had just turned eight, a misbegotten initiative by Casper and Esther occurred at home — at 22 Drolet, within earshot of the abattoir. It survives not as a memory but as an imprecise record:

> *On the 12th day of January February 1906*
> *Died Stillborn child of Casper*
> *Rutenberg and Ester Malke*
> *And was buried in the oversense*
> *of A. adler*

In traditional Judaism, a stillborn birth is observed in solitude and silence. The saying of Kaddish, the sitting of shiva, and other rituals of mourning are reserved for those who live beyond the gestation period of a rabbit — thirty days. Casper and Esther's lost child seemingly was buried nameless and without belongings, its gender unacknowledged. Moses, eventually the dispossessed Jockey Fleming, would assume names enough for two. As Casper and Esther suppressed mourning, Moses likely was taking notes, observing how the unexpected could lead either to grief or a bigger win at the races. Just blocks away at McGill, my grandfather Simon, a recent graduate, was engrossed in the study of abnormalities.

The stillbirth coincided, too, with the opening of Dominion Park, a Coney Island on Montreal's waterfront with a roller-coaster ride ending in a tunnel dubbed "Dante's Inferno." Other entertainments featured scaled-down representations of death and disaster: the Johnstown dam burst and the San Francisco earthquake. No less compelling were the Infant Incubators, where trained nurses oversaw heated, oxygenated tanks sheltering newborns with a tenuous hold on life. Other attractions included Myth City, the Crystal Maze, Shoot-the-Chutes, the Laughing Gallery. A boy could lose himself in the darkened funhouses and find himself in their looking glasses, his image distorted beyond recognition. At the centre of it all stood a 125-foot tower illuminated by seven thousand bulbs and a searchlight that rotated day and night, casting its beam indiscriminately over the surging crowds.

$\longleftarrow$

For me to understand Jockey Fleming's longings, which were both unbounded and ethereal, required research beyond the scant findings from my parents' basement. From my own home I took to the internet — to sites public and intangible that yielded curiously intimate particulars. I was looking not to retrieve memories but to discover things never known. Things my mother and grandparents perhaps had chosen not to know. The business of Jockey was perplexing, and already I felt obliged to modify an earlier opinion: *Jockey Fleming is Moses Rutenberg.* This I changed to the following:

Jockey Fleming is Moses Rutenberg in name alone.

Moses Rutenberg was born in the 1890s; Maurice, my grandfather, at the turn of the twentieth century. But Moses, not Maurice, became the innovator. It's he who deserves credit for self-determination, for refusing to abide by the dictum that the family had no luck. His inventiveness came from within, from his natural leanings, and from without, from the city he inhabited. In particular, Montreal in the war years allowed Moses Rutenberg to fulfill the promise of Jockey Fleming.

As elsewhere, in Montreal the anxiety of war fostered revelry. Already a source of illicit gambling and cheap whiskey in the twenties and thirties, Montreal in the mid-forties hosted some two hundred gambling dens, plus nightclubs and blind pigs. At the Samovar, the El Morocco, and the Tic-Toc Club, hustlers like Moses Rutenberg dodged Apache dancers and knife throwers. Nearby, in the Chez When Room, the newspaperman Dink Carroll, among the several literary endorsers of Jockey Fleming, drank in the lounge owned by the two prize-fighters Slitkins and Slotkins. Late nights ended at Bens Delicatessen, garlic sausage only ten cents, "The Breath of a Nation."

This was Freddie the Count's Montreal, Hickey the Lightman's, Oscar the Hammer's. Alongside Charlie the Horse, Jockey Fleming added to his already considerable reputation in a city open for business, where credit accrued not merely to the honourable but to those with an aptitude for the cover-up.

Jockey's agreement with the times continued into the postwar years, when both he and Maurice appeared outwardly respectable. Jockey, in one newspaper photo, might even have passed for an investigative journalist or a tenured professor. He had the same studied tilt to the head, the sleep-deprived eyes behind clearly articulated glasses, the same tweedy allure. Maurice, in his portrait from the same era, appeared to be modelling himself after the Rumba King and romancer Xavier Cugat. The photo at Old Orchard Beach shows him entirely in white

— bronze faced in a boxy jacket with loose-legged trousers, leaning against a car with a provocatively curved hood. At nearly fifty, he appeared barely older than at thirty-two, when he was documented holding his first baby girl in her parka, his hands cinched about her waist, her face as flat and fur rimmed as a capuchin monkey's.

One of Maurice's two daughters or his wife, Rose, must have snapped the picture at the beach that summer after the miners' strike at Asbestos. For Maurice in his household of women — a sanctuary of tulle, corsages, and giggled secrets — the tear gas, pummellings, and abductions at the mines eight miles away would have felt eight miles too close. Pugilism wasn't his natural milieu but Jockey's. The presence of women, Jockey's principal exclusion, was his younger brother's defining trait.

Jockey Fleming is not Maurice Rutenberg.

While Jockey was flouting Quebec's Napoleonic Code, Carol, one of his two dispossessed nieces, was poring over a birthday gift, the booklet *Edvard Grieg: The Story of the Boy Who Made Music in the Land of the Midnight Sun.* The younger brother, whose bunchy nose and bald pate weren't prophetic of female beauty, had produced two stunners — in the parlance of the time, "dolls" or "Judies." Carol, born six years after her sister, excelled at music, Latin poetry, history, and art. Rene, my mother, distinguished herself as a belle, her straight, thick hair as shiny black as obsidian, her first date a Toronto boy called Milton Sky. When it came to family, Jockey rejected simile and couldn't have pictured himself to be "like" either of the girls. In fact, both nieces qualified as young equestrians, and not merely in their imaginings.

In the postwar years, Carol's mounts were *Duchess, Pearl,* and *Tony,* all dark horses. My mother, at the same stables, rode *Golden Kay,* brown with a white diamond on the forehead. Carol wore a checked riding coat, my mother a jacket of a uniform shade with a suede vest the colour of fire beneath.

The stables where the sisters rode were located less than an hour's drive from Montreal, on what, in the nineteenth century, would have been termed the "right side" of the Malaria Line, the boundary between the more wholesome St. Lawrence lowlands of Quebec and the mosquito-ridden swamplands of southern Ontario. There both girls became disciples of Mrs. Beresford, who taught them to ride cowboy style, legs parted. They were photographed extensively on horseback but always motionless, never in a canter or a gallop, the photographer unwittingly casting a shadow. The hazy shape belonged to Maurice Rutenberg. The mounted girls belonged to him also, foretold in the only surviving photo of his mother, Esther Susnitsky, her aloneness shared with a miniature jockey riding sidesaddle.

For his part, Jockey Fleming remained engaged in the track. Foremost on his mind was the move at Blue Bonnets to institute saliva testing of horses. "What's going to happen to some of them old hop-heads out at the track," he demanded of Jim Coleman, one of his more regular amanuenses. "It looks as if they'll have to ship to Cuba or give themselves up at the Canada Packers' Plant." Simultaneously, but not in response, my mother had written in her diary, Went out with *Greg T. riding Charlemagne. Not bad, eh?*

Greg T. became a regular in my mother's diary as she approached twenty. *July 27: Greg — horseback riding, movies! September 3: Riding — Hunt Club. Greg. September 15: Greg — Bill's Bridle.* Although an able rider of an all-black steed, Greg T. in no way qualified as a jockey. His muscular arms were as shapely and burnished as a woman's thighs, his poundage more than a racehorse could bear. Rene Rutenberg was besotted. For sixty years she kept in her diary a note he'd written on the back of a rain cheque for a two-way carwash: *I, Greg T., hereby guarantee that Renée Rutenberg not do any harm to the horse on Sunday morning at 11 a.m.* Indeed, on September 20 she wrote *Nearly died.*

Followed by *Greg proposed marriage*. And then, on October 5, *Broke of* [sic] *with Greg*. The final entry, printed in cobalt blue pencil and half captured in a broken circle, turned out to be the last in my mother's five-year diary. It signified, as well, a final break with riding, Mrs. Beresford, and the Malaria Line. My mother, like the Jockey without a horse, had been in the business of chronicling her personal history. Yet my mother had always relied on her own hand, Jockey on dictation to scribes. Moreover, my mother's jottings had filled more than a hundred pages, whereas Jockey, nearly three times her age, found that his life story in print had been reduced to six hundred words.

The Rutenbergs show a propensity for scribbling, which I've inherited down the female line. I've alluded before to my mother's exuberant note-taking, the hoard of directives, lists, and jottings she composed. Unbeknownst to her, her uncle Jockey also manufactured scribbles and written decrees, seen always with a tattered notebook in hand, renowned for communicating sought-after information via the medium of sealed envelopes.

My mother's writing ranged from the provocatively cryptic — *Eddie* [her brother-in-law]: *Oka cheese, never peace since Cain killed Abel, U.S meddling, dial Vietnam* — to the transparently banal — *Maine: no white necessary for navy outfit, red duster, bras can wash.* She composed on the backs of scorecards for the golf course, on the cardboard rectangles from Knee-Highs packages, on sheets from my father's prescription pad. Her notes were rarely disciplined in appearance but, rather, shot out in the unpredictable manner of fireworks, some as linear as Roman candles, others expansive like a chrysanthemum burst, some as wayward as poppers and snaps.

In my mother's later years the note-taking served as a form of remembering, whereas throughout her life it made for a release from the too-many thoughts in her head. More than anything, the impetus for the scribblings was to avert disaster. Not infrequently, they were addressed to me. For example, the fire drill she sent when I first moved away from home and was living in England in a postgraduate residence named after a Roman emperor: *Sloping ceilings* [underlined in red]. *Is the door locked to your neighbour's room? If possible, crawl with nose and mouth covered to the closest escape.* And on the second of two pages, an afterthought: *Building location good.*

So pervasive was my mother's anxiety that my father, Jockey's estranged nephew by marriage, would share with relative strangers the following prognosis for his wife: "She has so many worries, if she has one more, she won't be able to worry about it for a month." With no genuine release for her surplus of imagination, my mother as a young housewife became focused on absurdities. What if my father used the pink instead of the blue finger towel. What if the baked prune whip didn't congeal. The prospects equal to her anxiety — for example, the prospect of losing her memory — she didn't worry about enough.

In her later years my mother was rarely heard and too often denied the ability to listen. Her silence resulted from her mental impairment, her lapses into deafness from the flimsy lifespan of her hearing-aid batteries. I continued to visit monthly, both to oversee her care and to assure her she was loved and remembered. This time, as I entered her apartment, she was straining to hear an episode of *Property Virgins*. The Kalanchoe plant on her kitchen table, a succulent, was bone-dry.

"I'm confused," said my mother. "What's that number on the screen?" The TV mother and daughter were searching for an apartment, the daughter's first home away from home.

"It's the price this young lady wants to pay for her condo," I said too loudly, pulling my chair close to my mother's.

"I'd be happier if you had indoor parking," the *Property Virgin*'s mum said to her daughter.

"Don't worry, Mum, I can take care of myself."

My own mother's head began to tilt forward, spume dotting the side of her mouth. As usual, her lipstick had been applied unevenly so the coral pink overshot the vermilion zone.

As I was zipping up my jacket, one of my mother's eyes opened. "Don't go home alone. I want you to take a taxi." Then the eye snapped shut.

When still in command of herself, my mother's greatest fear had been losing a child, her only child — by necessity, me. "There's nothing worse," she'd said often and with conviction.

t͡

It's evident from the surviving photographs of Jockey's parents that they, like my mother, were consumed with worry. Esther is beset with fear, Casper tense and furtive, his face narrow as a lupine. Underlying their apprehension was the experience of pogroms, the hardships of immigration, the inadequacy of a Hebrew teacher's salary, the unacknowledged grief for a still-born child.

One generation down, the sources of anxiety remained real but were made more vivid by imagined circumstances. Maurice, my grandfather, lost his mother young and his money and car in the Great Depression, yet even in later years, when his life bore the regularity of prayer, he inclined to worry. He worried about the sugar content of his *mohn* cookie, about whether my onset of puberty had occurred at the appropriate time. He worried that his toenail might become ingrown. He admired more than anything the film *The Ten Commandments* starring Charlton Heston, in which Moses brought the law to the Jewish people. Simultaneously, he was mesmerized by Alan Jay Lerner and Frederick Loewe, whose musical *Gigi* celebrated the breaking of rules and the imperative of young love in Paris. Jockey's sympathies lay entirely with the *shiksa*. With Gigi. But that's not to say Jockey Fleming was spared the family impulse to anxiety.

If my grandfather's brother had chosen to live with neither possessions nor personal ties, it was presumably so he had nothing to lose and, by implication, far fewer things to worry about. In that respect, we may assert the following:

Moses Rutenberg is Moses Rutenberg.

More than once, Jockey was diagnosed with a mental disorder, most notably by the "medico" for the Toronto Hockey Club. Catching sight of the physician in a hotel lobby, Jockey pleaded with him, "Doc — psychoanalyze me."

The doctor considered him gravely. "I would say that you suffer from anxiety neurosis."

"Right!" hollered Jockey happily. "Dat's the same thing dey told me up at the asylum."

In the 1940s, the era when Jockey solicited his snap diagnosis from the hockey medic, anxiety neurosis was understood as a Freudian aberration. Specifically, it was believed to originate in abstinence and coitus interruptus, resulting in an excess of libido that was then discharged via sweating, ill temper, breathlessness, and even tachycardia. Jockey might have interpreted the same as "absence," "coitus interrupts us," "card attack," and "ad lib at Lido." Dink Carroll, who for decades conveyed the Jockey's pronouncements to the reading public, arrived at an alternative diagnosis to the medic's: dyslexia, or

"trouble with words." As the Jockey would have put it, however, medical evaluation wasn't Dink's "era." More in his line of
work were the "Toronto Argues."

Among the many conundrums of Jockey Fleming is this:
how such a fundamentally anxious individual chose a lifestyle
that, for most, would have induced uncontrollable anxiety.

Equilibrium, for Jockey, demanded performance, telling the
good-enough story — like the time he was mobbed by guys
hoping to buy tickets for a Saturday football game. The scene
attracted the notice of a police officer, who had trouble squar-
ing the ordinariness of Jockey with the fervour surrounding
him. When the policeman asked about Jockey's doings, Jockey
replied, "They're just trying to get my autograph and I can't
give it to them all." Before the official could formulate his disbelief, Jockey had hailed a taxicab and jumped into it.

It's no wonder Moses Rutenberg's family stored his personal
effects in a white envelope and not the chocolate box kept for
family photos at the beach. They didn't get the joke. For them,
Moses accounted not merely for shame, but also anxiety. In
particular, Maurice Rutenberg must have worried daily about
being mistaken for Jockey Fleming.

$t \frown$

Beyond the face, my grandfather shared with his brother the
situation of not owning a home, for the former a perceived
deficiency inciting deep shame. For my grandmother, the pes-
simism that took hold during the Great Depression, when so
many aspirations moved beyond reach, was amplified by the
ever-present threat of Jockey's reappearance in her life.

Jockey, for his part, remained as intent on denying his family as they were him. From the 1940s, when the first biography appeared, the solitariness of Jockey, his inability to define

himself through kin, put him on a par with survivors of cataclysms — earthquakes, tsunamis, mass extermination by the Nazis. But unlike those veterans of disaster, Jockey had exercised a choice. He'd abjured his recent past. Like a victim of dissociative fugue, a severe form of amnesia, he'd mislaid both his name and a chunk of his personal history, albeit voluntarily.

As a young scholar vying to establish connections between living plants and the fossil record, my grandfather Simon had concluded, "Different appearances at different levels represent consecutive stages of the same structure." Considered superficially, my life and Jockey's bore no resemblance to each other. Nonetheless, I too found myself deprived of near blood relatives — neither a father nor siblings, a vanishing mother. And, like Jockey, I would never make a parent.

For someone whose livelihood and associates could only be described as "off-colour," Jockey Fleming appeared surprisingly at ease among children. Of the several photos from the overnight bag — the sum of Jockey's surviving personal memorabilia in my possession — four out of five depict him in the company of boys: Sandy, Frankie, Danny. The Jockey, in a white shirt and striped trousers, reclines on a striped lounge chair, eyes shut, the preschoolers keeping a steady vigil over him. Sandy in short trousers with the belt pulled too tight, fists jammed into his pockets, an oversized army cap obscuring his forehead; the twins even younger and wearing identical pale overalls. These aren't the Jockey's own boys, not his blood, but among them Jockey feels at home. Frankie, Danny, Sandy, Jockey.

$\overleftarrow{}\rule[0.4ex]{0.8em}{0.4pt}$

"Is that my daughter?" My mother directed the words not to me, but to Una, her caregiver.

I hadn't seen my mother for several weeks, and to my disappointment she squinted at me with recognition but little enthusiasm. "The trees are starting to flower," I announced. "Soon we'll be able to sit on your balcony."

So many people, so many subjects now, would trespass on my mother's composure: her late husband and parents; the cousins and friends whose phone calls she rebuffed; her uncle Jockey, who impersonated Santa at a Newark department store as the Nazis were occupying France and the Low Countries.

I considered the woman who'd given me life. Her skin was unblemished, her housedress spattered with spaghetti and meatballs. "Do you remember your little grand-cat?" I asked. My mother shook her head. "She sleeps eighteen hours a day. Just like you!"

My mother smiled, then slid one foot into her gaping white running shoe with the Velcro fastener. "I want to go to bed now."

⌐

To survive as Jockey meant a degree of verve that would have eluded his niece, my mother, in her later years. For a man with no fixed address, a propensity for overcrowded arenas, and an uncommonly high exposure to snow and ice, Jockey Fleming remained surprisingly resilient. Even a few years before his death, the "indomitable Jockey Fleming" was still taking his place ringside, shoulder to shoulder with hockey legend Henri Richard. In the end, Jockey died from a swift, unfaltering heart attack — and with his wits about him. And like Simon, Jockey timed his exit for a season of thin ice.

Understanding that death made for the single foregone conclusion, Jockey most likely didn't regard it as worthy of his anxiety. He must have been aware, though, that it would render him invisible, and when he hadn't yet commanded the audience he sought in the plush rooms of the El Morocco, Chinese Paradise, or Normandie Roof. For once my mother's uncle fostered a worthy aspiration. In the postwar era the entertainment profession in Canada drew numerous Jews, especially in Quebec, offering both a living and a way of countering the invisibility foisted upon European Jewry. Jockey exercised a legitimate claim to being an entertainer — not an Al Jolson, whose raccoon coat Jockey wore about town when his buddy Al was playing the Princess Theatre, but a standard gag man at prenuptial festivities and clubs of lesser distinction, the Colony Club or the Canadian Legion Hall. By his own count, my great-uncle performed at more than fifteen hundred stags. There, in the presence of an audience, he found himself genuinely at home.

Jockey's cachet only increased with the 1950 publication of Al Palmer's *Montreal Confidential*, and so, in the following years, he infiltrated the home of his estranged nieces by way of transistor radio or the TV set with rabbit ears. He was playing the Park Casino, making a guest appearance on Radio-Canada's *Carte Blanche*, broadcasting from the Showbar with Mr. and Miss Music.

Montreal in the 1950s: The diners, mostly parties of four, are seated at round tables encircling the stage. Linen napkins in the form of perfect cones dot the tabletops like starched white topiary. The waiters wear long-sleeved white shirts and silky black bowties. On stage, showgirls in sequined bikini tops and transparent hula skirts are finishing their routine, their breasts and feathered headpieces quivering in unison.

MC: And now, please welcome a Montreal treasure, famed raconteur and one of this city's savviest operators, the jockey without a horse — Mr. Jockey Fleming!

Jockey, seated among the audience, breaks into a gallop, vaulting over the velvet rope to assume his position on stage. He whin-

nies. The women toast him with their mai tais, the men with their Canadian Clubs straight up.

Jockey: Welcome, welcome! Say, you pal [points to a man with a bald pate and florid complexion], ya' heard this one? Little Jewish guy tells his wife he don't want to be kosher no more. Why? Because he has to bring home the bacon! Whoa, Nelly! A bum spends all his time in book-joints. When he finally goes to jail, they put him in charge of the library. Giddy-up!

Jockey prances on an imaginary mount. He wears a shirt of vivid colour — "loud," some would call it — emblazoned with names and pictures of famous racehorses and their riders.

Jockey [again]: Here's one for ya'. A guy has a pretty, a real doll. So why does he give her up? Because she always puts him down!

The MC motions for Jockey to wrap it up.

Jockey [finale]: And now, ladies and gents, a song for you.

Jockey launches into his signature tune, "Deep in the Heart of Texas," in what one naysayer has called "the world's worst baritone." Twirling an imaginary lasso, he canters offstage to rapturous applause.

At home, the nieces are removing their makeup after date night. My mother writes in her diary, *B kept letting his hands wander and we necked. I thought he would lose all respect.* In a year she'll be photographed wearing a mortar board. A fully qualified teacher, she'll dangle iridescent balls from a classroom Christmas tree for children with names like Gitel Rudansky, Hymie Glitman, and Brian Slepchick. Several years later she'll emerge a bride.

←⟍

Jockey was absent from the 1955 wedding of Rene Rutenberg to Dr. Archie Kirsch, when Maurice, wearing white gloves, a black top hat, and a spray of white carnation, escorted his older daughter to the *chuppah*, an imprecise look in his eyes.

That summer, the first of my parents' marriage, turned out to be the hottest in fifty years. Following their honeymoon in Virginia Beach, the newlyweds moved into their semi-detached house with its freshly excavated basement. In a home movie from the era, my mother, smiling and ebullient, her arms and legs moving too fast, is planting a rose bush in the back garden, surrounded by the skeletons of half-built houses. She wears tortoiseshell glasses and a subtly printed blouse, dark Bermudas, and flats that offset her porcelain calves. Round the front of the house, my grandparents are tugging a little girl — not me — down the concrete steps that decades later would serve as a maternity den for skunks. The front and garage doors are painted the harsh blue of fluorite, a mineral common to industry.

At the end of that year, to mark their first anniversary, my father presented my mother with a sapphire-and-diamond starburst brooch. Decades later the gifts had stopped, and my father, when he sought to undermine his wife, summoned up a name, "Your uncle Jockey."

In pondering my mother's uncle, I'd developed many assertions but few convictions:

Moses Rutenberg is Moses Rutenberg.

Jockey Fleming is not Jockey Fleming.

Jockey Fleming is Moses Rutenberg.

Since, put together, these afforded no logical outcome, I opted for elaboration and not an overarching conclusion. To my notebook I added:

Jockey Fleming is not Kid Oblay.

In fact, there were times when Jockey Fleming wished to be Kid Oblay and Kid Oblay, Jockey Fleming, and other times when the Kid was the Jock and the Jock, the Kid, especially when they were Moses Rutenberg and Lazarus Goldberg and the tin cup with lead pencils turned to gold.

Some forty years after the gimmick at Craig and Main, the National Film Board was recruiting talent for its short *Montreal by Night*. The story line, little more than a front for an after-dark tour of the city's nightclubs, Ferris wheels, and croquet pitch, celebrated a couple in love: Colette and Jacques. Colette was said to resemble every other Canadian girl in hoping soon to be married. No similar ambitions were articulated for Jacques, a Clark Gable lookalike.

There was no obvious role in *Montreal by Night* for either Jockey Fleming or Kid Oblay. Both prided themselves on their status as fastidious bachelors, with Oblay on record as having said, "Only crazy people get married." Yet in a film where the two leads are mute throughout, the Kid was awarded a speaking part consisting of one question and two interjections. A putative American tourist in a sloppy coat and a formless white cap like a melting marshmallow, a slick cigar between his lips, he inquires of two primly attired gendarmes, "Where is Dominion Square?" In answer to their inaudible reply and elaborate gesticulations, Oblay delivers his final lines, "Yeah [pause] yeah." As for Jockey, he didn't even make an extra.

Although Moses and Lazarus both rated as featherweights, their lifelong rivalry can be described as vigorous and without girlish innuendo. Al Palmer pronounced Jockey to be the more famous and "slightly more colorful" of the two characters. Still and all, in the 1954 contest for Mayor of Peel Street, Kid Oblay featured as the lone candidate and self-professed victor; his platform, to rid Dominion Square of its pigeons, plus Jockey Fleming. Oblay relented on the last point, tacitly acknowledging that without Fleming, he was barely the Kid. Meanwhile, Jockey assumed the title of "Peel Street Historian," a position implying better and longer memory than that of mayor.

Truth is, the rivalry between Fleming and Oblay once involved a trusted collaboration. In the Roaring Twenties, when the Billy Rose song "Hello Montreal" memorialized the city's blind pigs, barbotte parlours, and saucy madams, Moses and Lazarus forged a history they would later choose to forget. That each served as a reminder to the other perhaps underscored their mutual animosity.

Montreal in the nineteen teens and twenties counted as an important entrance point and marketplace for illicit drugs. By 1923 the RCMP were familiar with a Montreal criminal ring led by Harry Davis, a Russian by birth, of whom it was said, "[he] could have related one of the most authentic and factual stories of the activities in the night life and the underworld of this metropolis." In Davis's employ was a man the RCMP designated the "small Jew": "The drug is delivered by a small Jew . . . the car is met by the same small Jew and delivery effected . . . the runner, the small Jew, who always carries his coat on his arm, having the bottle of drugs in the coat . . ."

Two years later, Lazarus Goldberg, a sometime associate of Harry Davis, was charged first with drug sales and second with threatening a witness in a narcotics trial. He and his associates were sentenced to three years in the penitentiary. It would be easy to assume that Kid Oblay was the "small Jew" of the 1923 RCMP report. In fact, police had identified the small Jew runner as Jockie [sic] Fleming.

As early as the nineteen teens — in Jockey's non-fact-based history, his era as a singing waiter — Lazarus Goldberg and Moses Rutenberg were complicit in the trafficking of heroin, opium, and morphine. Their direct supervisor, Eddie Baker, aka "Kid Baker," an amateur boxer born in Russia and Jockey's former opponent in the ring, defied the Crown Prosecutor with his sleek evasions at trial:

> *Crown*: "Are you not the king of the drug men?"
> *Baker*: "I wish I were, but I am not."
> . . .
> *Crown*: "You are not known as a 'fixer' in that pedlars' district?"
> *Baker*: "No."

The jury, the purported "masters of the fact," were flummoxed by Baker's denied truths. He, along with Oblay and Jockey Fleming, was well known to RCMP surveillance.

Of the two lesser players, Oblay became the higher ranking, a *gownick*, a Jewish drug trafficker, with repeat convictions, whereas Jockey served principally as a *mekler*, a go-between. Work, for Jockey, involved slipping opium, as much as five ounces, to customers in slowed-down cars. The bottle hidden under his coat, the small Jew jumped into the car, the exchange was made, the buyers jumped out.

Between July 4 and October 28, 1923, the RCMP, posted near St. Lawrence Main, amassed "more than enough evidence . . . to arrest and convict Davis, Baker, and their cronies." Whether Jockey served time for his transgressions remains a fact awaiting validation. Also in the realm of unknowing is whether this episode of Moses's life accounted for the shame he inspired in his family, the stubborn disgrace ordaining that Jockey never could be reconciled with Moses.

As ever, Jockey didn't conform to type. Jewish criminals in the Diaspora were considered to be a relative rarity. In this era, moreover, begging or vagrancy or crimes of "moral turpitude" disqualified would-be immigrants to Canada from consideration. Jockey's wrongdoings weren't confined to dispensing drugs. He was known also to smoke opium in China-town, accompanied by showgirls from the Gayety Theatre. Had Moses been applying for admission to the country, Jockey's transgressions would have counted him out.

Without question, Jockey was dealing drugs as his younger brother came of age. For his part, Maurice had acquired a con-vertible he drove all the way to Lac Supérieur, along deserted roads hedged by rough cliffs and birch trees with the girth of broom poles. While his older brother dispensed hop, Maurice was wading into frigid lakes or angling for trout, the dozen or so fish aligned neatly on a wooden plank, tail-side down, heads severed.

Casper, invariably in Montreal, continued his forlorn prayers on behalf of his children. That Moses had blossomed into a *shlemiel*, a misfit, he must have grasped. The precepts of Montreal's Yiddish theatre — the importance of honesty, the imprecations against gambling and befriending people of bad character — clearly had been lost on Moses. When Casper died on May 9, 1923, his middle son was under constant RCMP sur-veillance and would soon be identified by his assumed name. The overwhelming insult, presumably not lost on the "small Jew runner," was this — that the horseless jockey had been brought down by the mounted police.

Maurice, while scrutinizing his older brother's face — his own face — must have felt as I did when examining my pater-nal grandfather's lantern slides: Both Simon and Jockey ren-dered the familiar unrecognizable. The man known to the RCMP wasn't Moses Rutenberg but Jockey Fleming.

Forty years later my grandfather would too often point at me, an elementary school pupil, and say to my mother, "The kid's a freeloader." Maybe he was confusing me with his brother. I did, however, share with Jockey at least one essential trait: the tendency to subterfuge. In my case, the habit of concealment arose not because I'd done anything wrong, but because for my mother the very acts of living and breathing entailed insupportable risks.

"And don't believe anything Kid Oblay tells you about me. You hear?" Such was Jockey Fleming's directive to Don Bell when in 1972 the Jock allowed Bell to undertake *The Autobiography of Jockey Fleming*. Following the principle of reciprocity, Bell also gave Jockey the opportunity to sum up Oblay, which Jockey did, calling Kid "a very nervous type of fellow," but "very kind-hearted." Inevitably, a criticism accompanied the "boost." In Jockey's view, Oblay simply didn't "understand the right part of life." Meanwhile the Kid, in his role as informant, made sure to excise Jockey's doings in the Roaring Twenties. To rat on Moses would have meant tarring Lazarus.

More surprising was the compliant ignorance, or amnesty, that columnists accorded to the Peel Street Historian when it came to his first manhood. "The jockey says he first went to Montreal as a singing waiter in the Frolics," wrote Jim Coleman, taking care to attribute the account of Jockey's early years to Jockey and not Jim Coleman. Al Palmer, a one-time police reporter with robust connections to the underworld, said merely, "[Fleming's] early history is rather fogged but it is generally believed that he is out of Newark, N.J."

For the most part Jockey had successfully obliterated his deep past, much as dementia banishes once-intact memories. But in the French press, at least, evidence of Jockey's continuing links to the Montreal underworld appeared as late as fall 1950, when he was summoned as a witness to a trial involving police corruption — specifically, police collusion with the owners of bordellos. In two French-language reports detailing the trial, published in *Le Canada*, Jockey unusually is identified by his birth name, Moses Rutenberg, and is said to have been granted an alternative date for his testimony in deference to the Jewish New Year. The more numerous English-language chroniclers of Jockey Fleming generally were less explicit, though one source from the 1960s designates Jockey the "singing Jew."

As with so much concerning Jockey, the questions frequently appear more genuine than the answers. I can counter the rumours about Moses Rutenberg's early manhood with a few facts: Jockey Fleming launched his doubtful collaboration with Eddie Baker soon after Esther Rutenberg's death and in the wake of the First World War. At this time his elder brother, Max, an army reservist with adequate hearing in both left and right ears, remained overseas in London but was prohibited from joining a combat unit. The reason? "Classified." And there's this: Along with his criminal past, Jockey's family background ranked among his most cherished blind spots.

⌐⟍

In their circumspect omissions from Jockey's obituaries and eulogy, rabbis and journalists shared a rare common ground. Dink Carroll wrote, "[In Jockey's] philosophy of 'Live and let live,' there were just bad guys and good guys. The bad guys were those who had no time for him, and the good guys were those who did." More vulnerable to hyperbole, Rabbi Denburg, among the most renowned Montreal rabbis of the era, told the live audience in the chapel at Paperman's funeral parlour how Moses Rutenberg appeared among us as other people do, "but he was really one of the angels." As the days grew longer and a visit to Jockey's grave became possible, I was to find the wording on my great-uncle's headstone as deliberately selective.

A crowd was assembling inside the front gates of the De la Savane Cemetery in Montreal as my husband and I pulled up in our rental car. "Are you here for the Gipschitz unveiling?" asked a woman in a dark hat as gently undulating as a stingray. Then she noted our attire and frowned. Both of us wore rumpled shorts and open-toe sandals, the cracked leather of our binocular straps pulled taut across our T-shirts. We'd just come down from the mountain, where we'd observed a flock of black-throated greens.

Like my father, Jockey was buried at the margins of a cemetery abutting secular ground, the views both crummy and majestic. That Maurice himself had overseen Jockey's inscription and burial I'd no doubt. The wording on the headstone turned out to be short, almost prim: IN MEMORY OF MOSES RUTENBERG / BELOVED BROTHER AND DEAR UNCLE / JAN. 3, 1898–APRIL 21, 1974. The death date, inexplicably, was wrong — three days too late — and "Dear Uncle" almost certainly betrayed a lie, a practice otherwise unknown to my grandfather. Equally noteworthy were the scant affiliations, along with the missing reference to Jockey Fleming himself. Moses Rutenberg had expressed a wish to be buried in the Irishman's cemetery, "the last place the devil will look for a Jew," and under his assumed name.

"Look at this!" I poked my husband in the ribs as we stood before the grave, our respective toes flush with the granite base. "Jockey was a Kohen — from the line of Jewish priests."

We leaned forward, the better to see the carving at the apex of the headstone: two hands touching at the thumbs and forefingers, the Star of David in the space between. The fingers on the granite hands appeared perfectly smooth. Jockey's own hands, reportedly like "monkey's paws," wouldn't have met their standard.

"I would have done this differently," I said.

"How so?"

"I would have written 'Fatalistic hustler.'"

Before we left the cemetery I scooped up a couple of stones and laid them on my great-uncle's grave — tokens of my visit. Then I retreated to the rental car. Jockey had a theory about himself: "Everything that Fleming touches turns to rubble."

Later that same day I tried to visit my mother but found her already asleep when I arrived.

"I'm sorry," whispered Una. "I couldn't hold her any longer."

"Never mind." Instinctively I bent down to straighten the pile of magazines on the Lucite coffee table — always the same few, never read and increasingly superannuated. Darlene, Una's "relief," had left her diary of my mother open on the table. The pages revealed were out of date.

Mrs. Kirsch, diarrhea this morning. Mashed banana.
Mrs. Kirsch finds brisket tough.
Mrs. Kirsch's daughter here. Didn't stay long.

On my way out I peered into my mother's bedroom, where she lay on the diagonal, one foot covered with a crocheted throw belonging to her mother, the other foot more brazen in its dirty white sock. My mother had been a lifelong proponent of bleach.

"You'd never guess who I went to see today," I murmured too softly to be heard above the whir of the convection fan.

In the elevator on the way down I pondered the epitaph on my great-uncle's footstone, "GONE BUT NOT FORGOTTEN." Jockey had enjoyed a special kinship with the one-liner.

So many of the nicknames attributed to Jockey imply something missing. The horseless rider. The dismounted dragoon. The dismounted horseman of Peel Street. For my grandfather's older brother, the greatest losses consisted in his lifelong forfeits: family, the company of true friends, tranquility, a permanent address. And yet Jockey's death must be considered remarkable for what he left behind: the size and number of obituaries inspired by his final disappearance — one admirer noted the Jock had got a "bigger write-up in the paper than Bronfman [the whiskey baron]" did when he died — along with the book chapters and newspaper and magazine columns accumulated throughout his adult life.

Also noteworthy were the rumours that persisted beyond Jockey Fleming's death. Kid Oblay, Jockey's significant rival, continued to believe the Jock had a treasure stashed away somewhere, which he, the Kid, hoped to tunnel into. Others thought my mother's uncle himself was invariably on the lookout for a find. Jim Coleman, for example, said Jockey was always searching for the end of the rainbow.

I say Jockey served as a measure of other people's largesse. To give to Jockey enhanced the stature of the donor, but where the money went — how my great-uncle spent or dispensed it — will never be accounted for. In the end, all I discovered some forty years after Jockey's death was the white envelope in the brown leatherette suitcase buried in a forgotten corner of my mother's basement — not treasure, but taboo. According to my dictionary, "treasure" can be either "sacred" or "accursed." I remind you that Moses Rutenberg was descended from holy men.

Jockey Fleming didn't occupy the overnight bag alone. From the same suitcase I recovered the evidence of Jockey's estranged niece Carol — the booklet on Edvard Grieg with a related essay by Carol at the rear, the photographs on mounts

Pearl, Duchess, and *Tony,* the younger sister's wedding portraits. Like Jockey, Carol had inspired in her parents a desire to cache her possessions, for reasons as contrasting as they were potent.

Such was my grandparents' buried treasure, then — a hoard prohibited to me until after my mother had lost her memory. And so I take my instruction now from the suitcase, from its unwritten commentary on life and the afterlife. It cautions me that treasure and taboo may be separate but the same. Both are secret. Hidden. Both are lonely.

CHAPTER FIVE

Lake Pátzcuaro

MORE THAN ANY OTHER SEQUENCE IN THE MOVIE CAROL *and Marvin's Wedding*, I watch time and again the beginning — the December morning when the grass is still green and without snow cover, and my mother's sister descends the steps of 4885 Queen Mary Road with her best friend and her parents at her side. Two children are standing by, one in a red hat, as my grandfather ushers the women into a chauffeur-driven chrome and black sedan. The day seems neither bright nor dark and is dry yet windy. Carol holds her short veil tight as she prepares for her last ride under her father's name.

As the film progresses, there's no moment when the groom lifts the veil and the bride's face is revealed. *Carol and Marvin's Wedding* favours the before and after, the unidentified cameraman excluded from the inner sanctuary of the synagogue. And peculiar to this film is the extent of black. The men, naturally, wear black tuxes, but the women too have opted for black — close-fitting, knee-length black dresses with black pillbox hats, a few hats with fine netting that extends over the eyes. At the wedding reception the younger women drink pale pink cocktails.

As the double doors open and Carol and Marvin make their way through the dense crowd, she's radiant, he more reticent. Sixteen years her senior and an established businessman, he looks at times as though he's being sidelined at his own wedding. A lithe young man in dark glasses plays exuberantly at a small keyboard. The camera pans to the high table, where my father, red-faced, is cramming something elongated into his mouth. Beside him, his wife, my mother, is resplendent in gold lamé. As Carol and Marvin prepare to kiss, my grandfather fumbles for a cigarette, lighting up as the kiss is consummated. The only food that merits a close-up is the wedding cake. It exhibits no plastic bride and groom for storage in a dresser drawer. Instead, the apex of the cake is a bent bough of pale pink roses that will shed their petals but have been spared their thorns.

Twelve minutes into the thirteen-minute film, everyone's leaving. *Mazel tov*, they must be saying. *Thank you, and congratulations on your* simcha. *Such a beautiful couple*, kine-ahora. *May you be blessed with children.* The older guests wouldn't have taken the future, theirs or anyone else's, for granted. Most were Eastern European Jews, speakers of Yiddish, by 1960 a language in decline and, in the instance of this film, not even heard. The film itself had remained viable only because my mother kept it for decades in a blackened cupboard beside medications that regulated her cholesterol and her mood.

Carol's never seen throwing her bouquet. In the last glimpse of the newlyweds, both are unsmiling. Solemn. The movie ends abruptly, with a momentary lapse into darkness and then the recovery of light, the final image an unknown thumbprint on a section of blank film.

Less than five years after the filming of Carol and Marvin's union, the female lead, my mother's only sibling, has been withdrawn.

My mother, before she lost her memory, assumed I had no recall of her sister. "This is where my sister collapsed before she miscarried," she'd say to me, her only child, as we drove past the prim turf of the Westmount Lawn Bowling Club on the approach to Greene Avenue, or "My sister was a rebel. She never let our parents boss her around." Always in these statements my mother referred to Carol as "my sister" or "my late sister," never as "your aunt." And although my mother loved to embellish stories — a favourite involved her repartee with a priest in Bruges, Belgium, who summoned her to venerate the reliquary of the Holy Blood — the accounts of her sister were uncharacteristically sparse. Facts without panache.

That I was four and a half at the time of my aunt Carol's death, an age when children are known readily to form lasting memories, had bypassed my mother. Even children approaching two are now believed to retain memories extending as far back as six months. As toddlers or older infants, we allegedly create and retrieve memories that later become lost to us. As adults, we typically are able to recall a first memory from no earlier than the age of three and a half, when our sentences rarely exceed several words and our interrogations are characterized by "Why?" and "What?"

Befitting early childhood, my sparse recollections of my aunt Carol remain inseparable from gifts. The toilet seat shaped like a swan. The set of chocolate paints wrapped in the same opalescent foils as tiny Easter eggs. Even the final memory — days, possibly hours, before my aunt's death — is tinged with generosity. I'm four years old and sitting in the hospital atrium, a room of tall proportions imbued with greenish light, not far from where my grandfather Simon had collected specimens in the cold season. A half century later I can still remember my impulse to be anywhere but there. Only once I enter the room where my aunt is sitting up in bed, the sheet folded neatly against her empty belly, I'm offered an assortment of chocolates — orange fondant, hazelnut cluster, and my favourite, because it's pink, strawberry cream.

After this, as in *Carol and Marvin's Wedding*, the images end too abruptly. The loss of Carol's unborn child, my aunt's own death at twenty-six and its immediate aftermath, the way it must have perturbed my home life, the grief encompassing me even though from a situation not fully understood, the fact that my father had helped to oversee my aunt's medical care, the burden of her parents my mother had to assume — from this time of privation and broken expectations I can retrieve nothing. If only I could recover such memories, however painful, they would rate as treasures.

Had I been a few years older at the time of Carol's death, her tragedy might have troubled me longer and more overtly. Instead, for almost fifty years, until my mother was nearing the end of her own life, I gave little thought to my aunt and how her death had reformulated my young mother's future. At the very mention of my aunt's name I fell silent or directed the conversation elsewhere, to a present Carol wasn't privileged to share.

$\longleftarrow$

By the time I finally began to wonder about my aunt Carol, I was travelling to Montreal every few weeks to remind my own mother that she had a daughter. It had been eighteen months since I'd confined my mother to assisted living, and I no longer had her house to preoccupy me, nor did I have the advantage of companionship. The friends who'd helped with the dismantling of my mother's house had returned to their respective homes, as had my husband. My mother herself had become my pursuit, my composure undermined as I observed she was speaking less and sleeping more. Annie, the night-sitter, gave me detailed accounts from notes she scribbled by flashlight. "Oh yes, she gets up in the night. She thinks it's mealtime. I give her a snack, but fast. She has no patience."

My mother's declining awareness brought a single advantage for me. It had become easier to investigate Carol, a subject now removed from my mother's remembrance of her distant past. Having discovered so much about Simon and Jockey, the apparent facts and the enduring mysteries, I'd grown intensely curious about my mother's sister and the relationship between the two daughters. While still in possession of my mother's house, I'd recovered a confusion of loose photos of Carol — from my grandparents' leatherette suitcase or my mother's stash kept in a padded silk glovebox the colour of offal. Yet in my mother's apartment sat various family albums, along with several unexplored boxes of memorabilia I'd transferred from the family home. All of these, I ventured, might afford a more coherent narrative of Carol's too-short life.

"I was only just getting to know my sister when she died," my mother had told me more than once as I was growing up. She was referring to the six-year age difference between the girls, a gap substantial enough to prevent their feeling like contemporaries. The evidence lies in *The Story of My Life* — my mother's black photo album with gilt lettering — assembled, I imagine, from middle childhood through to early adulthood. There the older sister allocated no space to Carol's birth, infancy, and first years. Instead, on the pages coinciding with her mother's pregnancy, my mother pasted in coy snapshots of herself, an only child, in a bathing suit at Old Orchard Beach, the captions *Daddy's pin-up* and *What a pose!* On the page opposite, Carol appears for the first time without explanation and fully formed. She must be two or three, dressed in a romper exposing her sturdy arms and legs, a pale sunbonnet concealing her lush hair. The older sister, my mother, grasps her charge firmly by the hand.

The backdrop to the photograph of the young sisters is the family apartment, a brick midrise in the newly fashionable quarter of Snowdon, in the English-speaking West End of Montreal, where Jews with enough money were beginning to move for their own betterment. There, for sixteen years, the girls were to share a bedroom of modest proportions, a nearness that didn't preclude their leading somewhat distant lives.

The two girls weren't separated merely by age but also by political and socio-economic currents. My mother's early formative years were spent in a predominantly immigrant community of Yiddish speakers, Carol's in a milieu where English-speaking Canadian-born Jews were becoming the majority. Unlike her older sister, a premature infant born during and shaped by the Depression, a period of escalating anti-Semitism, Carol came of age during years of increasing affluence and lessening discrimination against Montreal's Jewish minority. As well, the hardship and anxiety of the war years, for my mother uncomfortably within memory, were for Carol more out of reach. So too would have been the recollection of their mother's extensive hospitalization — for the older sister a vivid memory.

In fall 1941, the war ongoing and revelations about the plight of European Jewry just months away, the girls' mother had nearly died from fibroids of the uterus and then a post-surgical infection that confined her to hospital for several months. Some seventy years later, as my own mother drowsed in assisted living, I recovered from a Corticelli Hosiery box with the face of a perplexed cat on the lid a drawing that Carol, a child of three, had sent to her mother in the still-new Jewish General Hospital. It depicted an apple that looked like a cherry and a banana that looked like a yam. Also in the envelope, addressed to room 452, was a letter from my mother, aged nine:

November 1941

Dear Mother,

   How are you.
   When are you coming home?
   The family is lonesome for you.
   Carol is a very good girl.
                        With love,
                        Rene and Carol

That same year the girls' mother acquired a Singer Feather-weight, a gleaming black machine with Hellenic-inspired gold trim. When I'd retrieved this sewing machine and accessories from my mother's basement, the narrow tube of motor lubricant was no longer full; the bottle-green instruction booklet with the orange *S* was irreversibly bent and frayed from use, the inside front page marred by a declaration in block print: CAROL RUTEN BERG WAS H ERE. From early on, Carol shared neither her older sister's tentativeness nor her uncle Jockey's propensity to disappear.

"We never had a lot of money, but Granny always kept the apartment nice," my mother frequently told me as I was growing up. The scarcity of funds hadn't stopped her mother sewing fashionable clothes for her girls on the Singer Feather-weight — calf-length gingham dresses with puff sleeves, flared skirts, and pinched waists. I discovered in my mother's basement not only my grandmother's sewing machine, but also the cream wicker sewing box. The buttons inside are pale yellow, white, or smoke. To this day, three needles of contrasting size remain plunged into the rose silk pincushion on the underside of the lid. The box, now mine, in most ways aspires to nothing more than everyday life: the fraying threads, the small repairs, the effort to keep things, if not new, at least viable. The sewing box conceals a secret of which the daughters must have been aware. It's a musical sewing box, wound from the underside to produce a halting, delicately shaded tune that would have captivated both girls.

The older daughter had at one time exhibited a genuine aptitude for music, as had Carol, who won Distinction in the "Junior Piano" contest of the Arts and Letters Festival in March 1951. Six years earlier, Rene's examiner for Toronto Conservatory Grade III piano had rated her a "musical candidate," graduating her with Honours. Her musette was *nicely played*; her "Soldier's March" exhibited *fine rhythm*. Less satisfactory was "Tally-Ho!" *Well played (but a few slips of memory).*

ℓ

As my mother dozed in the apartment of her old age, the second and final apartment she ever was to occupy, I studied photos of her and her younger sister at Lac Supérieur. The family was solvent enough in the 1940s, it seemed, to go on summer holiday by car. In one picture the sisters are joined together by a length of wire with a dead fish suspended by the mouth, each girl smiling for the camera, immaculate in a frock and white ankle socks, each wearing braids tied with bows. They look to be six and twelve. In another photo in the same sequence the girls have ventured into the lake, each wearing a tight-fitting pale bathing cap, each clutching one of their father's hands. Carol is thrashing on her back, her feet churning the water; Rene is crouching and tranquil and, like her father, smiling broadly.

By the late forties the family of four was continually crossing the border for summer vacation, motoring to the beach at Plattsburgh, New York State, a place of assignations for my adolescent mother and her coterie of friends. While, in Montreal,

Jockey Fleming was bemoaning his exclusion from the short film *Montreal by Night*, Carol was posing for the camera in pale shorts and a matching ruffle top before rows of uniform vacation bungalows. The bungalows were small and neat, with A-line roofs and modest screen porches, and looked as though nothing eventful could ever happen in them. Nearby, however, Charles Donovan, a lineman for the Ticonderoga Electric & Power Company, fell forty feet from a power pole into an occupied baby carriage. Unpredictably, the baby emerged unhurt and Donovan was only slightly injured. Like everyone summering in the small town on Lake Champlain, the girls would have heard about the Plattsburgh Miracle, an event from which the older sister might have extracted the lesson that life was risky, the younger that calamities could give rise to a happy ending.

As my mother herself told it, she endured fears and phobias that didn't afflict the younger sister. In the 1945 edition of *Fundamentals of Psychiatry* belonging to my father, fears and phobias are defined as "a symbolic representation of material which cannot be faced in consciousness." Such fears, the volume continues, "may be derived from the emotional traumata of childhood." It wouldn't have occurred to my father, a thirty-year-old physician tasked with treating, among others, victims of the war, that the diagnostic guidelines might pertain to his future wife, at the time a gawky thirteen-year-old. But they pointed, nonetheless, to an early trauma underlying the older sister's sense of threat. Perhaps the trauma amounted to no more than her confinement to an incubator as befit a premature baby, a disquieting severance from her parents. Carol, in contrast, exhibited the confidence of an infant carried to full term.

My mother, whenever alluding to her sister, mostly had emphasized the age difference and character traits that kept them apart. Still, in the loose photographs recovered from my mother's basement, I could also detect an undeniable and unsurprising physical closeness between the sisters as children. In one photo, the infant Carol, propped on a window ledge, rests against Rene's back, Carol's tiny fingers plunged into her older sister's hair; in another, the older sister, her legs straddled, grips the nearly bald, barefoot one-year-old under the arms as she prepares to swing her back and forth. The first colour photo dates from 1946, when Carol and Rene are respectively eight and fourteen. In this studio portrait from the waist up, each girl wears an identical celadon blazer over a blouse that ties with a bow, and a celadon hair band or ribbon over glossy brown curls, the sisters positioned shoulder to shoulder and very nearly cheek to cheek.

↶

The Story of My Life, my mother's album, was compelling enough that I wanted to make it my own — that is, to remove it away to my own home. When I returned to the album in Toronto, the Second World War was over and gaiety restored, the older sister now part of a crowd, a gang of friends and boyfriends. At Old Orchard Beach in 1950, in a fitted white hip-length jacket, a matching white midi skirt, and lacy black flats, Rene poses for a shot she captions *Sophistication*.

In relation to her family, my mother, a characteristic teenager, had entered a state of oblivion — less a failure to recall her family than a failure to pay them any attention. The five-year diary, kept only from 1951 to '52, is devoted almost entirely to my mother's dizzying array of suitors. *I went out tonight with D. Never have I liked a fellow so much. He is just too terrific. Yet in some ways, he is way above me. . . . G can't distinguish between love & like and he told me he is beginning to fall. This was at the lookout. . . . B is just gorgeous and what a dresser. Could I ever go for him in a big way. He spends money like H20. . . . J made vegetable soup and baked beans I cut pickles Bread etc. He's so handy.* Only once does the girls' father feature. *By the time I got in it was 2:30. Dad was standing with the*

broomstick. *He told me I would have to break my date for tomorrow*
night & I knew my name would be mud.

Unsurprisingly, the younger sister, however much obliterated in the older sister's universe, was mesmerized by her sibling. According to Carol's best friend, the two younger girls sat
enthralled as my mother primped for date nights. "Rene was
gorgeous," Carol's friend told me a few years ago. "We thought
she was a queen."

By 1951, Rene's at the helm of a new convertible. In 1952 she
poses with Rose, her mother, at the Macdonald College graduation from the School for Teachers. Carol is nowhere to be seen.
The older sister begins to wear glamorous sunglasses with
cat's-eye frames. She's dating Greg, the horseman. She and
her friends are participating in a gag at Ruby Foo's Restaurant.
The photo is labelled *In the Act*, and my mother, wearing a curly
blonde wig, is laughing unrestrainedly.

If my mother in some respects paid little attention to her sister in life, the same could be said after death — at least in ways
that were evident to me. In truth, I'm not sure I ever saw my
mother look at any of her sister's possessions, not even Carol's
Sweet Sixteen album.

Nothing in the photos and mementos assembled by Carol
hints at the disarray that would mark the end of her short life.
The album, while pretty, is also deliberate. On the front page
are pasted in place cards for Carol and her boyfriend, Mickey,
two gold matchboxes inscribed with the letter *C*, a white cocktail napkin also embossed with *C*. The arrangement of photos
is both chronological and incremental: Carol alone, Carol and
Mickey, Carol and Mickey with Rose and Maurice and Rene,
Carol overlooking an avenue of girls, their flared skirts lilting
as though stirred by a wind. On the tables of the Normandie

Room, glasses are stuffed with cigarettes, small elevated dishes are piled with mints and cookies, chocolates are set out neatly on trays, and paper parasols bob in tumblers filled with water. In one photo the sisters, in kitten heels, stand the same height, both with delicate waists, swanlike necks, oval faces with well-defined jaw lines, unflinching dark eyes, and loosely curled hair parted asymmetrically.

Carol didn't share her older sister's passion for captioning. The photos in the Sweet Sixteen album are unannotated.

$\longleftarrow$

My mother didn't merely compose her own captions but was drawn, also, to headlines fashioned by others. Scattered around her apartment were some of the newspaper clippings she'd amassed over a lifetime and was reluctant to forfeit: "Endless Love: Centenarians married for 72 years," "No hospital is an island when it comes to Y2K bug," "Study says housewives an endangered species," "Gourd drying can take time." On this latest spring visit to my mother in assisted living, the headlines reminded me of the range of interests she'd once embraced. Now it seemed our conversation was confined to the functionality of her hearing-aid batteries, the state of her potted plants, and the compiling of her shrinking grocery lists. Without exception, she requested Sanka Instant Coffee, navel oranges, All-Bran cereal, Jarlsberg skimmed milk cheese, and 1% milk.

"That's it?" I asked.

"Corn."

"And what else?"

"Corn."

Some of the things my mother omitted to tell me at this time weren't necessarily the casualties of memory loss but were deemed irrelevant. Her needs now paralleled those of the simplest organism: air, water, food, a suitable habitat, and sunlight. The last was proving the most difficult to deliver. Once again, my mother was retreating to bed.

↼⟍

My mother herself was well versed in the essentials of life, having briefly studied first-year biological sciences at McGill before defecting to the School for Teachers at Macdonald College. During her foray as a scientist she had excelled in the Law of Moments and Composition of Forces but faltered at the dissection table, where a live fish bolted from her grasp. Ultimately, she demonstrated neither the skill nor the academic resolve of her younger sister, also eventually a student of anatomy and the life sciences.

Carol's graduation ceremony in May 1958 marked a return for the older sister to the university to which she'd been admitted seven years earlier. To qualify for their diploma in physical therapy, my aunt and her classmates — among them Grace Noreen Treen, Mable England, and Leba Starr — had mastered electrotherapy, botany and zoology, and Basic Conditions. They were to become practitioners of the movement sciences. The blue-and-yellow graduation hoods worn in their discipline evoked the male yellow-crowned euphonia, a neotropical bird of dry scrub, and would soon be exchanged for whites. In their heavily starched uniforms with autonomous buttons that had to be attached like cufflinks, the young women practitioners were close to immobilized.

At her sister's graduation my mother sat beside her mother-in-law, who sat, in turn, beside my mother's mother, each sporting an oversized bow or hat. Carol was presented with a book prize — *Cunningham's Text-Book of Anatomy* — for her first-place finish in the physiotherapy program. At the conclusion of a ceremony on the central lawn of McGill University, her all-female class of graduates sang "God Save the Queen." Then they planted a tree of unknown genus.

I have several relics from that day in May, when tents and folding chairs obscured the central playing field of the university, and the wind lifted the hem of my aunt's graduation gown, exposing her white pencil skirt beneath. The item that weighs most is *Cunningham's*. Its photos and diagrams represent the connective tissues, bones, and organs that lie just beneath the skin: vermiform appendix, cranial landmarks, and arachnoid mater.

The single item that weighs least is a Double 8 film in its original box of school bus orange. I've viewed the several minutes of footage perhaps a dozen times, and always I note my errors of memory or failures of perception from the prior screening — a confusion as basic as whether, in the first moments, my mother's younger sister is approaching or returning from the podium (she's returning) and whether, at any time, she holds the book prize in her hands (she doesn't). There are discontinuities, so Carol's receiving of her diploma is missing — only the lead-up and the aftermath are recorded. Her lips move throughout but produce no sound. Inarguably, she's self-possessed, resolute — qualities evident from the still photographs of the same occasion. Where the short film overtakes the photos is in elucidating the purposefulness and vigour of Carol's stride, the lilt of her shoulders as she walks in dark pumps, her smile and easy change of direction when she opts for a wrong turn upon stepping down from the podium.

The final remnant of Carol's graduation is her diploma encased in a red cardboard tube. On graduation day this item, once awarded, seemingly never left her hands. When her mother, my grandmother, suggests relieving her of it, Carol shakes her head — no. Eventually the diploma came to me, not by intent but because for decades it had lain undisturbed in my grandparents' faux leather suitcase, first in their apartment and then in my mother's basement. I can tell you that it has the pleasing heft of a dog's bone and, like old fur, smells musty.

If I'd apprehended something of Jockey by his exclusions, I was becoming familiar with Carol from her exceptions. Most everything available to me about my aunt, the visual and hand-written evidence, had happened at a remove from her everyday life. Too often I glimpsed Carol on holiday, away from home, or at the milestones of her Sweet Sixteen, graduation, and wedding — according to recent findings about the "reminiscence bump," precisely the kinds of events from the time of life most likely to be remembered. As we age, we recall disproportionately the vivid episodes from late adolescence and early adulthood. What remains to me of Carol, then, consists of what she herself might eventually have remembered. The rest, the day-to-day routines and ever-changing minutiae that both shape and consume us, I can't and don't know.

In the years Carol came of age, the late 1950s and early '60s, the winning slogan fashioned by the Quebec Liberal Party was "It's time for a change." Led by the reformer Jean Lesage, the Liberals assumed power in 1960 when Montreal itself was in flux, with the construction of the six-lane Champlain Bridge under way and the Dorval airport expansion nearing completion. Soon after, millions of passengers began to fly abroad. The women wore miniskirts over tights patterned with dots or ivy and carried white leatherette totes as cabin baggage. Champagne was served on board. Carol by now had distinguished herself as a career woman, featured in the newspaper for her work at a Physical Medicine unit demonstrating wrist and finger exercises to strengthen joint range. With an income of her own and an eagerness to embrace the new, she began flying passenger class to the Caribbean. In this, my mother, the older sister, tailed the younger by almost a decade, apprehensive of flying as she was of so many other enticements.

My mother chose instead the stay-at-home travel of Expo 67 denied to her sister. The theme of the Universal Exposition was Man and His World, and the variety of pavilions included Man the Creator, Man the Provider, Resources for Man, Man and the Universe, Man in Control? My parents and I walked so much at Expo that by late summer, after we were done with Canadian Pulp and Paper and approaching Uganda, "Cradle of the Nile," my mother's hip seized up with bursitis and we had to be ferried back to the Welcome Pavilion by golf cart.

Carol herself experienced merely the run-up to Man and His World. At the time of her death in January 1965, the pavilions were half realized — notions on paper bereft of physical expression — while the mid-river sites of îles Notre-Dame and Sainte-Hélène were nearing completion. She lived only long enough to observe how those artificial islands imposed changes on the plenitude and flow of the river.

The optimism of Man and His World must have felt at odds with the disaster that had befallen my mother and her parents two years before. And there was soon to be another loss. Malca, my father's mother, born in the Russian Pale of Settlement, died in the opening weeks of the Universal Exposition and was buried on the mountain in Montreal affording views over Expo. Yet for all the family's sorrows, Man and His World made for a mesmerizing excursion into the here and now. Even my mother, besieged as she was, took pains to handwrite in her Expo passport the names of the pavilions that had denied her an official stamp.

Despite my mother's failing memory and physical resilience, or maybe because of them, I'd decided to undertake a visit with her to the family graves. I hoped the short excursion out of the city and along the shore of Lake Saint-Louis would briefly give my mother relief from her routines at assisted living, where each day she insisted on taking her pills according to the same colour spectrum: white, pink, orange, then orange again, culminating in green. Blinds in her apartment had to be fully extended, even during daylight hours. Frequently she sought my advice about the order in which to eat the food on her plate. Did potato trump chicken? Should a pea supersede a cherry tomato?

I was familiar with the cemetery from previous visits when my mother still served as the driver and navigator. From these I knew that the arrangement of the graves conformed to the burial instructions left by my grandfather in a sealed envelope. *Mom in the middle,* he'd instructed his surviving daughter. *She carried her until birth — also much more sentimental — still keeps things of hers. So somehow feels closer. Dad on the other side.* My grandfather had resigned himself to Carol's death in a way that never became possible for his wife. In response to one of my grandmother's embittered remarks about Carol, he once said in my presence, "That was a long time ago."

"Would you like to get out of the car?" I asked my mother as we pulled into the cemetery. She'd scarcely looked out the window as we skirted the shoreline of Lake Saint-Louis, for decades one of her most cherished waterside drives. Now, in response to my suggestion she exit the car, my mother shook her head. I had her dressed in a navy nylon jacket, my father's, on this moderately cool spring day.

"Where are we?" More and more my mother had come to resemble my father in Southampton as he unwittingly prepared for the D-Day landing. "We had a hut there that had all maps of France," he said. "But it had different names, you see. Instead of being Caen, it was Berlin."

Unlike my father, my mother was unwilling to deploy. "I want to stay here."

"That's fine."

I locked her in and set off towards the graves. Her parents' burial sites were bright, almost carefree, with clumps of yellow and purple pansies, whereas Carol's exhibited only a mound of loose earth, as though she'd recently been interred. For several years someone unknown to me had been paying for the maintenance of her grave. No longer, apparently. *Note to myself: Check on planting in perpetuity.*

I returned to the car, where my mother was dozing in my father's zip-up jacket, her head angled like a nestling's awaiting a worm. I tapped her gently on the shoulder. "Let's get you some Chinese food."

She was unperturbed that evening as she addressed her eggplant beef hotpot. The next morning, however, I found her tearful and disturbed.

"What is it?" I asked. "What's wrong?"

"Dreams."

I slept through my aunt Carol's wedding, my toes curled around a string of plastic balls arranged across the top of my crib. While she was honeymooning in Jamaica, I lay naked on my changing table, clasping a foot in one hand.

On December 4, 1960, six months after my birth, Carol had married Marvin Silver, formerly known as Hiyo Silver, a bomber pilot in the Second World War. Their guests at the wedding luncheon partook of fresh fruit cocktail *au Maraschin, poulet rôti farci, rissolées* potatoes, salad Panuche, and *petits fours*. The wedding invitation was the pink of frost-tinged white hydrangea.

Tiger Moths, Spitfires, Masters, and Hurricanes were among the planes Marvin Silver flew for the RAF and RCAF after he shipped to England in 1943. His first missions originated in Grimbergen, outside Brussels, where he performed rail bombing and escort flying, his aircraft routinely loaded with bombs surpassing the weight of a grizzly bear. For all this, I recall him as a gentle man — sixteen years Carol's senior and statuesque, with a bar mitzvah boy voice that undercut his considerable height.

For their honeymoon in December 1960, Carol and Marvin chose Jamaica. *Just a short note to let you know how we are faring in both Jamaica and wedlock. What a paradise. And marriage is not too bad either!* Sent on December 7, the card must have reached my parents around December 13, 1960, or 24th of Kislev 5721 — the first night of Chanukah, when my mother would have been preparing meat *halishkes* and pea soup with hominy as prescribed by the Jewish cookbook *A Treasure for My Daughter*. The card Carol had chosen was titled "Bongo Bill play that drum again!" and portrayed a musician, elongated and barefoot, with a straw hat textured and shaped like a peanut, and the fingers of each hand spread wide like the fronds of a fern. *It is a little quiet now but we don't mind — it gives you a chance to get to know the natives a little better*, wrote Carol. Her much-older friend Jean Kaufman, who met Carol on the flight to Jamaica, immediately recognized in the newlywed *an unusual personality that was brilliant and extraordinary.*

The final pages of *A Treasure for My Daughter* were a concession to the non-festive season, including a fail-safe recipe for antipasto: "Place lettuce on each plate. Place on the lettuce a slice each of tomato, cucumber, hard-boiled egg, and salami. Add 3 stuffed anchovies and 1 tbsp. diced beets."

The burnished newlyweds were home for Christmas. "My sister blacked out on her honeymoon in Jamaica," my mother once told me. She couldn't say why.

The text of postcards is generally as brief and inscrutable as that of wedding announcements:

> *The bride was formerly Miss Carol Rutenberg, daughter of Mr. and Mrs. Maurice Rutenberg; the groom is the son of the late Mr. and Mrs. Alex N. Silver.*

> *Just a note to say hello. Marvellous flight. Having a wonderful time. The weather is absolutely gorgeous.*

But in contrast to wedding notices, the words and images of postcards are often at odds. Pronouncements about the weather appear on the backs of cards showing men in straw hats singing, "Yellow bird, / Up high in banana tree." Admissions of sunburn are paired with images of the flame tree, or royal poinciana. The essential facts about the flame tree, printed in mouse type at the top of the card, indicate the season of profuse flowering is late spring and early summer. The postmark on the card is dated February 21, 1963 — midwinter.

In the six or seven cards I have from my aunt Carol, always in a round, controlled hand, the word *good* is almost indistinguishable from the word *food*, and the second sentence invariably alludes to the weather. Among the only words from my aunt in my possession, these are the ephemera that have proved lasting. They stand alongside her childhood essay on the composer Edvard Grieg (*he was short and had a slight stoop, his eyes were of the deepest blue*), the soundlessly mouthed words in the wedding and graduation films, and recipe cards. Not unlike my father's treasure, none of these are addressed to me.

Carol's words in print, adding up to no more than a long poem or a short short story, were withheld from me in my childhood home. Instead I retrieved this evidence of my aunt decades later as I was rummaging through my mother's apartment while she half watched *Property Virgins* on Home & Garden TV. The postcards from the Caribbean were stored in a cardboard box that yielded, also, a newspaper clipping from my father's golf triumph, "Dr. Kirsch bags Elmridge Eagle," and instructions on how to survive a tornado: "In open country: Seek shelter indoors. If there's no time, lie flat in the nearest depression such as a ditch or culvert, and cover your head with your arms." All of these items my mother kept for me to find.

The postcards revealed to me that in 1963, precisely a year after I'd mastered the songs "Billy Boy" and "The Farmer in the Dell," my aunt Carol and her husband, Marvin, were island-hopping in the Caribbean. *Well we have really made the rounds the last few days,* wrote my twenty-five-year-old aunt to my mother. *We were in Guadeloupe (left after 4 days), Barbados (left after 2 days — we couldn't get into a decent hotel), Antigua and Puerto Rico. We finally arrived in Jamaica yesterday.* The card Carol sent was from Guadeloupe but posted in Jamaica, its stamp showing the head of Queen Elizabeth beside a sprig of ackee.

In the first of the series, from Guadeloupe, a card both composed and sent there, Carol wrote, *Having a wonderful time. Bought some perfume — very reasonable. We both have bad sunburns.* The reverse side shows the Soufrière volcano from Saint-Claude, with a two-storey white house carelessly thrust into the path of prospective lava flows.

Carol hadn't sent any postcards during her too-short passage through Barbados, an island sometimes likened in shape to a pear or a leg of mutton. Her last communication from the trip — the last in my mother's possession — was addressed to Malca, my mother's mother-in-law. In this card, mailed from Jamaica, the bad sunburns alluded to in Guadeloupe have become more deliberate tans. *Give Sharon a kiss for me,* the card ends. *Regards to all.*

Another memento of my aunt, a metal recipe box with a hinged lid, bespeaks wifely solicitude and domestic duty. Its pink sides exhibit a pepper mill, a cruet, and a salad bowl frothing with lettuce, each item depicted in lime green and cross-hatched for artistic effect. The recipes within are varied and abundant: *Mimi's Blueberry Cake, Cocoa Peanut Logs, Hermits, Jam Thumbprints, Ring-a-Lings*. For fowl, *Superior Fried Chicken*. Each recipe is written in a controlled hand so much like my mother's early writing, the title in capital letters, underscored twice, followed by the ingredients and instructions separated from the rest by a line space. In format, the recipes are near indistinguishable from the experiments in my mother's lab book, only with *flour* replacing *caliper*, and *Carnation evaporated milk, mercury in a glass thermometer*.

These index cards supplemented *A Treasure for My Daughter*, a cookbook that might equally have been titled *A Daughter to Treasure*. The book's modus operandi consists of dialogues between Hadassah, a young Jewish woman on the eve of marriage, and Mother, whose name we are never told. Recipes follow. In the Chanukah section, as the two polish the menorah, Hadassah exclaims, "I am so glad to be your daughter!" to which Mother replies, "Thank you, Hadassah, dear. I am happy indeed, that you are not reticent about these matters with me." The section concludes with recipes for Cole Slaw, together with Sour Cream and Cheese Pancakes.

The book and its impetus were relatively new when my grandmother purchased a copy for her first-born, less so by the time Carol was ready for the same. *A Treasure* originated in 1950 as a charitable venture, its purpose to safeguard the traditions of Jewish home life, its proceeds to rehabilitate Jewish war victims. My mother, who came of age in the early 1950s,

responded more readily to Hadassah's dutiful young woman-
hood than did Carol, though one entry in my mother's diary
suggests her obedience to convention might have arisen as
much from circumstance as from absolute preference: *I really
don't want to get married*, wrote the nineteen-year-old, *but heck
when you think of having a fiancé someone who you respect and has
respect for you, someone to trust, someone who will be faithful, the idea
of not having to sit and wait till someone calls so you won't have to stay
in on a Sat nite. Well, it sounds wonderful.*

Carol, six years her sister's junior, an accomplished swim-
mer and an adventurous water skier, inarguably rated as the
bolder personality, well suited to seizing the increasing opportunities for women that would have been less available to her
sister. In the estimation of an older cousin, "Carol was her own
manager," quite unlike her self-doubting older sibling, a pal-
lid, finicky girl who'd had to submit to treatments under a sun
lamp at the Shriners' children's hospital.

When my mother told me that I was "like her late sister"
— an admission that I little resembled my own mother — the
assertion stood not merely as a compliment but as a regret. She
was commending me for my initiative and self-reliance while
despairing of my hesitations about having a child. Never in her
expressions of disappointment did she acknowledge her own
one-time reluctance to embrace motherhood, a position she
shared with her sister. In defiance of the times, my mother had
resisted pregnancy for five years after her wedding.

Carol's best friend, who got pregnant first and carried her
own baby to term, recalls my aunt saying, "What would you
want to have a baby for?" Carol had married in a short dress
offset by a short veil, neither of them inhibiting. There were
islands to visit, limbs to rehabilitate, friendships to establish.
But Carol eventually became pregnant by choice, and in her
effort to bear a child, she succeeded only in making Marvin

a widower. Following her collapse mid-pregnancy near her apartment on Greene Avenue, she miscarried, rallied, and then, under the care of a locum obstetrician, died. "I think Carol had an undiagnosed disorder of the blood," her best friend said decades later. "She was shooting clots. The nurses were sitting on her chest trying to stop them."

"You'd better come," Carol had told her friend in a phone call from the hospital. "I'm not going to make it." She was aware of her impending death in a way my mother, more than a half century later, was unable to register her own decline. The sisters' mother, in contrast, showed a predilection for wrongly anticipating her own end. *Take care of your precious child*, wrote my grandmother in her old age to my mother, her surviving daughter. *To thine own self be true.* She wrote the words from her nursing home one night when she thought she was dying — a false premonition, the tenacity of life a disappointment.

t⟶

The nurse, Svetlana, an immigrant from Russia, had just withdrawn from my mother's apartment as I entered. My mother's hair was desiccated and uncombed, her features compressed. Nothing, in fact, could have prepared me for this version of my mother. "I'm getting a lot of cawas," she said, looking straight at me before lapsing into sounds with no resemblance to words.

A year or two earlier, a neuropsychiatrist, after evaluating my mother without me present, had diagnosed her as language-impaired. In fact, my mother never lost the ability to speak and be spoken to. Until the time of her death, the capacity to express herself and to comprehend remained one of the core elements of her identity that linked her to her former unimpaired self. On her better days she remained capable, too, of manipulating words to produce irony or humour as she continued to inquire after her "grand-cat" or designated herself an "old crock." Her performance before the neuropsychiatrist, then, had indicated nothing more than stress at being interrogated too early in the morning in an unfamiliar environment and without the assurance of her daughter present.

Now, however, my mother's ability to speak, even in monosyllables, genuinely had vanished. She enunciated only one coherent word, "Stupid," aimed at Darlene, her care aide. It was I, not my mother, who apologized.

It seemed to me as though my mother were no longer herself, although, in practice, who else could she be? My discomfort implied only that my mother no longer met my expectations.

Despite suggestions of a stroke, a urinary tract infection, accompanied by delirium, was diagnosed, and the patient was removed to hospital. Once my mother was stabilized and asleep and no longer in need of me, I returned to her apartment, intent on seizing the opportunity to investigate freely. There I found among her keepsakes several postcards from Mexico predating Carol's engagement to Marvin.

Only a year before she honeymooned in Jamaica, Carol was dating Rafael, a different suitor, in Mexico City. *This City is just beautiful*, she wrote to her older sister in her first postcard at altitude. *Needless to say, the weather couldn't be better*. On the front of the card is the University City library, its square tower faced with a mosaic in browns and terra cottas exhibiting a sombre moon and startled sun. My mother's sister promises to write again soon. *I'm running around like an idiot. I'm off on a date now*. Carol was on her way to meet Rafael, whose name in Hebrew means "God has healed."

"When Carol and I were about twenty-one, we travelled to Mexico," my aunt's best friend explained. "There were these Jewish doctors Carol had met at home when she was interning in physio. One of them was crazy about her and the other had a crush on me. *Oy vey*, were they rich! Their families in Mexico had many servants."

"What happened?" I asked.

"Are you kidding? We weren't going to live in Mexico!"

The photo Rafael gave Carol from that evening in 1959 — black and white and in a cardboard presentation folder — was never intended for me. On the inside cover the young doctor has composed a note: *I hope that you will never forget this night and your friend, Rafael.* The meal is just beginning or just over. Glasses, some of them half full, are balanced on clean plates. Carol and Rafael sit side by side at a small round table, lips compressed, shoulders nearly touching. The young doctor looks solemn, almost ill-tempered, a rare and challenging cast of face for a man with a small knob of a nose, sumptuous cheeks, and a rosebud mouth.

Carol's trip to Mexico proved to be her last, also her first. For the younger sister, twenty-one and with the illusion of a long life before her, Mexico's more troubling aspects likely eluded her. All the same, in 1959, the year of Carol's visit, air pollution in Mexico City was depriving babies of breath, and beyond the city, nature itself had come under threat. In the state of Michoacán, the yellow rail was making its last stand — a bird so furtive that the missing evidence of its life bore a strong resemblance to its extinction.

Predictably, the few communications Carol sent to Rene from Mexico suggest a young woman enthralled by the present. *Sorry I haven't written more often but we've been so busy running around — needless to say we are having an absolute ball*, she wrote her older sister. The postcard, a photograph of the fishermen of

Lake Pátzcuaro and the only one of Carol's cards in black and white, is dated December 15th. The photo itself alludes to neither year nor season and could just as easily have been taken a month earlier as decades before. Each of the four fishermen is adrift, his butterfly net balanced on the prow of his boat, his long spear or oar resting lengthwise. On a branch that extends over the boats blooms an orchid, an epiphyte taking nothing from the host tree. *We have met dolls wherever we go,* continued my aunt. *We've really been getting around.* For her Sweet Sixteen corsage, Carol had worn an orchid.

Aspects of the young woman's geography were impaired. To her older sister, she described being in a *small town about 600 miles away from Mexico City*. In fact, Pátzcuaro is only about 200 miles away, the slow and difficult access through mountain passes encouraging the aggrandizement of distance. After the error came a declaration: *It is one of the most beautiful places I have ever seen.*

No album exerts a greater hold on me than the pictures of my aunt at Lake Pátzcuaro. She walks with confidence among the stout, thick-waisted women at the local market, her slacks and cardigan at odds with their pale knee-length dresses. She stands before the cattail marshes ringing the lake, unencumbered by Rafael and not yet anticipating Marvin. She wonders at the fishermen with their *mariposas*, their butterfly nets, all the while fingering the narrow silver-rimmed pin on her sweater with its fragment of shimmering butterfly wing. Her tidbit of blue morpho. All the pictures in this album I commit to memory, caring not in the least that they exist only in my imagination. At Lake Pátzcuaro, fact invites disbelief and invention tangles with credibility.

I've been in this condition ever since I read a sentence in Wikitravel: "The natives believe that the lake is the place where the barrier between life and death is the thinnest."

The yellow rail Carol likely never saw is now locally extinct, and the slender-billed grackle, an endemic, almost certainly so. The lake itself became tainted with runoff from the leather industry, while the cattle grazing on its shores damaged the natural scrub. As early as the 1990s, one researcher suggested creating a new Lake Pátzcuaro near the ruins of the old — an artificial lake and wetlands mimicking the native species and aquatic communities that once were.

Carol's single advantage in dying young was this: She didn't live long enough to witness the near death of one of the most beautiful places she'd ever seen. *Returning to the city on Thurs*, she wrote to her sister from the lake. And then, *I'm just thrilled with the news!* She could only have been alluding to the news of my conception.

$\longleftarrow$

"Limited" designates the vocabulary of grief, equally the vocabulary of postcards. *Deep sorrow. Profound sorrow. Deepest regret. Shocked and grieved. An untimely and tragic loss.* So read the expressions of sympathy sent to my thirty-three-year-old mother in her bright, still-new split-level house — a house in a neighbourhood that had obliterated farmland, and with it the management of life and death belonging to animal husbandry. The notes were written almost always by women, on plain or monogrammed paper. All the writers were middle-aged or older, none of them contemporaries of the deceased. Many called my mother's loss *beyond understanding* and their own sentiments *beyond words.* They chose English alone to express the inexpressible, not once referring to my aunt's untimely death as a *hartsvaitik* or to her family's ensuing woes as a genuine *tsoriss*. In abandoning what was for many their mother tongue, or at least the language of the familiar, they were perhaps asserting their lack of intimacy with such an event. The *simcha* of pregnancy gone so irreparably wrong.

We hope that for Sharon's sake you bear up under this terrible blow and that time will soften your great burden of grief and suffering, wrote my Uncle Eddie, my father's brother, from New York City. He figured among the few men bold enough to put their feelings into words. Another father and husband, a family friend, said to Carol's parents, *Being a father of two daughters, having known yours since their infancy, I can identify with you at this moment of great sorrow; it's sad and shocking and so very unnecessary but one must accept reality no matter how painful.* The author was the brother of Louis Muhlstock, the Depression-era artist renowned for his depictions of human misery.

It's worth noting that nowhere in these stacks of cards, where people struggled to find words for the unspeakable, is there an enunciation by Jockey Fleming, my grandfather's brother. Although the book of condolences contains signatures in the hundreds, neither Jockey Fleming nor Moses Rutenberg wrote his name there. Any evidence of me is similarly missing. Like my great-uncle Jockey, an unacknowledged member of the family, I presumably was absent from Carol's funeral. My parents likely would have wanted to spare me the unsuppressed expressions of grief upon my aunt Carol's death.

My mother responded to the loss of her sister with lists and templates, or at least these are the only elements of her response known to me with certainty. She never told me how she reacted to the news of her sister's death or whether she was in fact with Carol at the time, nor did she describe the immediate aftermath, that moment when my mother's own life was altered irreversibly, everything that came before irretrievable. But she kept the artifacts, whether through sentiment or neglect or in the hopes that I would one day recover what she was missing or had chosen not to remember.

And so, in nondescript boxes in my mother's apartment, I discovered lists of food people sent for the shiva: nuts and figs from Aunt Ruth, chocolate from Aunt Belle, a fruit basket from the Stock Exchange Traders' Association, cheese bagels from cousin Syd, bread and soup from neighbour Martha. Other family and friends shied away from snacks and appetizers but paid for the planting of commemorative trees in Israel. My mother kept, too, a list of all the sympathy cards and letters received, the total numbering a hundred. And there is a list of gifts sent to Carol in hospital, when she still was expected to recover: pink and red poppies, travelling jewel case, Aquamarine body and hand lotion, dressing gown, pill box, book, nightie, neck pillow, handkerchief, bed jacket. My mother created a template for the thank-you notes acknowledging these gifts — a letter as formulaic and impartial as the expressions of sympathy were heartfelt.

> *Dear* —
> *Carole was delighted with the lovely ____ you sent her . . .*
> *Many thanks for your thoughtfulness.*

The older sister had been discreet, apparently, about the reason for Carol's hospitalization. In my mother's archives I retrieved a letter from Carol's great friend Jean Kaufman, first met on the plane to Jamaica as Carol and Marvin were embarking on their life together. To the older sister, Jean writes, *It was very thoughtful of you to write me, but I was so sorry to hear that Carol has been so ill. Though you didn't say what her illness was, I can imagine, and I'm sure that she and Marvin must be quite disappointed.* Jean finishes by saying she hopes *the New Year will bring the family happiness and health*. Unbeknownst to her, she composed the letter on the day of Carol's death and mailed it out posthumously.

My mother did share with me one thing about her response to Carol's tragedy. "I didn't mourn my sister's death until years later," she said. I was never aware of this process, although, by implication, I must have been in middle childhood or older when my mother finally acknowledged the loss of her sister and the child she was carrying. Although I felt in some respects I knew my mother too well, in this respect I realize I scarcely knew her at all.

In the first photograph of me taken after my aunt's death, I'm not myself — I'm the little Dutch girl. This is not invention. Someone has written in block capitals under the photo, RUTH AND LITTLE DUTCH GIRL, FEB. 65.

Ruth is my au pair from the Netherlands, a strawberry blonde in fitted slacks and a powder-blue V-neck sweater, who's as tall seated as I am standing. Ruth's bed in my parents' home is covered with a spread the blues and whites of Delftware. I'm clad in a *hoofddeksel* and *klompen* — a Dutch bonnet like a nun's wimple and turquoise wooden shoes. The little Dutch girl is smiling.

It's widely accepted that four- and five-year-olds are incapable of distinguishing between make-believe and reality. Most likely I was too young to understand the irreversibility of Carol's disappearance — either that or my parents somehow succeeded in shielding me from the calamity. And having only just grown up herself, my aunt, a young adult, presumably didn't play a large role in my day-to-day life. Throughout the four and a half years our lives coincided, she was engaged or newly married, island-hopping in the Caribbean, assisting her husband in his shoe boutiques, setting up a new home, and eventually preparing to start a family. Strikingly, I've discovered no photographs of Carol and me to elucidate our bond or to clarify her frame of mind in her final years. Not a single image of the two of us together appears in the entire archive of family photos. Based on visual evidence alone, our relationship didn't exist. Like the city itself, our connection was subject to rapid change that left no trace.

By 1965, the year of Carol's death, horse dealers had withdrawn from Montreal as had the blacksmiths who served them. Cars, once a luxury, had become routine. Yiddish was spoken less and less, and the hundreds of farms on the Island of Montreal had been sacrificed to suburbs. The farm meadow where I walked with my father behind my childhood home counted, I realize now, as a relic. By the time I turned four it had vanished, along with the future my family had envisaged for itself — a predictable future including my aunt and her newborn child. The belief in an assured future proved to be as selective as slides viewed under a microscope or imprecise memories formed long ago.

t⌐

In her final years, Carol might have been suffering from an illness of which my father alone among the broader family would have been aware. If this is a fact, his young sister-in-law must have asked for his discretion. My mother and her parents knew nothing and may have had only one reason for suspicion — that Carol had blacked out on her honeymoon. It was in the aftermath of Carol's death, my mother confided to me during my teen years, that she overheard my father talking on the phone to another medical professional. Overheard — or more likely she was eavesdropping. "Did you tell them about the MS?" my mother thought she heard as she hid behind a door left ajar. Whatever my father communicated to the neutral party on the phone, he didn't share with his wife, sister of the deceased, nor did Marvin, now a widower, reveal Carol's secret to her family — if indeed she'd had a secret at all.

Regardless of my father's feeling about Carol's death — and he never spoke of the tragedy to me — he surely never found release from it. Each morning he woke up to the sight of Carol's bereaved sister — like his own daughter, an only child — and too often he was confronted with her bereaved parents. His relationship with my grandmother reportedly had always been combative — a clash of strong personalities, said an older cousin — and presumably became even more volatile after Carol's death. So awkward were the pair's exchanges that when my grandparents came to our house for dinner, my father routinely left the table before the fruit salad and macaroons.

If Carol did have an underlying medical condition, my father might have warned her of the risks of pregnancy or even advised against it, but he was neither her gynecologist nor among the doctors responsible for her care in hospital. Marvin apparently did not hold my father accountable for the loss and was generous enough in the months after Carol's death to acknowledge family occasions. Among the possessions in a cardboard box in my mother's apartment, beside the several postcards from her sister, was tucked away a Canadian Pacific telegram. The paper is stamped *Apr 4 1:55 PM '65*, followed by the typewritten words, FD *Montreal* QUE *April 4 1965 / Mr Mrs A Kirsch / Montreal* QUE */ Many happy returns on your tenth anniversary Love / Marvin*. Two months later, for my fifth birthday, my uncle Marvin gave me a doll, the last of his gifts to me on record. Then he went away without going anywhere at all.

For my mother, the routine absence of her brother-in-law from her life became a decades-long habit. Several years after

Carol's death, Marvin had remarried, by all accounts happily. Apart from rare and awkward visits to Marvin's shoe store during my adolescence — visits sometimes resulting in no purchases — my mother and I never saw my uncle. Those visits took place during a time of political unease, the era of Quebec separatism, when the Parti Québécois was devising a referendum on the option to secede from Canada. My parents' car licence plates soon bore an established Quebec motto, *Je me souviens*, I remember.

Some thirty-odd years later, Marvin developed dementia and, like his one-time brother-in-law, my father, was accepted into the veterans hospital just outside Montreal in Sainte-Anne-de-Bellevue, where he died in 2010. In my adult life, my single encounter with him took place at my father's shiva, when Marvin summoned the grace and courage to appear at my mother's house. After a decades-long silence, we exchanged just a few words. *Hello. Thank you for coming. How are you? I'm sorry for your loss.* All the same, I recognized how the sight of me, and my mother, revived his sadness at the loss of his young wife and unborn child. It was perhaps only at the veterans hospital, amid survivors of war, that my former uncle was finally released from memories he otherwise couldn't disperse.

There are few people alive now who might tell me about Carol, and they themselves would be relying on memories aged by more than a half century, dating back to the era of Avon Ladies and Tupperware parties, the death of Marilyn Monroe, and the first man in space. Such recollections, as described by Jonathan Foster in his book *Memory*, "may contain some actual elements of the past" but, taken as a whole, make for "an imperfect re-construction of the past located in the present."

Equally, my own way of making sense of Carol is as circumscribed as my cognition at the time of her death: I'm stymied by images without continuity and my limited recall of the past, marked by an exaggerated sense of the physicality of objects, endowed with a propensity to imagine detail beyond artifacts and hearsay. Only in one respect do I possess an adult understanding of my aunt: the damage inflicted by her tragedy.

For my grandmother in particular, the death of her younger daughter represented a loss that she couldn't assimilate. She found neither instruction nor comfort in *A Treasure for My Daughter*, the single volume she'd presented to both girls. There, the treasure's a cultural inheritance, a way of life, an identity expressed in dialogue between mother and daughter. It's both personal and collective, from mother to daughter, but also from one generation of Jewish women to the next. Such a treasure makes for an insurance against loss.

But my grandmother, not surprisingly, remained inconsolable. In her drawer she kept hidden the final birthday card sent to her by Carol and Marvin. On the outside are three red carnations interspersed with blue butterflies and layered with glitter; inside, a pop-up crepe paper heart. It was a birthday–Valentine's Day card, my grandmother having chosen February 14 as her nominal birthday because her parents couldn't recall the date. The youngest of their many children, she was in all likelihood an accident that eventually gave rise to a tragedy.

↰

The memory of her sister and its overlay of regret accompanied my mother, too, throughout the years. Arguably her most extensive, and perhaps most intense, relationship with her sister was posthumous — the forty-eight years when she remembered or might have remembered Carol or continued to suffer the consequences of her death versus the near twenty-seven years when both sisters shared their lives.

The older sister spent too much of her adult life trying to compensate her parents for their irremediable loss, organizing a fortieth anniversary party, driving them to the beach at Ogunquit in Maine, laying a Passover table with too few places. In *The Story of My Life*, my mother's photo album, the first pictures she affixed to the pages were of herself as an infant; the final ones, of herself or her new husband on a beach of fine sand littered with outcroppings of rock. That she stopped documenting her own life as mine began wasn't random. Although, like Carol, she'd had reservations about motherhood, in the end it was not my birth but her sister's death that undermined my mother's claim to her own existence. It might have confirmed, as well, her inclination not to risk bearing another child — a decision otherwise prompted by my mother's Rh-negative blood type, together with my father's advanced age. The older sister's life thus was determined by the death of the younger sister in the way her father's was determined by his missing brother. For as long as I knew my grandfather, his *modus vivendi* had been to do no wrong. My mother and her father rarely spoke to me about Carol or Jockey, nor did they share anything about the family origins, a condition I later came to see as an inheritance of willed forgetfulness.

In my mother's final years, it had become too late to ask the questions. Conversation with her was nearing the limitations of a postcard, the responsibility borne by a single speaker with a presumed or hoped-for audience.

Outside my mother's building, the blunt stems and tightly sealed buds of the early tulips were beginning to breach the half-frozen soil as they did every spring and would continue to do without relying on memory as we understand it.

As I entered her apartment, my mother stared at me. "I didn't think you were coming today," she said before refocusing her attention on the salsa competitors on her TV screen. The dancing partners wore tight-fitting Lycra garments of black and fuchsia, their sequins twinkling ferociously under the strobe lighting. On her upper bodice, the female dancer sported an oversized polyester rose.

"This lady and gentleman look very nice," I said with well-rehearsed insincerity.

My mother nodded. She herself was in a peach-coloured housedress with floral trim, rumpled white ankle socks, and white New Balance running shoes fastened with Velcro.

"Let's visit a bit," I suggested to my mother as the dancing ceased. "I'm going to water your Kalanchoe, and maybe then we'll look at some photos."

"If you say so."

In her final months in her own home my mother had turned the framed photographs of her husband, her parents, and her sister towards the wall in a gesture of deliberate forgetting. Now, close to two years later, I decided to look with her at her wedding album, at the professional photos taken just before "Dr. and Mrs. Kirsch left for Washington, Virginia, and the Southern States, the bride travelling in a blue tweed suit under a matching cashmere topcoat and wearing a white hat, black patent leather accessories, and a corsage bouquet of white orchids."

We started with my mother herself, unblemished and regal in her Simonetta of Rome wedding gown, a collar of fine pearls around her neck. So perfect, so unreal, did she appear that a museum curator viewing the photo referred to her as "a mannequin." Then came my father, dapper in top hat and tails, a white carnation pinned to his lapel. He was seated at a leather-topped desk with metal studs, one hand securing the marriage certificate, the other poised to sign. To his side, the rabbi looked on approvingly.

Eventually the pages fell open at a picture of Carol, the younger girl anticipating the older in the wedding procession, a maiden to the mature bride. "[She] wore a frock of white lace over pink taffeta, with a bustle effect. She carried a muff of pink roses and white stephanotis and wore a coronet of matching flowers." Like all the wedding photographs, the picture was black and white and encased in stiff plastic.

I glanced at my mother fearfully, but she appeared composed. "Do you know who this is?" I asked.

My mother took a brief look at the portrait. And then she said with the impartiality reserved for victims of collisions on the late-night news, "Is she the one who died?"

CHAPTER SIX

Counterclockwise

Bean Clemen

☐ No Repeat   Repeat 1 -

IT WAS ON HOLIDAYS TO FLORIDA THAT MY PARENTS MADE UP for the loss of my mother's sister by enjoying the benefits of extended family with my father's two brothers. Florida, for my parents, carried the reassurance of a safe place — a haven that satisfied the aspirations of my mother's fridge magnet titled "Renee's Florida Beachfront Property." It was where my father and mother fulfilled their urge to be "on the water," she by gazing out over the Gulf from the hotel balcony, he by roaming the beach in search of shells. The Sunshine State was where my parents together bought cheap gas and engaged in unchecked overeating, gorging on New York–style cheesecake, frequenting the early bird special at Mother Applebee's, casting aside kosher law to indulge in snow crab claws at a dockside shack where the waiters tied plastic bibs around the necks of wizened patrons. It was on a beach in Florida, one occasionally tainted by red tide, that my lifelong relationship with my parents suffered an irreversible shift.

As my parents grew older, my husband and I began the practice of joining them annually for a few days in Florida, as much to spend time with them as to visit with more rarely encountered members of the family. Not infrequently we accompanied my father on his beach walks while he scavenged for shells. In his early eighties then, my father suffered from compressed discs in his back and balance that could be considered at best precarious. He always wore one of two bathing outfits with trunks and a matching shirt, the one ochre and white, the other indigo and white. The pattern on each resembled a network of veins and capillaries, with the bottoms the inverse colours of the tops.

On this midwinter day in Florida, after my father had stooped without mishap to claim a whelk of modest proportions, he grinned at my husband and me, content with his find. Then, nonchalantly, he asked, "Are you two thinking of getting married any time soon?"

I scanned the face of my father, a perennial joker, for evidence he was joking. There was none. Half anguished, half incredulous, I replied, "We are married. You know that. We've been married for more than ten years."

My father appeared serene. "Well, then, are you thinking of having children?"

"Let's go back to the hotel," I said, "and we'll scrub down your whelk in the bathtub."

My father's lapse wasn't entirely without precedent. For at least a year he'd been repeating himself, too often at intervals of just a few seconds. "Did I ever tell you what the principal asked on my first day at Westmount High? 'The name's Kirsch, you say?' the principal asked me. 'Any relation to Edward and Leonard?' 'They're my brothers, sir,' I said. 'Any more at home?' he asked. 'No, sir.' 'Well, thank God for that!'" Typically, my father related the same joke or anecdote at least three times, until my husband and I could supply the punchline ourselves.

Uncharacteristically, my father had also begun scribbling notes to himself, a practice otherwise claimed by my mother.

Simon 1949, he wrote, *Malca 1967, Lionel 1944, Leonard 1993*, itemizing the death dates of his parents, cousin, and brother. He began to record, also, the intricacies of his pensions and annuities, the previously undisclosed location of his income tax returns. It must have been amid this frenzy of recording that my father endeavoured to tell me for the final time about the treasure, although I realize now the word *treasure* was never his but mine. He referred to it, invariably, as "something under the bedroom carpet." We were walking on the pesticide-laced lawn of a resort by Lake Simcoe, an easy drive north of Toronto, when my father pulled me aside to remind me of the "something," along with the essentials of his retirement plan. Still in my thirties, I was neither as responsive nor as reassuring as I should have been. Although chagrined by my father's declining faculties, I felt resentful, too, that this parent, from my youthful standpoint, was anticipating the end of his life. When we returned to Toronto later that same day, my father urinated into the flowerbed in front of my townhouse.

In hindsight, then, the ten words my father pronounced on the Florida beach — the same beach where he imagined himself to be during his last moments of consciousness in intensive care — were arguably a logical conclusion to the confusion and misdemeanours of the preceding year. But logic didn't prevail. Like many families tipping over into a crisis, we inclined to optimism, attributing my father's irregular behaviours and thinking patterns to a more wholesome form of natural decline. The mental lapses were obscured, too, by a co-occurring condition, a neurological disorder presenting as double vision and difficulties eating, which led to overall weakness accompanied by a degree of befuddlement. Oddly enough, my father as a medical intern in 1939 had written a paper on precisely this disorder but later failed to diagnose it in himself.

In the end, what my mother, my husband, and I had observed in my father in the lead-up to his blunder on the Florida beach wasn't nearly enough to undermine the ruthlessness of that moment. For the first time my father had misplaced a verifiable fact, an actuality confirmed daily for over a decade, the irrefutable reality of my marriage. As soon as I returned to the hotel and shared my father's harrowing misstep with my mother, she and I became a twosome complicit in his management and care. There would be no more genuine sparring between my parents. Worthwhile argument presumes and necessitates a grasp of the facts.

From my mother I learned that the community health service would send a nurse gratis to clip my father's toenails. The summer after my father's undeniable memory lapse, as he and I sat on the back balcony overlooking his garden, his toenails were immaculate, his spirits level.

"Your beans have done well," I said to my father, "and look how many bees are in your garden."

"The thing is, it's been a good season," my father said. He sat opposite me in one of two folding chairs with fake basket weave supported by a metal frame. His wore his favourite hat, a baseball cap from the golf course with the club name in raised silk letters, and a grease-stained blue zip-up windbreaker my mother would store in the cedar closet and eventually adopt as her own.

I couldn't have guessed then that the time I spent with my father in his final uninterrupted year at home would serve as a rehearsal for my interactions with my mother some ten years later. I chose in both instances the path of non-complexity, focusing conversation on the present and the readily observable, resorting to silence when I sensed my parents' fatigue, dispensing false assurances. It was as though my father and I were looking at each other through a peephole, each of us privy to only a partial view of the other — just enough to validate identity and confer a sense of well-being.

A similar withholding prevailed in my exchanges with my mother as we considered my father's predicament. Whereas my mother previously had kept me under a microscope, exaggerating my every move and perceiving in me *specimen of daughter, only child, only grandchild, childless wife* — a cluster of forlorn designations — now my father merited the more powerful scrutiny. Almost always, she and I discussed my father's memory loss in the context of the care needed and the direct burden my mother was experiencing, never the existential dimensions nor the sadness imposed. Most often, my mother valued my opinion and took heed of my advice.

"I'm at the end of my rope," my mother would tell me long distance over the phone, although in practice she coped well, as she so often did when confronted with a real rather than an imaginary threat. Nonetheless, her desperation and fatigue were genuine. As my husband and I discovered when we occasionally stayed the weekend to allow my mother respite, my father, who previously had slept soundly through the night — a skill acquired both in the army and during his shifts as a medical intern — had become restive. His was a deeply personal sense of time. At 3 a.m. my bedroom door would squeak open and I'd observe, through sleep-inflamed eyes, the detritus of my father — a once-robust man turned gaunt, his boxer shorts hanging in curtain folds around his thighs, his eyes as dilated and unblinking as a barn owl's.

"Is it time for breakfast now?" he'd ask.

"Not yet. Go back to bed." Had he been eighty years younger, I might have laughed.

"Tell me how you skied to school," I once asked my father when he was still in possession of his faculties.

"We had a big blizzard," he said. "The streets were covered in snow. Mind you, I used to ski like that in the Laurentians before they had a rope tow. We climbed up one hill and skied down the next. You had to be strong."

I'd found a photograph of him, one of a quartet of skiers, clad in a belted dark jumpsuit layered over a turtleneck sweater, offset by a semi-structured white tam. His mittens, pneumatic and rounded like boxing gloves, implied the power in his hands.

Throughout his life my father had demonstrated resilience. As the youngest of three brothers, he learned early how to scrap, playing defence in hockey and cultivating a powerful backhand in tennis. Of his wounding on Juno Beach on D-Day, he related, "Something hit me in the leg and it spun me around like a top about three times. So anyway, I held up my finger ... and said, 'One wound strike.' And I kept on working ..." He was recovered by VE Day, wearing his mother's necklace of three interlinked leaves as he celebrated with the crowds in London. Upon his return home from the Second World War, my father tended to Jewish refugees with numbers imprinted on their skin. He employed neither a receptionist nor a nurse in his medical practice because he remained intent on following his own rules.

My father didn't retire from medicine until he turned seventy-six and, in his early sixties, after the Parti Québécois came to power, was required to sit an exam proving his ability to minister to patients in French. English speakers of my father's generation perversely were never schooled in the language of Quebec's majority. Even so, my father gamely studied for one of the final exams he'd ever sit, rehearsing aloud the names of body members, organs, and digits: *les cuisses* (the thighs), *la foie* (the liver), *le gros orteil* (the big toe). "You know," he told me in the aftermath of his successful result, "all my French-Canadian patients say they have *les yeux pers.*" My father seemed to have trouble grasping the precise nature of this blue-green, or hazel, although his own eyes conformed to the same description. Then again, he was colour-blind.

When, a couple of decades after his French exam, my father began to lose track of his memory, he maintained the same silence on the subject as my mother and I. I didn't know, and still don't, whether his silence flagged a conscious secret he didn't wish to confide in us or a genuine lack of awareness of his condition, which might have evolved gradually and become second nature to him. Perhaps his illness counted as a perverse form of treasure — an enigma to be buried and kept from view.

Similarly, I've no idea whether, in the early stages of dementia, my father sought medical advice. On his better days, and in some respects, not a lot had changed. Mostly, my father still kissed me and shook hands with my husband when we arrived from out of town. He watched reruns of *The Lawrence Welk Show* and drank Schweppes ginger ale from the bottle. If my mother was out of view, he slipped me and my husband a cheque, counselling us to buy a "really BIG TV, but don't tell Rene." Only once, when I was folding laundry in his bedroom, did my father allude to "forgetting things." "It's frightening," he added, looking towards the back yard, where his beans were ascending their poles in the only direction they could go, counterclockwise.

Too startled to muster an adequate response, I said to him merely, "How are you feeling?"

"Fair."

To this day, my inability to engage him counts as one of my most remarkable failures.

⌐⟶

One of my final gestures for my father was to read aloud to him a recipe for brownies from a lifestyle magazine. "Three tablespoons of butter, one teaspoon of vanilla extract, one cup of confectioner's sugar." My father had lost consciousness and, in all likelihood, couldn't hear what I was saying, but I kept on just in case — "one-third of a cup unsweetened cocoa powder, a quarter teaspoon of salt" — and because I hoped he might recognize the sound of my voice and glean comfort from it. A tray of uneaten hospital food was perched on the table by my father's bedside. His GP, a long-time friend, had already come by to declare that my father couldn't possibly survive. "His organs are failing," Dr. Nieman said, with the rare mastery of fact specific to the medical profession.

I leaned forward to assess my father's breathing, which was regular, then laid a hand on his arm. "And here's how you make them. 'Grease and flour an eight-inch square pan ... Spread batter ... Bake in a preheated oven ... Do not overcook.'"

Food would become equally essential to my overtures to my mother in her final year. For Passover, the Feast of Freedom, I baked her a jelly roll from *A Treasure for My Daughter* — a concoction of potato starch, sugar, eggs, lemon juice, matzo cake flour, and fruit jelly. My husband wrapped the cake tightly in foil, and it travelled with me on the little plane from Toronto, which reared and lunged like a startled filly until we rose above the clouds. On the descent into Montreal, parcels of woodland, sombre without their leaves, were lit by brilliant sunshine.

When I arrived at my mother's apartment, Darlene was preparing to serve a festive meal assembled on a tray from the communal kitchen downstairs. My mother looked up as I entered, apparently unsurprised to see me. "Sit here, sweetheart," Darlene said to my mother, patting the chair. She cut up all the elements of the too-large servings: hard-boiled egg, matzo ball soup, gefilte fish with a lettuce leaf, roast chicken leg with a half sweet potato.

Over the years my mother had shared little with me about how she and her parents and sister had celebrated the holidays, expressing only the regret that she hadn't observed her mother, my grandmother, as she prepared her own mother's recipes from Kiev in the Ukraine. "Nu, Rene, what's with the lack of interest?" my grandmother asked my mother more than once. Her preparations of matzo ball soup and gefilte fish were nuanced, requiring both instinct and spontaneity.

In general, my mother had downplayed the religious rituals of her childhood, enthusing instead about the beach holidays in Plattsburgh or at Lac Supérieur. Later, in her early widowhood, she became fond of reminiscing about my father's wartime experiences, mesmerized by recollections that were not her own, and watched obsessively TV re-enactments of the D-Day landing.

Darlene appraised the leftovers on my mother's plate, then raised another spoonful to my mother's lips. "Chew, Rene. Chew."

"I've had enough," my mother said to no one in particular after having consumed a single matzo ball, several morsels of fish, and a portion of chicken thigh no bigger than a dishwasher tablet. She'd licked the lettuce leaf but swiftly returned it to the plate. The jelly roll remained untouched. Then came my mother's refrain, the aspect of her that remained most predictable: "I want to go to bed now."

I accompanied my mother to her bedroom, where I removed her top and bra and helped her into one of my father's old short-sleeved shirts that extended to her thighs. "Let's take off your trousers," I suggested. Next I unplugged the convection fan. A low of eight was expected that night. "Happy Passover," I said, "you're doing so well," feeling all the while as though I was eavesdropping on an insincerity volunteered by someone other than myself.

$\longleftarrow$

Many of my greatest acts of kindness towards my mother — or so I persuaded myself — involved concealment. In the years I struggled with emptying and selling her house, I kept from her other irreversible happenings — most notably, that both my mother-in-law and sister-in-law had died, my mother-in-law from heart disease and dementia, my sister-in-law from cancer. Since they lived in England and Denmark, respectively, my mother didn't register their absence. This withholding of facts or dispensing of partial truths was already so entrenched in my dealings with my mother that accommodating her memory loss proved easier than it might otherwise have been. My method implied not confrontation but evasion. I'd engaged in this habit for almost a half century, having learned from middle childhood to excise particulars that would stoke my mother's anxiety. Astonishingly, it never occurred to me to wonder whether my mother similarly hid anything from me.

In her final years, my mother was prone neither to secrecy nor to fabrication. Whereas my mother-in-law, in the early stages of forgetfulness, feigned competence, clambering onto a chair in slingback pumps to water geraniums or imagining herself once again to be the Latin mistress, "bringing to heel" unruly girls in a north London schoolroom, my mother merely declared, "I don't know what I'm doing." It was something she said often and with discomposure. In this respect she remained a reliable witness to her own plight. If she complained that her wrist ached or a care aide had made her cry or the kasha and bow ties were "lousy," I'd no reason to doubt her. To the last she never relinquished her grip on the fearful present.

My father, in contrast, largely kept silent about suspicions he might have had and braced for the skirmishes ahead, as befits an old soldier. Before he was removed to the hospital where he died, he lived for two months in a nursing home for veterans, receiving on Remembrance Day a card from an anonymous small child with a crepe paper poppy anchored to the page by a black plastic centre. My father by then had surrendered his recall of his military past and found even the caged parakeets in the downstairs aviary brought no solace.

In thinking back now on my parents in their years of declining awareness, their individualizing of reality, the specifics they misplaced and the confusion they engendered, I'm confronted by a fact I might have recognized long ago — that I myself was the practitioner of greatest insincerity. In relation to them, at least, and not entirely out of selfish motives, I acted as a peddler of omissions, obfuscation, and half actualities, a purveyor of the very methods that frustrated my inquiry into the nature and placement of the buried treasure or the missing recollections of Jockey, Simon, and Carol. A self-confessed liar, I never questioned my own entitlement to the truth.

Such was my obsession that I didn't wonder at the feasibility of excavating facts from inert objects, from the ephemera of old photographs or words in print. I've since become alert to the obvious — that when exercising even the most intense scrutiny, when aiming for the highest levels of disclosure, we can discern at best only partial truths. My grandfather Simon's early childhood in Vilkomir is verifiable only in my imagination. Jockey's preference for beginning the narrative of his life. midway through implies a fragment. Carol's story offers the counterbalance to his, a beginning deprived of its end, her final illness apparently undiagnosed.

My great-uncle Jockey, a renowned fantasist, found his moxie in the negotiation of volatile and unverifiable facts. Yet one of his preferred aphorisms, "There ain't no such thing as a sure thing," betrayed his status as a realist. My mother and my grandfather Simon were of a different ilk. Like Simon, the father-in-law she never knew, my mother became a connoisseur of minutiae. The dropout biology student and the professor — both sought truth in magnification, my mother in crocheted Kleenex-box covers and the scheme for condiments in her fridge, Simon in the cells and vascular bundles of common bracken. But the danger of magnification is it misses out the rest. The treasure may remain unseen. The purpose of obsession, medically speaking, may be to direct attention away from something when, by implication, the true subject lies elsewhere. It's too easy to become estranged from what matters.

From the time I was old enough to reach upwards, my father kept a treasury of small objects in the top drawer of his man's dresser. Assembled neatly were magnifying glasses, blank prescription pads, boxes of playing cards, faded letters, coins, desiccated stamp pads, and TripTik maps from the Canadian Automobile Association in which each page illustrated a discrete segment of the journey.

When my father moved into the veterans nursing home in what proved to be the final months of his life, he'd lost his mobility after a series of small strokes and had to be lifted in and out of bed by a sort of crane, as though he were an element in a building under construction or perhaps, more forebodingly, demolition. Almost worse still, my father was assigned to the dementia unit, a lockdown where he was deprived of his favourite objects and thereby of whatever memories they might have roused. Forbidden were his seashells, framed family photos, military medals, segments of lava and coral, anything that in the hands of his hungrier or more mobile inmates could be either launched as a weapon or inappropriately swallowed. One of the only items I managed to introduce for him was a photo of the orphaned pelican chick Sunbeam, in a cardboard frame. She'd been rescued by an animal shelter in Florida with funds my mother and I had donated in my father's name. The caption underneath her photo stated, "Although Sunbeam has been raised in captivity, she will rightly take her place in the wild as soon as she is strong enough to fish and survive on her own."

My father's specimens weren't complicit in their own destiny. The fragments of shell or mineral or grains of sand captured in a sterile bottle were removed without permission from their places of origin and the natural processes to which they belonged. This creating of specimens renders them outside time but assigns them a place within memory, as long as memory prevails — each specimen a reminder of a destination possibly never to be frequented again.

It troubled me deeply that my father had become estranged from his own objects and, in particular, his nature specimens, the collecting of which was a direct legacy from Simon, his father. The son's ways both revealed and renewed those of the father, the allure of samples evident in my father's sequestering of small objects and even his eating habits. Before his confinement in the lockdown unit, no pleasure for him could surpass the buffet, where a miniature eggroll, a dollop of egg salad, and a slice of chicken bologna with a side of lemon meringue pie far exceeded the gratification of a single serving on a plate.

For Simon, the sections of common bracken gathered for viewing under a microscope or by means of a magic lantern assumed a different and more impersonal meaning. In them he sought examples of a class or group, and yet, perversely, the basis for his research was irregularities, those examples flouting the rules of the larger whole. The word *truth*, originating in Old English *triewth*, means "faithfulness" or "constancy." Simon's samples presumably complied with the law of irregularities but showed themselves unfaithful to the broader rules of the median or norm. They were both responsive to the truth and dissenters from it.

My own quest for particulars — of the buried treasure, of the lost family members as revealed through their objects — was perhaps exhibiting a similar faith in the way fragments can satisfy or illuminate the whole. Naively, I never considered the hazards that might ensue from a successful quest, how the truth might prove hard to believe or accept, and untruth or ignorance less so. My fear surrounded not finding the treasure, an eventuality that came to pass and left me having to acknowledge how there may be appeasement in unknowing. A specimen, as much as an individual life, defends a hoard of secrets.

CHAPTER SEVEN

The Possibilities Are Fantastic

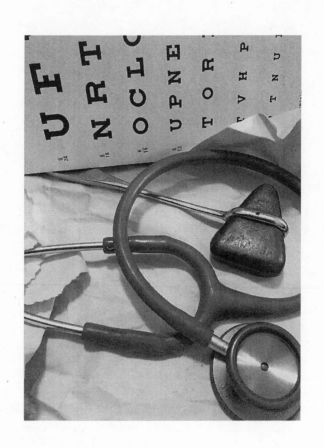

In a semi-private room adjoining the hallway where Darlene and I conversed, my mother lay dying beside a scrupulously clean woman with glassy blue eyes whose face she would never see. A muted pink curtain separated one patient from the other. The woman was tended by Filipinas round the clock, and when occasionally she spoke, exhibited a low, refined voice.

As soon as my mother had entered palliative care, during the worst blizzard in decades, she began searching for coordinates. Not once did she wonder about the identity of the stranger behind the curtain, but too often she demanded from her hospital bed "Where am I?" The question invariably was succeeded by the appeal "I want to go home." In truth, the room my mother shared with a stranger at Mount Sinai Hospital was an easy drive from the home she'd commanded for more than fifty years, forty-six of them with my father. Even so, the hospital and its rituals afforded no recognition. Here my mother no longer was able to resist the hands of strangers. Gloved fingers touched and probed her, striving for tenderness but practising science. At Mount Sinai, my mother had become unlike herself.

To placate my mother I brought her vanilla ice cream in Dixie cups, free and always at the ready in the patients' freezer-fridge. One day as my mother was licking clean the tiny wooden spoon, a candy-striper entered the room.

"Are you the daughter?" she asked, noting me seated by the bedside.

"Yes."

"And why not! She's a nice little lady. She deserves to have a daughter."

I nodded my acknowledgment. Despite the anxiety and grief that pervaded me, whether in my mother's presence or during the hours and days spent away from her, I discovered myself frequently unable to sleep and even less able to cry. Too often I was alone in the city of my birth, without my husband or others by my side. In the absence of company, I read and reread emails from friends in Toronto. One woman's son had developed an allergy to dragon rolls. Another's financial adviser was pushing for a move into consumer staples. At night, to encourage sleep, I began devouring mysteries about curates impaled on altarpieces and cat burglars found murdered in Venetian lagoons. It seemed that confronting my mother's situation — inevitably, my own situation — perversely entailed willing my thoughts elsewhere.

$\longleftarrow$

The beginning of the truth had been delivered to me months earlier on a cloudless day in Washington, DC — via phone, long distance, by an administrator familiar from my mother's eighteen months in assisted living. My mother had been admitted to hospital with dangerously low hemoglobin. I was on vacation. She was short of oxygen.

"Maybe I should leave straight away," I said to my husband, my hands clenched, my own chest tightening. The lounge we stood in, though not in a hospital, exuded that same off-dry smell of cleaning agents.

"They told you to stay here," he replied, enforcing calm. "Let's just wait for the results."

The second phone call, from a specialist, came soon and was marred by poor reception: "... markers ... latest scan ... individuals your mother's age ... more often than not...." The specialist sneezed.

"Bless you," I said.

"We may be looking at cancer," he said.

In a nearby forsythia hedge, a catbird discharged a pungent meow.

I quickly booked the next available flight to Montreal. Then I withdrew for hours to a remote, tangled garden where a dog tick found its way between my breasts. Before I'd noticed or could brush it off, it had pierced me with its harpoon-like mouth and was rapidly becoming engorged with my blood. The head gardener, a PhD in entomology, removed the tick with tweezers as I lay supine on a bench with the entire grounds staff looking on.

"A tick isn't an insect," she explained. "It's only got two body segments." She held up the mite poised between the tweezers. "And eight legs." Then the head gardener–entomologist placed the tick — smaller than a cultivated blueberry — under her microscope for all to view. I can no longer recall whether it was alive or dead.

⟵

During the first months of my mother's subjugation, when scans and tests proliferated but she'd not yet been admitted to Mount Sinai, I began to formulate a new search. The treasure in this instance assumed the guise of my grandfather's house — a house other than the once-familiar Victorian in Lower Westmount. In the *Canadian Jewish Review*, I'd found evidence that during the war years my grandfather had commissioned a different home or homes in Petit Lac Long from Mr. Arthur Cyr, "the best-known building contractor in the Laurentian Mountains."

As I resolved to search for my grandfather's house, it never occurred to me to do otherwise. Undoubtedly my impulse to find the house on Petit Lac Long harked back to my failure to locate my father's treasure, which, possibly, entailed a failure of recognition. My inability to acknowledge a genuine treasure right before my eyes. In hindsight, I believe I was searching, also, for commonalities — a dissolving of boundaries between Simon's Baltic origins and the Laurentian landscape he later claimed as his. And as much as my search was invigorated by a yearning for messages from the past, it acquired value, too, as a detour from the present. Within weeks of her diagnosis, on the most fecund days of early summer, my mother no longer went outdoors and scarcely left her apartment. As her life became more circumscribed, her body refusing any opportunity for recovery, I was looking for a view.

Perhaps it was no surprise, then, that I became mesmerized by a structure that predated my mother's own life and surely would supersede it, something made of more durable materials than human flesh and bone. The Laurentian Mountains themselves, where the house was to be found, rank among the most ancient mountain ranges in the world.

Searching for my grandfather's house didn't serve merely as a tantalizing distraction. Instead, the quest soon became entangled with my own survival. Whereas my mother and I, in our long association, had become accustomed to noting our considerable differences, in my growing tendency to obsession and the sense of purposefulness it conferred, I became my mother's daughter.

To accelerate the search for the missing house, I emailed a doyenne of the Jewish community in nearby Sainte-Agathe. Her reply came quickly: *Call my friend. She knows all the history. She's ninety-one and is amazing.*

I called her friend. "My husband would know," she told me. "He knows everything."

"Let's ask him."

"He's deceased."

On my day trip to Petit Lac Long, which I undertook as my mother was languishing in assisted living, I carried, as always, my cellphone, in readiness for a call from her caregivers. Since my mother's diagnosis, the imperative to expose my whereabouts at all times had returned me to my years of living at home, when she pinpointed my every move. Then, as now, her undue concern for me arose from a surplus of love.

As I neared the lake, I pulled over by a small bridge spanning a stream. Beside it, stands of conifers were in distress. This I deduced from the degree of brown where there should have been green and from the depth of resin. "The substance called resin has been known for a long time," wrote my grandfather Simon in a scientific paper read by Professor Nicholls to the Royal Society of Canada, "and is described by Theophrastus and Aristotle as the life sap of certain trees."

I can personally say more about resin: It clings to your fingers, and when fossilized forms amber, which stills fragments of plants and animals in time. Debate about resin, so compelling in my grandfather's time, was neutralized long ago. The substance plays no role in nourishing conifers but serves rather as a sealant or antiseptic, an agent to ward off outsiders aiming to penetrate wounded or otherwise vulnerable areas of a tree. I met a number of people at Petit Lac Long, but not one of them, I felt, could have discoursed on resin. They were impartial to conifers, finding intrigue in water wings and the better cuts of brisket.

Once I'd reached the end of the lakeside drive, I doubled back to the gravel parking area leading to a scrap of public beach, where several plump teenaged girls — *zaftig*, my mother would have called them — sprawled in lounge chairs. They paid me no heed, whereas the elders seated on the dock, their pale legs dangling in the water, scrutinized me from head to toe.

"Can I help?" asked one man, not unpleasantly. He was bare-chested, his belly arrayed with damp grey hair like seaweed stranded on a beach.

"My grandfather Simon Kirsch had a house on this lake. In the early forties. I was hoping to find it."

"What's this?" The woman approaching was middle-aged but svelte and wore a one-piece maillot and round sunglasses. I noticed suddenly how the folded plastic chairs on the sand had names like *Cohen* and *Lipschitz* written on them in indelible ink.

The woman gestured towards the dock and the several wooden cottages bordering the sand. "This beach is for the families in these houses."

"Oh, I'm sorry. I was only trying to find my grandfather's house from a long time ago."

The property owners stood impassive in their bathing suits.

"Would you mind if I took a few photos of the lake?" I inquired.

"Feel free," said the older man before clasping his grandson's hand. The boy had sidled up to him. "We're going to have a look at the rocket."

"Thanks again," I said to the woman in the maillot, who remained nearby.

She shrugged. "What did you take from us, anyway? A breath of air?"

As I drove for a final time over the little bridge, I craned my neck to look at the suppurating conifers. It has to be acknowledged that dieback in a conifer can originate in a trauma one or two seasons earlier. Whatever had assailed the spruce trees by the bridge might no longer be present, the browning needles an effect bereft of a cause.

t⟶

I'd like to believe that towards the end of her life my mother was freed from the sense of menace that pervaded her younger years. Instead, the objects of her anxiety became more and more removed from other people's and her own truth. For brief intervals she profited from a false serenity. She feared neither her own mortality nor the loss of those close to her, in part because she was unable to apprehend her own illness. But more often than not she was fretful, her refrain "I don't know what I'm doing" becoming a catch-all for "I can't do what you're asking" or "I no longer understand where I am or where I'm going" and then evolving into the single certainty "I want to go to bed." Sleep had become my mother's medium, her waking a brief recess. Darlene merely said, "My lady's going down."

On Darlene's orders I made trips to the drugstore to buy Nivea moisturizing lotion and Zincolac, which came in a cardboard box with a picture of a grinning naked baby splayed on a diaper. In the months leading up to my mother's admission to Mount Sinai, I stayed occasionally in an apartment hotel where too often I was startled in the night by randomly set clock radios or smoke alarms triggered by occupants who'd burned toast. During my mother's brief spells of waking, I lavished her with smiles and reassurances, conveying the opposite of the grief and fear that threatened to subsume me. "It's all right," I told her time and again, though I would have been at a loss to identify what "it" was.

Several years earlier, when her confusion first became evident, my mother herself had alienated most family and long-standing friends by continually rebuffing their invitations and phone calls. Although I regretted her social withdrawal, I was forced to respect it. Even banal conversation could induce panic as she failed to recall this morning's news, yesterday's weather, her last meal, or the provenance of her flowering plant. Routine questions served only the purpose of making her remember that she couldn't remember. Now, understandably, none of the people she'd banished were aware of her condition, nor would my mother have felt equal to receiving them.

Whenever he could, my husband joined me in Montreal to visit my mother, who immediately recognized him as "her favourite son-in-law," a joke of her own invention that persisted in making her smile. Yet my husband, too, mostly was obliged to stay away for reasons that were unyielding. He needed to maintain his earnings as more and more I had to turn down contracts of my own, and both his teaching and consultancy involved travel elsewhere. Not inconsequential was illness in his own family overseas. And more palpably, before my mother's diagnosis we'd planned a basement renovation, and the work had now got under way, demanding oversight. Then there was this: When my mother died, my husband would need to suspend both the basement renovation and his work to join me in Montreal. The reality of time off now had to be measured against the certainty of time off in the near future.

↩

As a child, and like so many children, I yearned to hear the same story over and over, even though I knew the ending —

in particular because I knew the ending. The Cat in the Hat scattered "things" everywhere — a cup, a rake, milk, strings, a toy ship, a living fish — then magically restored them to their rightful place. The Velveteen Rabbit who longed to be "real" became so first when he garnered the adoration of his boy owner, and again when the nursery fairy saved him from burning, endowing him with hind legs to hop away.

The single story that pursued me now was my mother's, with only the ending to come, but I found no lust for rehearsing it. Nonetheless, this story I didn't want to hear, the story of my mother's impending death, imposed itself on me relentlessly by way of images in the prelude to sleep and during sleep itself. My mother's face bleeding. My mother's fingers shredding her blanket. My mother calling for me by name.

The more pervasive my mother's illness, the more she slept, the more I endured sleeplessness. In the opinion of the Johns Hopkins Medicine website, my unrelenting sleep deprivation put me at increased risk of obesity, cravings for sweet and starchy food, irritability, high blood pressure, fuzzy thinking, fatal car crashes, dementia. In practice, however, I was hypervigilant though not fully awake, and, by necessity, in command. And in my waking time, which ended up being most of the time, I continued to read about hoards — how burying objects, whether in the earth or in a streambed, might have served as a means of willing them an afterlife.

By now the search for my grandfather's house, a house lost not by design but by accident, had overwhelmed my obsession with finding my father's treasure. Nevertheless, this later search had evolved out of the earlier one and arguably made for its afterlife, even though my grandfather's house predated the original treasure. My father hadn't buried his hoard until 1955, some twelve years after Simon broke ground at Petit Lac Long. In a photo of my father from this era, he's seated on a rock at Little Beach in Ogunquit, legs spread wide, wearing mesh sand shoes with black knee socks. His hair close cropped, his eyes invisible behind sunglasses, the newlywed, perennially seasick, is smiling at the North Atlantic. Without a doubt, he has already buried the treasure.

Bored of pondering lost opportunities and researching my own vulnerabilities, I conducted fruitless Web searches for the house in the Laurentians. When I'd exhausted all prospects in English, I switched to French. The first of my keywords, "Simon Kirsch *and* Maison Petit Lac Long," yielded nothing. I streamlined my search terms, which produced a hit: La Maison Simon Kirsh. My grandfather's surname, and my own, minus the *c*.

t ⌐

I could no longer venture far. My mother's condition was worsening, and she was alternately restless and unresponsive. "What do you want?" Darlene told her not unkindly. "You're not going anywhere. You're in your bed."

At night, in my rented room, I reviewed a letter from my mother dated November 1990, the words on the envelope, *If I cannot act for myself, instructions enclosed.* Although not specifically addressed to me, the letter ended *Love, Mom,* implicating me as the sole recipient:

> *If there is a chance that a clinic elsewhere out of Quebec would be able to help me, then I would want you to try.*
> *I have seen people who were told they would never lead a normal life recover enough that their families still enjoy whatever they can contribute. You could seek several opinions.*

Aware that no doctor could restore my mother's vitality, I sought none. Instead, I drafted an inquiry about the house that aspired to my paternal grandfather's name.

Whatever its genuine identity, La Maison Simon Kirsh in no way pretended to be the house at Petit Lac Long. Over time I'd formed only a vague image of the country home built for my grandfather by Mr. Arthur Cyr — a house in stone or wood, possibly with an A-line roof, modest in scale — but imagined more vividly its setting — on or by a lake, in the shelter of fir trees. A birch grove flourished nearby, and in its understory, generations of common bracken. Conversely, La Maison Simon Kirsh was situated in a prosperous neighbourhood on a higher slope of Montreal's so-called mountain, thereby exempting it from wildness. Categorized as Art Deco, it was an edifice of defiant geometries.

In composing my inquiry to Art Deco Montreal, I drew on the letter-writing skills inherited from my mother, who composed liberally. In particular, my mother had frequently penned notes to my father as a means of avoiding argument. These envelopes deposited on my father's man's dresser harboured criticisms or appeals — my mother wanted my father to address her more politely in the company of friends, she wanted to redecorate the living room and would need an allowance, she requested that my father play less golf and gin rummy and spend more time at home. I'm not aware that my father ever replied in writing to these entreaties. Often he filled his mouth with Liquorice Allsorts.

The representative from Art Deco Montreal was more forth-coming with words. *The architects Shorey and Ritchie had the home built for Simon Kirsh who was the first owner of the home in 1934*, he wrote. *Therefore if your grandfather lived there, the house bears his name.*

It was out of the question that Simon should have occupied the house bearing a semblance of his surname. Outremont, the mountainside location of Maison Simon Kirsh, was claimed in that era by the overlords of the schmatte trade — affluent factory owners like the fictitious entrepreneur David Levinsky.

The north slope of Mount Royal harboured, as well, several of Montreal's most desirable cemeteries. In fact, this mountain, despite its hold on the prosperous and the dead, rated as no more than a pluton, a large body of intrusive igneous rock. Of this, Simon might have been aware. In 1925 he'd moved his family "on the flat" to the Victorian house in Lower Westmount where, twenty-four years later, surrounded by academics, small businessmen, and young professionals, he'd died in the bathtub. His final move, the one he undertook alone, was to the cemetery just a few blocks uphill from Maison Simon Kirsh.

My mother was admitted to Mount Sinai in the final days of the old year and had been there several weeks when her right leg swelled up. She'd become so thin that the normal leg looked atrophied, the swollen leg normal. In the inexactitude of the two legs, she now resembled her mother, Rose, whose withered right leg had resulted from a club foot. But my mother compared herself neither to her progenitors nor to her former self. She simply was.

For my part, I could barely countenance the woman before me, who bore little resemblance to the widow my husband and I had chaperoned to the South of France for her seventieth birthday. On that trip, strapped into a beige maxi-length raincoat with a half cape at the back and a belted waistline, exhibiting a bouffant hairdo sustained by spray, and wearing oversized truncated square glasses, my mother had cared little for sleep and showed herself impervious to anxiety, as she so often did when removed from her own home.

"Don't worry," I'd told her as my husband was struggling to find the reverse gear after having mistakenly driven our Peugeot onto the tram tracks in Montpellier.

"What's to worry," my mother replied, refreshing her lipstick as the tram hurtled towards us.

Later that day I photographed her at our *gîte* near Mont Sainte-Victoire, where she sat smiling before a plate of ratatouille and a full glass of wine. The scene was staged (my mother never drank alcohol), but the contentment genuine.

Throughout her life my mother had been searching for the calm she attained in that *gîte* near Cézanne's iconic mountain. Ten years later, half the size and with faltering executive skills, she was casting about for connections and reassurances that involved me and others in ever-more-elaborate lies.

Now my mother had begun to ask for her mother. "I need her telephone number," she told Darlene.

"Don't worry, sweetheart, I'll get it for you tomorrow."

The head nurse, when she heard about my mother's request, said it might be significant. "People nearing the end often speak to the dead," she explained. "Then again, it could be the dementia." She returned to the nurses' station, where a bouquet of white lilies, so often a sign of hope or resurrection, here bespoke the gratitude of a grieving family. A hoard of silver coins, I'd read, could indicate great wealth or irremediable loss.

$\longleftarrow$

The house that almost certainly hadn't belonged to my grandfather was notable for its irregularities. According to my research, the structure combined a range of styles, approaching Art Deco in its geometry while rejecting "ornamental exuberance"; hinting in its horizontal lines at German Expressionism yet distinct in its "compact nature"; exhibiting similarities with Dutch neoplasticism, but "without dogmatism and sometimes in a more rational manner." The house was identified also as "rare." The authorities had rated it nationally and provincially "very rare" for its era (1930–50), "very rare" among buildings surviving from this time, "very rare" in its stylistic attributes. Maison Simon Kirsh qualified as a specimen and, as such, was credible as the production of a man of science.

The status assigned to Maison Simon Kirsh was presented as fact, as though rarity could be severed from opinion. And yet my parents, when travelling, regularly had amassed common objects that back home assumed the guise of rarities. From Nassau, pale, fast-flowing sand worthy of an hourglass. In Lanzarote, black sand from lava beaches where hawkers sold hand-embroidered tablecloths slung over the backs of camels. A sliver of agate from Mexico. My parents nested the objects in orange-and-white Sunflight carry-on bags, ensuring their safe passage through Security and Immigration. Once home my mother and father printed the names and provenance of the sand and semi-precious stones on masking tape, secured the samples in labelled containers, and put them in the basement. However much ignored, the specimens that had outlived their purpose became, for my parents, displaced treasures.

From such accidents of retrieval and possession, I inferred that the house at Petit Lac Long might be not unlike my parents' forgotten specimens or my father's buried treasure. It, too, might still exist. The reputation of treasure may be based on lies and misunderstandings. Memory can confuse or be misplaced. I refer you to the colour *pink*. Pink, in childhood, counted as my favourite colour, but it was also pink — a pink stain — that foretold my mother's final illness. In a sense, all my efforts were aimed at restoring my original sense of pink.

To my queries regarding my mother's illness — nature, duration, manner of death — the palliative care doctor had several candid replies: "I don't know," "I really couldn't say," "It's impossible to be sure." Patients who appear frail may linger for months. Others who look more robust can disappear in an instant. "But your mother's vital signs are stable," she offered by way of factual appeasement. I'd learned that more women than men were drawn to palliative medicine, women being somehow better equipped to confront disorder and the inability to sustain life.

I took care, also, to solicit my mother's opinion. "You're doing all right?" I asked time and again, clasping her hand as I sat by her bedside or inquiring over the telephone.

"They tell me so."

Throughout her adult life my mother had surrounded herself with vivacious pictures and ornaments — 3-D orange and yellow mushrooms in scored Lucite, a miniature clay cockerel with red hearts for wings and one-dimensional yellow feet traced onto a cerulean base, a print of nuns blowing smoke out of their haloes. Here in the palliative care room, against the metal sheen of the bed frame and beneath the overexposed lighting, her illness stood out as the only thing evocative of life.

$\longleftarrow$

"Walk on the side of the road facing traffic so oncoming headlights keep you illuminated." "While you're enjoying the blue-plate special at your favorite restaurant, Madam, the chap at the next table is rifling through your purse." More and more I rummaged through my mother's newspaper clippings in the hopes of finding advice that would keep me safe. To foster serenity, I dabbled in old advertising slogans and headlines from the online archives of the *Montreal Gazette* and *Canadian Jewish Review*. "Men's and Women's spring coats: a thorough cleaning, then correct pressing, will put them in shape for use once more" was reassuring. "Mrs. H. Wener, Oxford Avenue, is visiting Mrs. Samuel J. Cohen of Regina" was comfortingly not open to debate.

As well, I pored over decades-old articles about Outremont. One of these, "Valuation Roll is cause of breeze," dated from October 20, 1932, three weeks in advance of my mother's birth. The report's lead sentence commanded my attention: "Protest of Dr. Simon Kirsch against his land assessment, as levied by the city of Outremont, occasioned a sharp verbal clash on the subject of valuations between Ald. Ernest Pitt and the majority of the municipal council." Here was an indirect revelation that my grandfather had owned land in Outremont, and just two years before the appearance of Maison Simon Kirsh.

I soon established online that in 1929 Henri Duverger had sold to Simon Kirsch several extensive lots in Outremont: 15-29-1 to 4, all facing onto Pagnuelo. The address of Maison Simon Kirsh happened to be 12 Pagnuelo.

$$\longleftarrow$$

Once again my mother had become unresponsive. She lay impassive in her paper hospital gown on her side of the pink curtain, neither dead nor wholly alive, unmoved by language but capable of sensing pain.

"From a medical viewpoint, she's not comatose," a nurse told me.

"She's not producing urine," countered Darlene. "That's not a good sign." She was watching coverage of a nor'easter on CNN and turned up the volume as soon as the nurse had left the room. Beside Darlene sat a limp sandwich in a cardboard triangle. The TV reporter's orange hood had blown off, her soaked head as slick as a mollusc.

Back at my room, dry-mouthed and impotent, I paced. With little to be done for my mother, the natural outlet for my restlessness became Maison Simon Kirsh. Willing my thoughts towards the *style moderne*, I visualized, instead of an inflatable blood pressure cuff, a cornice, instead of a hospital curtain, a "guillotine" or sash window.

I arranged an appointment with the archivist for Outremont. The interview was to be held over the phone and — a worrisome prospect — in French. My vocabulary in the language that wasn't my mother tongue had never extended to architectural discourse. In French class at school, we'd concentrated on the novella *Le Torrent* by the Quebec writer Anne Hébert, whose central character, François Perreault, became deaf (*sourd*) when his mother struck him with a key ring (*trousseau de clefs*). To everyone's satisfaction, François's mother later was kicked to death (*piétinée à mort*) by a horse.

"So, you say your grandfather was a *courtier immobilier*, a real estate agent, in the thirties and forties?" the archivist began.

"To be honest," I replied, "he was more of a *promoteur*, a developer." I'd learned and rehearsed the core terminology in advance of our chat, and so far the exchange wasn't trying my newly acquired lexicon. "I'm wondering," I continued, "whether you might have background materials for 12 Pagnuelo, like a *maquette* or even a *plan d'implantation?*"

"I'd have to verify."

"Monsieur?"

"*Oui?*"

"Is there a lot number for Maison Simon Kirsh?"

He consulted his notes. "Yes, but I can't make it out *précisément*. It's either 15-15 or 15-18."

In front of me were the lot numbers for my grandfather's landholdings on Pagnuelo, all of them in the 15-20s. "Is it possible that the lot number could have changed?"

"*Ah non*, that would be most irregular."

My mother had woken up, and her ascites, the store of fluid in her abdominal cavity, was unrelieved. Neither her attending physician nor the liver specialist wished to intervene, though the palliative care doctor suggested reducing the pressure through an abdominal tap. The procedure carried a few risks, rare but grave occurrences — infection, peritonitis, hemorrhaging. The decision was mine.

"Do you trust me?" I asked my mother apropos of nothing in particular.

"Yes, but I don't know what I'm doing."

My mother's refrain echoed her favourite expression recorded more than a half century before in her high school yearbook: "But, I don't understand." Dementia, widely considered a degenerative disease, could be interpreted for my mother as a progression, the inevitable fulfillment of character traits that presented early in her life and clearly would persist through to her death. The fearfulness, anxiety, and agitation so often signifying dementia ranked among my mother's core attributes from an early age, when her pediatrician prescribed treatment under a sun lamp. In my mother, it seemed, the aptitude for dementia, the inclination towards it, was sown deep.

After I'd authorized the abdominal tap, Darlene and I waited in the corridor while the doctor undertook the procedure on my mother, who was gently sedated. Soon the doctor invited us back into the room, indicating six or seven sealed glass bottles filled to the brim with a clear yellow fluid. "That's how much was in there," she said. A casual observer might have mistaken the filled bottles for refreshments on a hot day.

I was finding it necessary to devote several days each week to my mother in spite of the expense and difficulty of travel to

Montreal. Her first weeks in palliative care had coincided with a series of record-breaking blizzards. So abundant was the snow early in the new year that the sidewalks near Mount Sinai became impassable, forcing me to walk on the road alongside heavy vehicles skidding on ice liquefying under a crust of salt. Once indoors, I could never rely on finding my mother awake. The fluid had returned to her abdomen. That it would stay away had always been understood as an outside chance.

I decided to undertake one last search for proof of my grandfather's ownership of 12 Pagnuelo. In the online archive for the *Canadian Jewish Review*, I entered several variations of "Kirsch AND 15-15 Pagnuelo." Nothing. "Search again," I implored. This time I keyed in "Kirsch AND 15-18 Pagnuelo," to which the database conceded "One result":

> July 22, 1927 — Marcus M. Sperber sold to Simon Kirsch lots nos. 15-18, 28, City of Outremont, measuring 200 by 166 to 170 feet, without buildings and fronting on Pagnuelo Avenue.

The result was as startling as the guidance in one of my mother's clippings about finding a suitable pair of sunglasses: "Look at a traffic light and make sure the colours are true," the article advised. "If you fail to stop for a red light, take them back."

In view of the daytime high, −17 C with a wind chill of −25, the meteorologists issued a single caution: "Don't go out." I wasn't to be deterred — not even when the walk was unrelievedly uphill, along a steep slope, the drifts thigh-deep. As I neared the cemetery where both Simon and my father lay concealed, all the graves appeared as one under an expanse of driven snow. The decorative bows on my synthetic grey parka had come undone, limp strands of nylon cleaving to the waist and pockets. Particles of ice coated my eyes, melting into a trickle of water down my cheeks. By my father's footstone I scrabbled to expose a few words — BELOVED HUSBAND FATHER BROTHER — each of the recessed letters filled with dainty granules. Beyond this I could achieve little here. Half-blinded and in a world where all sound had been subdued by whiteness, I prepared for the partial descent down the mountain and my first glimpse of Maison Simon Kirsh.

Earlier that day I'd left my mother drowsing at Mount Sinai. She was as unaware of Simon's Art Deco house as she'd become of most things outside her own comfort and immersion in sleep, and had she been aware, she no longer would have been interested. Although still alive, she was in most respects no longer participating in life. Her appetite remained sound, however. She regularly ate macaroni and ice cream and on occasion would warm to General Tso's chicken. The rest of the time, she slept.

In approaching my grandfather's house, I struggled to disengage from troubled thoughts of the woman who persisted in being my mother. Most likely she'd already told her last joke.

$\hookleftarrow$

My grandfather's house sat without affectation on a mountain slope of Outremont called Springgrove, which originally had belonged to the Sulpician order of priests, whose clothing was black and white. Like every surviving photograph of my grandfather in my possession, the house itself was black and white, as well as conforming in each respect to the property descriptions I'd read. I was grateful for its precocious minimalism, the abjuring of stone lions by the drive and pink flamingos on the front lawn.

The white stucco façade of Maison Simon Kirsh gave the appearance of serenity. On closer inspection, the right side revealed itself to be as scrupulously linear as the left was graciously curved, its rounded balcony evoking a ship's deck. For the door and window frames, the architects had selected black; the windows comprised subtly elongated rectangles, together with a saucy lone hexagon.

To design his house, my grandfather had chosen the architects Shorey & Ritchie, later to become celebrated for their Art Deco and Modernist structures. Yet Simon retained their services during the Great Depression, when the firm was obscure and commissions scarce. Once celebrated among his classmates for his self-assurance and his grin, my father's father inclined as readily to outré styles of architecture as to contentious theories about vascular bundles in the stems of common bracken. The rogue "avant-gardisme" of 12 Pagnuelo thus ranked as one of many dissensions that assured Simon he was genuinely himself.

Here, then, stood my grandfather's house, but for me to approach the front door would have been trespassing. I was mindful that Simon himself had never lived at 12 Pagnuelo, whether because it was beyond his reach financially, unsuitable for his family of several boys, or an experiment that failed to conform to his own taste. Whatever the reason, for him, as for me, the avant-garde house was one he'd occupied primarily in his imagination. Like my imagining of the family home in Lithuania, this house would inhabit me but continue to elude me. Even so, it existed as a physical structure — in stucco and transparent glass — only because my grandfather had commissioned it and watched it grow. Once he'd stepped inside the finished structure, ranging its rooms and inspecting the views from its windows, he gave the command that came second nature to him — "Simon says, 'Sell!'" I was possessed of no such entitlement. Instead, my inability to partake in this house mimicked my exclusion from my mother's daily labours and immersion in sleep. In its power of exile, Maison Simon Kirsh returned me to my mother's impending death.

There was one form of release, though, that I could exercise when standing before my grandfather's house. Twelve Pagnuelo furnished me with an opportunity for looking. The palliative care unit counts as a rare place where, for those outside the medical profession, observation is constrained, if not outright prohibited. Close-ups are not encouraged, panoramas not available, selfies not taken. When with my mother, I tried not to notice her arms barely thicker than yardsticks, the swell of her belly under the thin blanket, the way my presence at times furnished her no comfort as she retreated into a world of her own with wellsprings of agitation unknown to me. Similarly, I resolved not to look at any length at the other patients in the unit. No stance seemed appropriate. Neither encouragement nor pity. But my grandfather's house offered something I could look at with greed and with abandon, for as long as I liked, without fear of anyone looking back at me.

$\longleftarrow$

There was still my mother.

She'd begun to ask for her sister. I brought her instead a pot of rust chrysanthemums flowering out of season.

"You can relax now," I said. "Everything's all right."

"It's not all right."

Darlene adjusted my mother's blanket, then whispered to me, "I don't want to have to see her pass. I tell her, 'You go when I'm not here.'"

My mother had fallen back asleep.

I didn't share with Darlene the investigations that preoccupied me during the day, nor how they were a side effect of my mother's illness. Most recently I'd begun to pore over my father's stamp albums, especially *The Imperial Album for the Postage Stamps of the British Empire and Egypt*. It afforded a study in vanished countries and territories. Stamps for Hejaz and Sirmur, for Bechuanaland and the Orange River Colony. For the most part, my father had pasted the stamps in neatly, each one unwrinkled and perfectly straight.

The colours described in *The Imperial Album* were among the most nuanced I'd ever met with: *lake-red, rose-red, pale carmine-rose, dull vermilion,* and *rosy mauve* for Great Britain in the nineteenth century. Alternatively, Heligoland from 1876 to 1879 was distinguished by *vermilion aniline, bright green,* and *lemon*. My father, born in 1915, was both white and colour-blind. How he differentiated his stamps I couldn't say, but he seemed to falter suddenly with Gwalior, where he pasted in grey instead of carmine, and then with Newfoundland 1866, where he stuck down blue in lieu of dark brown. The stamps extended to 1927, when my father, at twelve, continued licking and pasting. His father would have recognized that aniline, an oily derivative of coal tar, is poisonous. He was beginning to acquire land in Outremont, including the lot for 12 Pagnuelo.

My materials on the built heritage of Outremont indicated a second Modernist house on Pagnuelo, also commissioned by my grandfather — number 43, a white stucco house with black trim built several years later than number 12 and distinguished for its "style and articulation." In the manner of a stillborn child, the second house wasn't dignified with a name.

Throughout the 1930s, as 12 and 43 Pagnuelo moved from drawings to inception, Simon Kirsch had kept busy. In this era when ads commonly appeared for "Milk, Table Cream and Whipping Cream from Tuberculin-Tested Herds," he sat on the board and house committee of the Mount Sinai Sanatorium. In 1934 — 5695 on the Jewish calendar — he watched as the final stone was laid at the Jewish General Hospital on the site for which he alone had argued. The solariums at the rear faced onto undeveloped land in the Laurentians — depending on one's point of view, a business prospect or a panacea.

During this same era, Simon Kirsch renewed his friendship with a butcher, Eddie Barkoff, and together they formed a partnership in the buying and selling of land. In 1948, Simon persuaded Eddie to view one thousand acres in Cap-de-la-Madeleine, Quebec, a wilderness at the junction of the Saint-Maurice and St. Lawrence rivers.

"One day I went to look at it," said Eddie, "a thousand acres of wild grass and sand, a big untouched area. I was disgusted. 'Simon,' I said, 'what am I doing in this god-forsaken place?'"

"Never mind," Simon told him. "This is the largest pulp and paper centre in the world and the possibilities are fantastic."

Eddie Barkoff acquired the thousand acres for a model town to feature health-enhancing worker housing, good sanitation, and ample green space — values shared by him and Simon. The one hundred cottages commissioned from the architect Harry Mayerovitch were erected in 1950, a year after Simon's death. Some thirty years earlier, Mayerovitch had served as the architect for the nameless house at 43 Pagnuelo.

Alleys, empty fields or other secluded areas offer the best vision on cloudy days. If a car stops to ask for directions, don't do it alone. Don't walk through yellow and orange tints. If you have to, don't get too close. It may be a mugger who wants your purse.

I'd been able to undertake few ventures in life without considering first my mother and her fears or the lies I'd felt obliged to tell her. From our earliest acquaintance she'd imposed constraints, monitoring my physical safety and, in her final years, unwittingly commanding care and attention beyond that required by a young child. In her parting act, however, she swiftly overturned the roles we'd evolved throughout our respective lifetimes. On the occasion of her death, my mother had become the one who engaged in subterfuge, the one who quietly and decisively stole away.

The last time I spoke to my mother, just hours before she took ill in the middle of the night, she'd sounded "chipper," as she herself might have said. "Sleep well," I advised her.

"You too," she replied brightly before hanging up the phone.

At 6 a.m. my phone rang, a call from palliative care. "Your mother took ill in the night," a familiar nurse said without prelude. "You'd better come."

"Could it be a false alarm?"

"For some patients, yes. For your mother, no."

"Can I speak to her?"

"Not really. She's — asleep."

My husband and I stumbled into whatever clothing came to hand, and without eating Weetabix or combing our hair we hastened to the airport, boarding the first available flight. Despite our best efforts, as our plane bobbed on the runway in Montreal, my mother died. She'd spent six weeks at Mount Sinai, an idea of a place once familiar to her from the film version of Exodus by Cecil B. DeMille, where Moses receives the commandments on a summit occluded by a reddish sky.

Mount Sinai was the name, too, of Simon's sanatorium at Prefontaine, with its formal gardens, potager, gazebo, and chicken farm — a complex that offered superior chances of recovery for tuberculars while doubling as an end-of-life sanctuary for the institution's failures. Until my mother became a ward of Mount Sinai Hospital, I'd never suspected a link between Simon's one-time facility and its Montreal namesake. Only as I was leaving the hospital on the day of my mother's admission had I noted my grandfather's name, twice, in raised gilt letters, on a plaque in the foyer:

> *Dr. Simon Kirsch Board of Directors*
> *Dr. Simon Kirsch House Committee*

My mother had died in the successor to the sanatorium at Prefontaine.

t⟶

In the same room where I'd first conversed with the palliative care doctor — the arrivals lounge that doubled, apparently, for departures — my mother lay on her back on a metal trolley. Immaculately clean, her hair brushed back, she was covered with a simple sheet. Already her skin was turning a waxy yellow.

My mother's cousin stood beside the body as my husband and I entered the room. Earlier that morning, as I was leaving for the airport, I'd phoned Thelma and asked her to go over as soon as possible, even though my mother was "asleep." "There she is," I said, referring not to Thelma but to my mother, and in the present tense. I touched my mother's arm lightly with one finger. She was neither warm nor cold. If she no longer was my mother, nor was she convincingly anyone else.

Tears came despite the disbelief. Thelma and my husband and I held one another, murmuring, *What happened? She went so fast. If only we'd arrived on time.* Then Thelma said aloud, "Where did all that blood come from?" I shook my head, unable to answer and unwilling to solicit more detail.

When the male attendants from the funeral parlour arrived to claim my mother's body, they brought the assurance she wouldn't be left alone. According to Jewish tradition, a *shomer*, or watcher, would remain by her side. Before burial, the ritual washing and dressing of the body by other women, the *taharah*, would take place. The sequence of washing is prescribed and would have satisfied my mother's obsession with order and hygiene. First the head, then the neck, the right hand, the right upper half of the body, the right lower half of the body, the right foot ... The women who undertake this task repeatedly wash their hands.

From my cellphone I called my oldest friend, who'd known my parents since the age of three. "She's gone," I said.

Outside the world was white. In the days following my mother's death, snow fell thickly on the grounds of Mount Sinai Hospital and on its very doorstep, quickly making invisible the footprints of anyone who entered there.

The orderly who turned over my mother's belongings days after her death might as well have been wearing sunglasses because he couldn't meet my eye. The bag he handed me was made of white plastic and contained a white cardigan, a chipped white enamel ring, a voided wallet, and an empty bud vase. I placed them in a drawer in my mother's soon-to-be-emptied apartment — a last-ditch assertion of continuity in a home that was only ever hers on loan.

It's said that objects in Iron Age and Roman Britain were confided to pits or ditches to signify the beginning or end of kinship with a building. With no memory of this precedent, my father had buried a treasure in the house built to his specifications. My fruitless search for that treasure, coinciding with my mother's loss of awareness, had concluded our relationship with the family home. The intrinsic value of the treasure my father buried in the split-level for his new bride was always secondary in my mind to its message. More pressing was to satisfy the accusation of its being there.

There was no longer anyone tailing me. Insofar as I now was absolved from the habit of lying, my mother's death marked my greater engagement with the truth. In other respects I failed to profit from my new freedom. Throughout my mother's illness — and for the first time in my life — I'd been beset by anxiety, placing me on a par with my mother herself. My heart had become susceptible to racing whenever I was en route to Mount Sinai, on a plane with the cabin pressure building, or, worse still, leaving my mother behind. I'd persuaded myself that the end of my mother's life would release me from the disquiet surrounding her illness. Instead, my apprehension worsened, a persistent emotion suddenly without a target.

Competing with my anxiety were sadness and a sense of disorientation. Because, according to Jewish custom, all jewellery is removed before burial, I now possessed my mother's wedding ring, two finely ridged gold bands that met in the middle, one ultimately superimposing itself upon the other. The ring had been crafted by a Jewish refugee from Czechoslovakia, my parents' next-door neighbour by virtue of a common wall. "A souvenir," the funeral director said as he'd handed the near-weightless object to me. It was the same ring present but not discernible in the photo of my parents waving goodbye to family and friends as they left their wedding supper, oblivious to where or how their decades-long argument would end.

There was one respect, though, in which my mother's death afforded undeniable relief: the certainty I hadn't predeceased her. If I hadn't satisfied my mother's aspiration for grandchildren, I also never fulfilled her worst fear. I hadn't imposed on her the tragedy her parents suffered in her sister. My very survival made for something I could regard as an achievement — a final gift, albeit one my mother was unable knowingly to receive.

It was only at my mother's funeral, some half century after Carol's, that I realized conclusively the loss of my aunt. In a formless beige sweater dress, I stood before the assembled crowd enumerating my mother's qualities — loyal, particular, humorous, imaginative, generous-hearted, receptive to beauty — with no one by my side to corroborate the facts. As the pallbearers, my husband among them, hoisted the coffin to carry my mother away, I made ready to follow. Alone. Moments later, Carol's best friend was the first to seize my arm and walk me down the aisle.

⌒

"Her belly's gone flat." Darlene had remarked on this after my mother's death, when briefly she'd joined me, my husband, and my mother's cousin before my mother's body was ushered away from Mount Sinai.

Darlene was a bulky woman and, if a boxer, would have qualified as a middleweight. While my mother had been turning smaller, Darlene, alongside her, had seemed to be growing larger, though I recognized the effect to be an optical illusion. Harder to account for was why clothing once worn by my mother now fit Darlene. On the day Darlene came over to help me sort my mother's belongings, she accepted the never-worn mauve plush bed jacket bought at a discount mall in Maine, the fine shearling boots with the foolproof grips, a folding black umbrella. Other items in my mother's apartment couldn't be repurposed. The signed and numbered colonial-style dining room set, according to an estate sale agent, was magnificent but worthless. Everyone wanted Danish Modern.

In the corridor outside my mother's apartment, trolley carts like the ones flight attendants use for duty-free rattled and then braked. "Mrs. Schwartz, pills are ready." "Mr. Essing, please take your tray." "Mrs. Guptman, time for your hygiene." The care aides worked to a tight schedule. The dinner menu for that night, posted beside the elevator, promised flank steak with kasha.

Six weeks earlier, my mother had left here for the last time in her stocking feet. There had been a novelty earlier that morning. Darlene, who picked up the receiver when I called, had refused to put my mother on the line. "My lady can't talk" was how she put it.

"Is she in the bathroom?"

"No, she's in my lap. She can't walk anymore." Darlene's tone was evenly robust — the same tone she used day in day out to inform me my mother had cleaned her plate or needed more Zincolac or had used the B-word. "We're on the floor," she added. "I called the nurse."

Earlier that same morning I'd conversed with my mother in a limited exchange that paired an imploration with a cheep of compliance.

"Sharon!" my mother had cried out.

"Yes!" I'd agreed instantly and aloud and from my bed. I hadn't understood the request nor can I remember it now, but I never hesitated to comply. The conversation happened on the edge of sleep or during sleep and took the form of dialogue but might have been a soliloquy.

Later that day the ambulance delivered my mother to Mount Sinai in her pyjamas.

⌐⌐

As I prepared to close down the apartment for the last time, not much remained — a softening orange in a Styrofoam container in the fridge, grip bars in the bathroom, a copy of the termination agreement for services that had included "cues, reminders and help to maintain dignity." More germane to my mother's life, her wished-for life, was the fridge magnet "Renee's Florida Beachfront Property." Renee with an extra *e*, maybe a trade-off for Kirsh missing a *c*. The fridge magnet consisted of a cardboard landscape — a sand spit intersected by a blue palm tree with the stature of a paper clip — with a teaspoonful of real sand and a real spiral seashell on a par with a pistachio nut. Both background and foreground were enclosed in a clear plastic sachet with a Ziploc top.

"The only thing they never had was a house," my mother occasionally had said to me of her parents. "But your grandmother made the apartment a home." My mother told me this while still in mid-life — a relative term. For my mother's sister, Carol, dead at twenty-six, mid-life amounted to her early teens.

⌐⌐

The bus serving my mother's neighbourhood has a varied clientele of Filipina aides coming off shift, ironic Jewish retirees clutching bags of bagels, and sullen young adults with lip studs and nostril screws. The rigid plastic seats are expertly moulded for comfort, the drivers never withhold a *Bonjour*. For these reasons, as well as for economy, I almost always caught this bus when travelling to and from the residence for assisted living.

Today, however, my last at my mother's apartment and with a load to transport, I called for a taxi. When the cab arrived, the driver was oddly familiar.

"Are you Sher?" I asked.

"No, but Sher's my friend. You know him?" Like Sher, the driver was Iranian, his English more heavily accented.

"He drove me. Once. I have his card."

Sher hadn't been just any driver. He was lean, with a face scarcely wider than a bookend and thick glasses above a nose that flared like a parrot tulip, and he'd picked me up as I was leaving my mother's house for the final time. We'd talked about the 747 Express bus to and from the airport, how it was damaging Sher's bottom line. "I should have moved to Toronto years ago," Sher told me. His friend, an Iranian engineer also now driving a taxi, had made the move, and for him, things were working out. Sher confused himself for a failure when, really, he was an exile.

I knew relatively little of Iran — about the Shah and the Ayatollah, of course, and more recently that the country was moving to revive its nuclear program. I knew the cuisine was liberal with pomegranate seeds, and I imagined there were apricots. I understood that there were black terns. They're a travelling species, breeding in one location and wintering in another, migrating over land and open water, belonging, ultimately, to no place.

I studied the back of the head of the taxi driver who wasn't Sher. His hair appeared coarse and sleek, as though made to repel water. Light sparked off the frames of his silver-rimmed glasses.

The driver, whose name I never asked, took an indirect route. We passed the preschool where I'd refused to take a nap and the high school where my mother swore all the kids were hooked on LSD. We drove past the memory of farmers' fields where my father had played fetch with a half-grown poodle I'd recognize only from photographs. We cruised the block where the fat boy two grades ahead told me he was planning to beat me up, until my mother phoned his mother and his mother confided to mine that her boy wasn't all right. Soon we'd be driving by the entrance to what I persisted in thinking of as my mother's street. There'd be no view of my mother's house. Bypassing her block had become a regular practice for me on my occasional walks through the neighbourhood. I stuck to the margins in the way cats do when confronted with an open space where they'd feel at risk.

At a red light the driver craned his neck to look at me. "So, you really know Sher?"

"Yes, I do."

"What's your name? I want to make sure I have the right customer."

"Sharon. But he won't know me."

The light changed, the driver stepped on the gas. "Sher's my best friend."

We took a crucial turn towards the train station. In my lap sat my mother's Lifeline, the box with the hinged panel she'd pressed twice daily to indicate to an impartial responder in an undisclosed location that she wasn't merely alive but okay. It had two settings, both of them now disabled, "Home" and "Away."

AFTERWORD

Malibu Apr 02

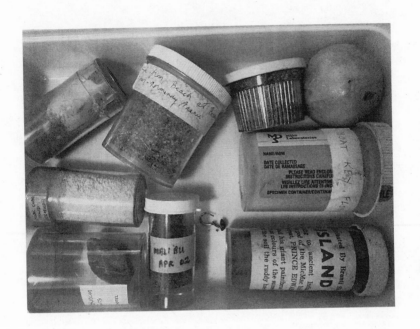

SHE'S A GOOD EGG." THAT'S WHAT MY MOTHER LIKED TO SAY OF other women she found worthy or congenial. In the year following my father's death, when my mother was grieving for my father but relishing her newly recovered freedom, I persuaded her to visit two women in California, a close friend and a cousin, both of whom were indisputably "good eggs."

My mother at this time was only seventy and robust, her hallmark stamina and proclivity for staying up late undiminished. The photographs from her trip, taken with the Canon Sure Shot she carried in a black canvas pouch with beige leather trim, were of the ocean and the desert. "The place in Palm Desert is just stunning," she said, referring to her friend's rancher with its floor-to-ceiling windows, modular furniture, and stripped-down courtyard. The so-called beach shots, in LA, were mostly of carpeted interiors with several generations of relatives crowded onto loveseats and dining room chairs — the cousin's elderly mother, adult children, and grandchildren. Nonetheless, my mother respected her own urge to be "by the water." In her album she pointed out a couple of beach scenes from Los Angeles County with a narrow arc of sand yielding to low bluffs scattered with coyote bush and canyons of lemonade sumac. There was no one present to take my mother's photograph, no evidence she'd been there.

Although I often think of my mother both sick and well, I rarely think of those weeks in California, the last fully autonomous trip she'd ever take. The way my mother lingers in me more typically entails honouring her many observances: plumping up the pillows on the sofa before I go to bed each night; slipping on one of her several rings, all of which fit my middle or ring finger; heeding warnings of danger from which she can no longer protect me, except through the precepts she instilled. I remember her when I occasionally extend the shaft of the 1950s telescope keychain she left behind and see through the eyepiece a woman I don't recognize. My mother from the neckline up, an unmarried virgin wearing a black spaghetti-strap bodice with a white carnation tucked behind her right ear.

For several years now I've had the sense of exhausting my parents' objects — that the items deemed lost would never be recovered and nothing further could be available to find. Even longer ago I'd reconciled myself to the reality that my father's treasure, the rumoured stash under the bedroom carpet, did not exist. And so I've redirected my attention to the things my parents taught me to value and which I continue to prize: tea with lemon, a funny story, eggrolls with plum sauce, the first snow. Inevitably, I've re-engaged, also, with the more mundane aspects of life. Grocery shopping and housework. Not by accident, then, when the weather recently fast-tracked from bathing suits to toques and scarves, I decided to sort through a pile of forgotten boxes in a corner of my kitchen. One of them contained items from my mother's house.

First I came upon the Expo 67 Visitor's Vademecum, or guide, which begins by describing Canada as a country on a map that "lies sprawled across the top half of North America," later supplies pointers about "Tipping and Gratuities" and "Poison-Control Centres," and eventually recommends shopping at the department store Dupuis Frères for "its colourful French atmosphere." Further delving into the box revealed a brochure from Galeria Cano in Colombia extolling the "legendary treasures from the land of 'El Dorado'" — matte gold nose rings shaped like maple samaras, squat sculptures with rectangular heads and hollowed-out horizontal slits simulating mouth and eyes. Other objects, the brochure cautioned, had been melted down, all traces of them vanished. I discovered in the box, too, remnants of day trips from Montreal, one of them to the Central Experimental Farm in Ottawa, where, from Winding Lane, the Crops Display Building came into view, a nod to forages, cereals, horticulture, and agronomy. The east of the site was bordered by the Rideau Canal, built to safeguard Canadian transit routes after the 1812 victory against the Americans.

All these items served as a reminder of my parents' fondness for locomotion and how, for much of her adult life, my mother had been more at home roaming her city, her country, or the world than the few rooms she inhabited in her final years. The smaller her outlook, it seemed, the greater her sense of disorientation. In her final months she could scarcely negotiate the relationship of her bedroom to her bathroom.

The box also contained a single postcard penned by my grandmother Rose. From Radium Hot Springs, BC. Dated August 11, 1961, it depicts a fenced-in rectangular pool of standard appearance accessed by a metal walkway leading into a building of monotonous grey brick. A low-security prison or a mental asylum, one might have thought. In the window for text, my grandmother, formulating her words before the death of her younger daughter and a mere fourteen months after the birth of her first and only grandchild, wrote this:

Dear Rene,
  This place is out of this world. We bathe in a hot pool full of minerals + then in a cool one. It has to be seen to be believe [sic].
    Love,
    Mother

When my mother returned home from her trip to California, she returned alone and to an empty house. My father had been dead for a year. I was living several hundred miles away in Toronto. Only the potato bugs in the basement made for a vital presence.

In spite of her obsession with order and hygiene, my mother could be slow to unpack, her suitcase of unwashed clothes propped open for weeks on a luggage stand before she dealt with them, suggesting as much preparations for a departure as a return. When eventually she got around to it, her preference was to do laundry by night. She did it in the semi-finished basement, encircled by my childhood eggshell compositions, the travel posters of places she'd never visit, a treadmill more telling of ambition than use, and a now-empty table with drawers that once concealed my father's revolver. In front of my rocking horse, Blaze, whose distinguishing trait consisted of producing a frenzy of motion without going anywhere, my mother unloaded her shirts soaked with perspiration and soiled knee-highs in a bid to make them clean.

One night, undetected and unseen, my mother brought something beyond dirty laundry down to the basement. A small, nondescript object. I won't say she *hid* it — *stored* would be more apt. For whom, I'm not sure.

Seven years after my mother's death I rarely hear her intoning "Don't touch that," and so when I noted the same apparently unremarkable item in a tray of like objects in the box in my kitchen, I removed the protective plastic sleeve without hesitation. Inside were seven or eight plastic pill jars with labels written in my mother's hand. The first one I examined, LONG BOAT KEY FLORIDA, was filled partway with fine sand the colour of unbleached sugar. The vial marked "Line up the arrows/Push off" contained *Sand from Beach at Bernières-sur-Mer — Normandy France*, granules the colour of standard pepper but with iridescent fragments of shell mingled in. In a small, squat jar, not for medication but for peach conserve, was showcased sand so black and dense that I took it to be from the volcanic beaches in the Canary Islands, though the source itself was unidentified.

The smallest jar of all — the only one that appeared unfamiliar — was the one that had caught my eye. This transparent pill bottle with a white plastic lid, filled just under halfway with mocha-coloured sand strewn with tiny splinters of wood or plant material, bore the label MALIBU APR 02. Here, in the palm of my hand, was my mother's final specimen, the lone sample of her widowhood and advancing age, a last proof of her lucidity, and a harking back to the biology student she once was. Of all my mother's belongings, this one, the late arrival, radiated the greatest shock, the simplest pleasure, and the most unreserved grief. I closed my hand around the small bottle, recognizing it for the treasure that it was.

Sources

Whereas the smallest objective originated in papers and memorabilia my parents refused to discard, I consulted and benefited from many other sources while writing the book. In particular, the principal characters, all of them inhabitants of Montreal in the twentieth century, led me somewhat accidentally to a selective history of the city and, more specifically, its Jewish heritage.

A starting point for my understanding of Montreal's overall history were two excellent temporary exhibitions: *Lives and Times of the Plateau*, Pointe-à-Callière museum of archaeology, October 23, 2013, to January 4, 2015; and *Scandale! Vice, crime et moralité à Montréal, 1940–1960*, Centre d'histoire de Montréal, November 15, 2013, to April 2, 2017. Also to be recommended for a pictorial history of Montreal is the McCord Museum's collection of historic photographs, available online. In book form, William Weintraub's *City Unique: Montreal Days and Nights in the 1940s and 1950s* (McClelland and Stewart, 1996) makes for an invaluable resource about the metropolis in two of its most vivid decades. Finally, *Lovell's Montreal Directory* (1842–1992), available online from Bibliothèque et Archives nationales du Québec (BAnQ), supplies extensive information about Montreal institutions and residents through the centuries, not least their addresses and professions.

The size and historical significance of Montreal's Jewish community mean that much on the city's Jewish heritage has been written or otherwise produced. The resources I drew upon, cited below, are not intended as a comprehensive list but rather reflect my selective reading for the purposes of this book. Before mentioning the relevant titles, I should give a nod to the McCord Museum exhibition *Shalom Montreal: Stories and Contributions of the Jewish Community*, May 3 to November 11, 2018, a fine introduction to Jewish life and achievement in the city during the twentieth century.

One of the most recent and highly informative overviews of Quebec Jewry is the French-language *Histoire des Juifs du Québec* by Pierre Anctil (Les éditions du Boréal, 2017), a long-time authority on the province's Jewish history. Also recommended for its wide-ranging approach is *From Immigration to*

Integration: The Canadian Jewish Experience; A Millennium Edition edited by Ruth Klein and Frank Dimant (Malcolm Lester for the Institute for International Affairs, B'nai Brith Canada, 2001). More specifically, *Juifs et Canadiens français dans la société Québécoise* (Septentrion, 1999) — a book of conference proceedings edited by Pierre Anctil, Ira Robinson, and Gérard Bouchard — explores the complex relationship between Quebec's Jews and French Canadians.

Some titles dedicated especially to the early history of Jewish immigration and settlement are *From the Ghetto to the Main: The Story of the Jews of Montreal* by Joe King (Montreal Jewish Publication Society, 2001), *Taking Root: The Origins of the Canadian Jewish Community* by Gerald Tulchinsky (Lester Publishing, 1992), *Montreal of Yesterday: Jewish Life in Montreal 1900–1920* by Israel Medres, translated from the Yiddish by Vivian Felsen (published in Yiddish, 1947; reprinted by Véhicule Press, 1998), and *Canada's Jews: A Social and Economic Study of the Jews in Canada in the 1930s* by Louis Rosenberg (McGill-Queen's University Press, 1993). *Heritage of a Patriarch: A Fresh Look at Nine of Canada's Earliest Jewish Families* by Anne Joseph (Septentrion, 1995) offers a valuable chronological account of Montreal's first Jewish settlers dating back to the eighteenth century and their successors to the present day. For an in-depth treatment of the Yiddish heritage of Montreal, *Jewish Roots, Canadian Soil: Yiddish Culture in Montreal, 1905–1945* by Rebecca Margolis (McGill-Queen's University Press, 2011) is indispensable. *The Gate of Heaven: The Story of Congregation Shaar Hashomayim of Montreal 1846–1996* by Rabbi Wilfred Shuchat (McGill-Queen's University Press, 2000) serves as a history of both a specific congregation and, more broadly, the city's Jewish community. For a history of Jewish burial in Montreal, I recommend *Sacred Ground on de la Savane: Montreal's Baron de Hirsch Cemetery* by Danny Kucharsky, with a portfolio of photographs by D.R. Cowles (Véhicule Press, 2008). Finally, for the life histories of specific individuals, see the two volumes produced by *The Canadian Jewish Times: A Biographical Dictionary of Canadian Jewry, 1897–1909* and *1909–1914*.

Before providing the essential sources for each of the chapters, I wish to acknowledge several excellent works I read on a completely different subject but also one essential to this book: the topic of memory. *Memory: A Very Short Introduction* by Jonathan K. Foster (Oxford University Press, 2009) offers a readable and enlightening gateway into this complex topic. For a more detailed account, see *Memory: The Key to Consciousness* by Richard F. Thompson and Stephen A. Madigan (Joseph Henry Press, 2005). A very recent work, *Lost and Found: Memory, Identity, and Who We Become When We're No Longer Ourselves* by Jules Montague (Sceptre, 2018), is essential reading, both scientific and philosophical, for anyone interested in how memory impairment affects identity. Another recent book about memory impairment and its revelations, this one centred on a single patient, is *Remembering: What 50 Years of Research with Famous Amnesia Patient H.M. Can Teach Us about Memory and How It Works* by Donald G. MacKay (Prometheus Books, 2019).

Epigraph
The first of the two quotations is from *Collecting Microscopes* by Gerard L'E. Turner, Christie's International Collectors Series (Mayflower Books, 1981). This book was especially helpful in introducing me to the basics of period microscopes, as detailed in Chapter Two, "Lantern Slides." The second quotation originates in the manual accompanying the Bausch & Lomb Optical Co. microscope depicted in the frontispiece. The manual is titled *Use and Care of the Microscope* by Edward Bausch and contains extracts from his text "Manipulation of the Microscope."

Chapter One: Treasure
Hoards: Hidden History by Eleanor Ghey (British Museum Press, 2015) proved instrumental here and in subsequent chapters in helping me ponder the concept and history of buried treasure. The description of my mother's wedding gown and bouquet comes from one of her own newspaper clippings, presumably from the *Montreal Star* or *Gazette*, but the source isn't identified. An anonymous suitor composed the unsigned acrostic poem, which includes a longer verse based on my mother's surname. My father's account of his experience as a "stretcher case" is from an unpublished interview about the Second World War and the D-Day landing he gave to Captain Raziel Zisman for the Queen's Own Rifles (Interviewee: Dr. Archie Kirsch, Medical Corps. Date of interview: 03/05/94). I'm most grateful to the regiment and Raziel Zisman for creating this record of my father's wartime experience in his own words. The italicized quotations relating to the GPR survey are from "Ground Penetrating Radar and Metal Detector Survey," a private report issued to me on February 18, 2011, by archaeologists Blake Williams and John Dunlop.

Chapter Two: Lantern Slides
Reconstructing the chronology of Simon's life and activities would have been daunting without the online archives of two newspapers, *The Canadian Jewish Chronicle*, available from Google News, and *Canadian Jewish Review*, available from Multicultural Canada, Simon Fraser University digitized newspapers. To this purpose, but to a much lesser extent, I also used several resources from Ancestry.com, including *Quebec Vital and Church Records, 1621-1967* (Drouin Collection).

For background to Jewish life in Lithuania during Simon's childhood, I read *Heshel's Kingdom* by Dan Jacobson (Hamish Hamilton, 1998), a moving account of the author's search for his own family history in the Pale of Settlement. I also benefited greatly from a visit to the permanent exhibition on pre-Holocaust Lithuanian Jewish life at the Tolerance Center of the Vilna Gaon State Jewish Museum in Vilnius, Lithuania, as well as from more generally touring that country following my mother's death. Finally, for an account of the Baltic timber trade in the late nineteenth century, I suggest *Forests and Forestry in Poland, Lithuania, the Ukraine, and the Baltic Provinces of Russia, with Notices of the Export of Timber from Memel, Dantzig, and Riga*, compiled by John Croumbie Brown (Dawson Brothers, 1885).

In Montreal, Mary Ellen Hood of the McGill Archives graciously made available to me the archival materials documenting Simon Kirsch as a student: the university calendars for 1907–08 and 1908–09, the convocation booklet from May 11, 1910, as well as Simon's student record and the *Old McGill* yearbooks. To round off my understanding of Simon's university years, I was fortunate to be able to locate both his master's and PhD theses online: *On the Development and Function of Certain Structures in the Stipe and Rhizome of* Pteris aquilina *and Other Pteridophytes* by Simon Kirsch, communicated by D.P. Penhallow in *Proceedings and Transactions of the Royal Society of Canada*, Third Series–Volume 1, Meeting of May 1907 (Copp-Clark, 1907); *The Origin and Development of Resin Canals in the Coniferae, with Special Reference to the Development of Thyloses and Their Correlation with the Thylosal Strands of the Pteridophytes* by Simon Kirsch, MA, PhD, Former Demonstrator in Botany, McGill University, Expert, Forest Service, U.S. Department of Agriculture, presented by Prof. A.G. Nicholls, MD, in *Proceedings and Transactions of the Royal Society of Canada*, Third Series–Volume 5, Meeting of May 1911. It is worth nothing that *Pteris aquilina* was the binomial routinely used for common bracken in Simon's era. However, the designation now in use is *Pteridium aquilinum*. Zev Moses, executive director of the Museum of Jewish Montreal, kindly helped me pinpoint Simon's home addresses during his years teaching at McGill, since the building numbers, and in some cases the street names themselves, have changed.

In seeking to understand the life and accomplishments of Simon's mentor at McGill, Professor David Pearce Penhallow, I consulted Suzanne Zeller's engaging entry on the botanist in *Dictionary of Canadian Biography*, Volume 13 (1901–1910). The single quote from Professor Penhallow ("internal structures … external morphology") and the words about his attachment to history are cited in a tribute to David Pearce Penhallow in *Proceedings and Transactions of the Royal Society of Canada*, Third Series–Volume 5, Meeting of May 1911, page ix; the sentence about internal structures originally appeared in Penhallow's book *A Manual of the North American Gymnosperms*.

For the material about Simon's microscope, I am deeply indebted to Dr. Boyd Suttie, an antiquarian and authority on period microscopes, who graciously identified the make and date of the Jug Handle, educated me about its parts and maintenance, and demonstrated its capabilities, all as a gesture of goodwill. Similarly, the scene in the Rock, Gem, Mineral, Fossil, and Meteorite Identification Clinic at the Royal Ontario Museum (referred to in the text by its informal name, "The Mineral Clinic") was based on consultations with two different experts, both of which took place in 2012. These free clinics, held several times a year, are an excellent resource and a welcome gift from the ROM and its specialists to the citizens of Toronto.

Details of Simon Kirsch's work at the U.S. Forest Service and his eventual departure are from the service's online "Pamphlets on Forest History: 1910–1914." Also essential to an understanding of his work environment were *The USDA Forest Service — The First Century*, FS-650, by Gerald W. Williams, PhD, Historical Analyst (*USDA* Forest Service, 2005), and *The Forest Products*

Laboratory: A Decennial Record 1910–1920, USDA Forest Service (Democrat Printing Company, 1921), digitized by University of Toronto. The description of the lumberjacks is inspired by period photographs of Wisconsin forestry in the online collection of the U.S. Forest Service. Finally, the Humboldt Redwoods Project, an online digital exhibition from Humboldt State University in California, informed the description of Simon and Malca's honeymoon in the Western states.

Aspects of Simon's real estate activity, especially the early years, were recorded in the *Quebec Official Gazette* and occasionally in *Le Devoir*, both accessible through the excellent online resource of the Quebec archives, Bibliothèque et Archives nationales du Québec (BAnQ). In aiming to understand Simon's transition from academe to real estate, I read my grandfather's own copy of *The Rise of David Levinsky* by Abraham Cahan (Grosset & Dunlap, 1917; quotes from pp. 481–82 and 511). It is worth mentioning that at least one commentator on the novel refers to Antomir as a fictitious place invented by Cahan. Simon's birth town, Vilkomir, is now known as Ukmerge.

Material about the situation of Jews at Canadian universities is covered in some of the general resources described above, including *Canada's Jews* and *Taking Root*, as well as in "McGill's 1926 Jewish ban" by N.D.P. McGill, Alexandre Edde, Vishwaa Ramakrishnan, and Celeste Cassidy in the *McGill Daily*, September 2, 2018; the phrasing "academically concentrated" is a quote from Dr. Ira Robinson, professor of Religion and Jewish Studies at Concordia University. In this same section, the details of Archie's bar mitzvah are from the *Jewish Chronicle* of November 2, 1928.

"Through the Years" *60th Anniversary Camp B'nai B'rith Grand Reunion Souvenir Program Book* (October 3, 1981) provides a useful overview of the camp and its origins. For the histories of the Jewish General and Mount Sinai Hospitals, I consulted *Our Tribute Everlasting: 50th Anniversary Sir Mortimer Davis Jewish General Hospital, 1934–1984* by Alexander Wright (Jewish General Hospital, 1984). Also invaluable to an understanding of Mount Sinai was the article "Architecture, Religion, and Tuberculosis in Sainte-Agathe-des-Monts, Quebec" by Annmarie Adams and Mary Anne Poutanen, *Scientia Canadensis*, 32, no. 1 (2009).

Janice Rosen, Archives Director at the Canadian Jewish Archives, and Hélène Vallée, Archives Assistant, were most obliging in sending me copies of memberships and death announcements for both Simon and Abraham Kirsch.

Chapter Three: *Shut Out the Yesterdays*

The booklet presented to my parents was *Bride and Groom: A Manual for Marriage* by Dr. Albert I. Gordon (United Synagogue of America, 1949). My mother possessed, as well, the 1955 edition of *The Jewish Home Beautiful* by Betty D. Greenberg and Althea O. Silverman (The National Women's League of the United Synagogue of America, 1955); the related quotation is from the "Music in the Home" section, p. 78. Later in this chapter, the two quotes come from *A Way of Life: An Address Delivered to Yale Students Sunday Evening, April 20, 1913* by William Osler. My father's edition was a special one prepared for McGill medical students entering their second year (privately printed for Burton's Limited, 1934). "Life is a habit …" appears on p. 4 and "Shut out the yesterdays …" on p. 14.

Chapter Four: The Right Part of Life

This exploration of my mother's uncle would not have been possible without the numerous chroniclers of Jockey Fleming who meticulously recorded both his words and his doings. In particular, two book chapters proved essential to my understanding of Jockey: "Characters, Characters — Never Any Normal People" by Al Palmer in *Montreal Confidential: The Low Down on the Big Town* (1950; reprinted by Véhicule Press, 2009) and "The Last of the Runyons" by Don Bell in *Saturday Night at the Bagel Factory* (McClelland and Stewart, 1972). Bell had already demonstrated an interest in Jockey Fleming several years earlier, when he published "Fifty Years as a Moocher" in the *Ottawa Journal*, April 30, 1969. I am indebted to both these writers for the precision and verve they brought to their portraits of the man they knew as Jockey Fleming.

In *Montreal Confidential*, Al Palmer, a writer for the *Montreal Herald* and later the *Montreal Gazette*, offers an essential portrait not merely of Jockey but also of the city he inhabited — the late-night clubs, casinos, bars, and restaurants, along with the sports personalities, the police, and Montreal's criminal element. Palmer also details the "territory" claimed by Jockey, his supposed origins and forms of employment, his status as Montreal's "One-Eyed Connolly," and his ongoing rivalry with Kid Oblay, including Kid's role in the film *Montreal by Night*. It's worth noting that Palmer's mystery *Sugar-Puss on Dorchester Street* (1949; reprinted by Véhicule Press, 2013) is an engaging read offering further insight into Montreal during the era of Jockey and Kid Oblay.

Without author Don Bell's efforts, I would not have known the story of Jockey assuming the guise of a blind boy; also from Bell are the hard-boiled egg joke, the revelation that Jockey's pension cheque was delivered to a strip-tease club, Jockey's admission to being so dumb in school that he couldn't even spell his name, Kid Oblay's belief that Jockey had a bundle stashed away somewhere, and Jockey's wish to be buried in the Irishman's cemetery. Not least, the chapter title "The Right Part of Life" originates in Jockey's own words quoted by Bell, winner of the Stephen Leacock Memorial Medal for Humour.

Among the newspapermen who regularly featured Jockey in their columns, Dink Carroll of the *Montreal Gazette* ranks among Fleming's greatest promoters. Carroll's final tribute to Jockey, "Passing of horseless Jockey leaves void on sports scene," *Montreal Gazette*, April 23, 1974, is especially illuminating, not least in its speculation that Jockey might have suffered from dyslexia; this same eulogy is the source of the "Live and let live" quote that appears later in the chapter. Also from Carroll's *Montreal Gazette* column Playing the Field are the following: Jockey's lie to the police that the crowds attempting to buy tickets from him were seeking his autograph (September 19, 1959); the revelation that Jockey was spending time in the Jewish Convalescent Hospital in Chomedey (November 6, 1965); and the reference to the "Singing Jew" (February 28, 1966).

Likewise, Jim Coleman's column in *The Globe and Mail* provides a wealth of information and rumour about Jockey, much of it during the 1940s. From that era comes the story of the Toronto Hockey Club medic (March 24, 1944); details of Texas Guinan's career, along with the phrase "the frigid clavicle" (March 26, 1946); the moniker "the dismounted dragoon" (February 11, 1949); and Jockey's inquiry "What's going to happen to some of them old hopheads out at the track?" (March 12, 1949). Jockey's account of how everything he touches "turns to rubble" is to be found in Jim Coleman's column in the *Ottawa Journal*, December 16, 1950.

In other articles, by a diversity of writers, the *Montreal Gazette* furnished much information about Jockey and his rival Kid Oblay, sometimes in the column "On and Off the Record." Oblay's assertion that "only crazy people get married" originates in the story "'Mayor of Peel Street' still punching as 89th birthday approaches" by Mike King, January 27, 1989. Also noteworthy is "Kid Oblay dies at 97: Character kept Peel and St. Catherine warm for more than 60 years" by Philip Fine, April 24, 1997. Jockey's ringside experience and the phrase "the indomitable Jockey Fleming" come from "Cleroux cuts Chase, wins in 9th," by Marvin Moss, January 31, 1969. More recently, on October 25, 2010, "Jockey Fleming — Montreal Legend" was featured on the blog Coolopolis Montreal.

Anecdotes about Jockey and his entourage appear also in publications such as the *Montreal Star* and *Montreal Herald*, neither of which was available for consultation online at the time of my research. To compound the difficulty of reviewing these sources, no index for the print editions was readily available in libraries. Fortunately, my mother left me a clipping of the *Montreal Star* obituary for her uncle Jockey, published on April 20, 1974; titled "Jockey Fleming rides no more," it provides a summary of Jockey's life, followed by excerpts from Don Bell's *Saturday Night at the Bagel Factory*. The summary is notable for publishing the names of Jockey's surviving family, including that of Maurice Rutenberg. As well, Rabbi Denburg's assessment of Jockey as "one of the angels" and the claim that the Jock got a "bigger write-up in the paper than Bronfman" both originate in Jim Stewart's *Montreal Star* column of April 22, 1974. Marie Grebenc's story "Colourful characters — we got 'em — just walk St. Catherine street, mister" — published in the *Montreal Herald* on May 15, 1953 — details Jockey's relationship with Maxie the Goon, plus the thirty men under Jockey's control.

The newspaper *The Canadian Jewish Times* turned out to be a valuable source of information about Jockey's extended family. The death notice for his Uncle Hiram was published there on November 29, 1907. To my knowledge, Jockey's own death was not reported in this Jewish publication, but it did receive coverage in papers as far away as the *Lethbridge Herald* ("Jockey Fleming dead at 75," no date).

On a much smaller scale, notices of Jockey's death, as well as stories about his antics, occasionally featured in French-language publications such as *Le Devoir*, *La Presse*, *Le Canada*, and *À propos*. For example, the announcements of Jockey's boxing matches with Kid Baker appear in *Le Devoir* (December 4, 1919) and *La Presse* (March 19, 1920); the reference to Jockey's composition "How I became a bum" in *Le Devoir* (February 24, 1921). All of these articles are accessible through the wonderful online resource of the Quebec archives, Bibliothèque et Archives nationales du Québec (BAnQ).

Piers Morgan's interview with Hugh Hefner and Crystal Harris was broadcast on CNN on February 27, 2011. The transcript of the interview is readily available online from CNN, as is the relevant part of the broadcast on YouTube.

The short film *Montreal by Night*, directed by Arthur Burrows and Jean Palardy (National Film Board, 1947), conveys the flavour of Jockey Fleming's Montreal, as well as a glimpse of Kid Oblay. For the more literal flavour of Montreal, I was fortunate to see the McCord Museum exhibition *Bens, the Legendary Deli*, June 19 to November 23, 2014.

Without Stephen Schneider's invaluable book *Iced: The Story of Organized Crime in Canada* (John Wiley & Sons, 2009), I would not have known about Jockey Fleming's involvement in drug dealing. In the related section of "The Right Part of Life," the material in quotation marks is verbatim from period RCMP reports quoted by Schneider. Also essential to understanding Jockey's criminal associates were a number of articles: "Immigrant Boy's Night Life Career Led to Narcotics, Prison, Racketeering" by J.E. Thomson, *Montreal Gazette*, July 26, 1946; "Heavy Barrage of Questions for Kid Baker: Judge Compliments Witness on Cleverness of Denials," *Montreal Gazette*, November 29, 1924; "Praise the work of Mounted Police," *Ottawa Journal*, December 4, 1925 (related to the sentencing of Kid Oblay and others for witness tampering); and "The day Montreal's crime king was killed" by Robert Walker in *Annals of Canadian Crime* (the quote "as hard to believe as to disbelieve" originated in this article, acquired through the Concordia Archives; the date is missing). Finally, Jockey's links to criminal activity and police corruption in the early 1950s are documented in two articles in the French publication *Le Canada*: "L'enquête sur le vice est ajournée à lundi prochain" by Jean-Paul Guérin (September 19, 1950) and "A l'enquête sur la police: Un avocat demande au tribunal d'intervenir près des journaux" (October 20, 1950).

The reference to "monkey's paws" appears in a novel, *The O'Briens* by Peter Behrens (House of Anansi, 2011), and reportedly refers to a character based on Jockey.

"Neurosis," *International Encyclopedia of the Social Sciences 1968*, Encyclopedia.com, is the source for the symptoms of neurosis.

Finally, the italicized passage on page 109 combines small details about Jockey derived from numerous sources, along with my own invention inspired by photographs and accounts from the period. The same applies to the italicized passage on pages 131 to 132, where even more of the scene is imagined.

Chapter Five: Lake Pátzcuaro
A book my mother gave me, *A Treasure for My Daughter: A Reference Book of Jewish Festivals with Menus and Recipes*, 2nd printing (Ethel Epstein Ein Chapter of Hadassah, Montreal, 1952), is cited in this chapter more than once. The dialogue between Hadassah and Mother appears on p. 59.

I discovered the account of the Plattsburgh Miracle in "Man falls 40 feet into baby carriage, winds up in hospital; baby unhurt," *Plattsburgh Press-Republican*, July 12, 1947.

Some of the details of the physiotherapy occupation in this era come from the 2008 Enid Graham lecture, "Physiotherapy — Leadership and Opportunities" by Joan M. Cleather, published in *Physiotherapy Canada*, 60, no. 4 (Fall 2008).

The information about Marvin Silver's wartime flying record originates in the online entry for "Flying Officer Marvin Silver," the Spitfire and Hurricane Memorial Museum, Marston, Kent, UK.

Details of the condition of Lake Pátzcuaro are from "Mexico: State of Michoacan," in the "Flooded Grasslands and Savannas" section of the World Wildlife Fund website, 2015.

Chapter Six: Counterclockwise
My father's account of his wounding on D-Day comes from the same unpublished interview with Captain Raziel Zisman for the Queen's Own Rifles cited in Chapter 1: Interviewee: Dr. Archie Kirsch, Medical Corps. Date of interview: 03/05/94.

Chapter Seven: The Possibilities Are Fantastic
The ad that alerted me to the house or houses commissioned by Simon Kirsch at Petit Lac Long appeared in the *Canadian Jewish Review*, April 3, 1942. My related brief email exchanges were with Ressa Nadler, July 12, 2012, and Rose Adelson, July 13, 2012.

The first correspondence concerning Maison Simon Kirsh was an email exchange with Jack Gaiptman, Art Deco Montreal, March 30, 2012. I am very grateful to Monsieur Leblanc from Outremont Centre d'archives for supplying me with the heritage assessment for Maison Simon Kirsh produced by Pierre-Richard Bisson et associés, architectes in 1992, together with devoting time on July 10, 2012, to a conversation about my search for the house. As well, Monsieur Leblanc kindly sent me the page for 43 Pagnuelo from "Fichier signalétique des bâtiments, Ville d'Outremont," a heritage report prepared by Pierre-Richard Bisson et associés, architectes, 1990. The translations from French for the assessments of 12 and 43 Pagnuelo, along with the related English-language paraphrase, are my own. Additionally, Robert Hill, writer and editor of the *Biographical Dictionary of Architects in Canada, 1800–1950*, generously corresponded with me about 12 Pagnuelo and sent me the related entry from *Les Résidences: Répertoire d'architecture traditionnelle sur le territoire de la*

Communauté urbaine de Montréal (CUM, 1987). In Hill's informative dictionary of architects, I consulted the entries dedicated to Shorey & Ritchie, along with that for Harry Mayerovitch, designer of 43 Pagnuelo.

The cautions about pedestrian safety and the risk of purse theft originate in my mother's clippings: "Stash that purse with peace of mind" by Harvey Enchin, *Montreal Gazette*, Tuesday, September 21, 1982, and "Bright sunlight is not the eye's best friend," Scripps Howard News Service, May 29, 1987. The ad for cleaning spring coats appears in *Canadian Jewish Review*, March 14, 1930, and details of Mrs. Wener's itinerary in *Canadian Jewish Review*, May 1, 1931.

My first inkling of Simon Kirsch's land holdings on Pagnuelo came from "Valuation Roll is cause of breeze / Real Estate Record / Motion of Aldermen Pitt and Grothe at Outremont voted down," *Montreal Gazette*, October 20, 1932.

The story of the model town in Cap-de-la-Madeleine and the related dialogue is as recalled by Edward Barkoff in "Rue Edward Barkoff, in city in Quebec, is street with a story," story and drawing by Lou Seligson. Once again, the material originates in one of my mother's clippings, with the source of publication uncertain. Possibly the article appeared in *Canadian Jewish News*, where Seligson worked from 1977, producing a column with text and caricatures. A thought-provoking interview with the architect Harry Mayerovitch, conducted by Annmarie Adams and David Covo on September 28, 1995, is available on the McGill.ca website.

The italicized text in the paragraph anticipating my mother's death is a scrambled version of single-line quotations from my mother's clippings, among them "Police have tips on avoiding muggers and purse-snatchers" (date and source unknown) and "Choose sunglasses that protect eyes," Canadian Press, April 23, 1988.

The Jewish Way in Death and Mourning by Maurice Lamm (Jonathan David Publishers, 1969) includes a comprehensive description of the ritual of the *taharah*.

Afterword: Malibu Apr 02
Quotes are from the Expo 67 Visitor's Vademecum.

List of Photographs

Photographs are by Sharon Kirsch with enhancements by Kathy Mills.

Frontispiece
Bausch & Lomb Jug Handle microscope belonging to Dr. Simon Kirsch, c. 1919/1920

Chapter One: Treasure
The small charm, or *fève*, discovered in the *galette des rois*, the cake with the buried treasure, February 2011

Chapter Two: Lantern Slides
Lantern slide depicting plant cells, property of Dr. Simon Kirsch, date unknown

Chapter Three: Shut Out the Yesterdays
Robin's nest built over outside light at home of Mrs. Rene Kirsch, spring 2011

Chapter Four: The Right Part of Life
Men's 1950s waistcoat button, moulded glass, collection of Sharon Kirsch; actual size 1.5 cm

Chapter Five: Lake Pátzcuaro
Postcard of fishermen on Lake Pátzcuaro, sent by Carol Rutenberg from Mexico, dated December 15, 1959

Chapter Six: Counterclockwise
Purple runner beans, or *Dolichos lablab*, grown and harvested by Dr. Archie Kirsch, handwriting by Dr. Archie Kirsch on his prescription pad (the spelling mistake betrays his advanced age)

Chapter Seven: *The Possibilities Are Fantastic*
   Stethoscope, plexor, and eye chart belonging to Dr. Archie Kirsch

Afterword: Malibu Apr 02
   Specimen jars containing sand and rock from travels of Dr. and Mrs. Archie Kirsch

Acknowledgments

Although *the smallest objective* counts in some important respects as an experiment in solitude, the experiences related, as well as the writing and making of the book, arose from the support and generosity of many people. Not least are those who make an appearance in its pages. To those friends who embraced the quest for treasure and furnished the necessary skills and apparatus, I offer my sincere and heartfelt thanks: David and Margaret; Kathy Mills; archaeologists Ron Williamson, Debbie Steiss, John Dunlop, and Blake Williams. I'm indebted, also, to Dr. Boyd Suttie, antiquarian, who so generously donated his time and expertise to explain the history and functioning of my grandfather's compound microscope. By delightful coincidence, the publication of *The Smallest Objective* marks the centenary of Simon's Jug Handle.

My gratitude extends, moreover, to my aunt's best friend, Lila Bergman, for sharing her recollections of Carol, and to Thelma Gearey, my mother's cousin, for her loyalty and dedication to both my parents. I wish to acknowledge, too, the case managers and care aides who tended my mother and eased her way in her final months and years. Theirs is a demanding and not adequately recognized profession. Similar thanks are owing to the medical staff and volunteers at the palliative care unit of Mount Sinai Hospital, Montreal.

Several friends were kind enough to read the manuscript in full or to assist with the illustrations and related website. Writer Sharon White of Philadelphia provided vital support and enthusiasm from start to finish, deftly appraising and commenting on numerous drafts. In Toronto, writer Maria Meindl took time out of her exceptionally demanding schedule to engage in a thoughtful and stimulating critique of a late draft. Monica Sandor, a versatile translator and editor based in Brussels, also kindly read through the manuscript when it was nearing completion, as did my husband, Mark, an astute critic. I'm especially grateful to Monica for her microscopic attention to the text as she undertook the scrutiny of each and every word. Jennifer Bell, my oldest friend, offered reassurance about the balance I hoped to achieve in the portrayals of my parents. Kathy Mills of Toronto, an accomplished photographer, generously spent several days improving all the photographs, ensuring that their definition, dark/light balance, and resolution met the standard for publication. Her light table made possible photography of the lantern slides. Not least, I wish to thank graphic designer Helen Dimitrijevic of Studio HD for the visual imagination she brought to the making of my website.

Turning to BC, I'm indebted to New Star Books for providing a home for *The Smallest Objective*. Rolf Maurer, publisher of New Star, undertook a rigorous and essential substantive edit of the manuscript, for which I'm most grateful. Undoubtedly, his efforts improved the work. Also at New Star Books, I wish to acknowledge Vladimir Cristache for his many valuable contributions ranging from administrative tasks to the elegant interior design and typesetting. For the second time I've had the pleasure of working with copy editor extraordinaire Audrey McClellan, who once again has done an impeccable job. Additionally, I thank Robin Mitchell Cranfield for her striking and inventive cover design.

I would be remiss if I didn't mention the several archivists who led me to sources that enhanced the book: Monsieur Leblanc from Outremont Centre d'archives and Mary Ellen Hood of the McGill Archives, along with Janice Rosen, Archives Director, and Hélène Vallée, Archives Assistant, at the Canadian Jewish Archives. Zev Moses, executive director of the Museum of Jewish Montreal, kindly helped me to pinpoint Simon's home addresses in instances where the house numbers and even the street names had changed. Robert Hill, writer and editor of the *Biographical Dictionary of Architects in Canada, 1800–1950*, generously corresponded with me about 12 Pagnuelo and sent me related materials. I am most grateful as well to the Queen's Own Rifles for allowing me to cite from the unpublished interview conducted for them by Raziel Zisman (03/05/94), in which my father described his experience of the D-Day landing as a medical officer with the regiment.

I began *The Smallest Objective* by studying possessions, and myself became possessed, claimed by my subjects. My mother died with few possessions and no inkling that she would become the subject of a book. My father, dead nearly twenty years now, scarcely was aware of me as a writer. For Carol, Jockey, and Simon, the surprise would be even greater. Carol knew me only as a toddler with few words, Jockey knew of me but didn't know me, Simon never knew of me at all. I like to think I have got to know them, however, at least a little, and insofar as this is possible. I acknowledge them all—my parents for everything they gave me during their lifetimes, not to mention the abundance of memories and artifacts they left behind, and Carol, Simon, and Jockey for enriching my life through the objects, publications, and anecdotes that have survived them.

Finally, I thank my husband, Mark, for always being there throughout the years of the living and the writing while allowing me the freedom, when necessary, to disappear.